The Quest for Consciousness

Interpreting Indian Knowledge Systems no. 1

The Quest for Consciousness

Indian and Cross-Cultural Perspectives

Volume I

Edited by

Adarasupally Nataraju

Munmun Chakraborty

Foreword by

Ram-Prasad Chakravarthi

DK PRINTWORLD

Publishers of Indian Traditions

Cataloging in Publication Data — DK
[Courtesy: D.K. Agencies (P) Ltd. <docinfo@dkagencies.com>]

The quest for consciousness : Indian and cross-cultural perspectives / edited by Adarasupally Nataraju, Munmun Chakraborty ; foreword by Chakravarthi Ram-Prasad.
volumes cm (Interpretating Indian knowledge systems; no. 1)
Includes bibliographical references.
ISBN 9788124612262

1. Consciousness. 2. Philosophy, Indic. I. Nataraju, Adarasupally, editor. II. Chakraborty, Munmun, 1988- editor.
III. Series: Interpreting Indian knowledge systems; no. 1.

LCC B105.C477Q47 2024 | DDC 128.2 23

ISBN: 978-81-246-1226-2

First published in India in 2024
Editors: Adarasupally Nataraju (b.1972); Munmun Chakraborty (b.1988)

Printed and published by:
D.K. Printworld (P) Ltd.
Regd. Office : "Vedaśrī", F-395, Sudarshan Park
ESI Hospital Metro Station, New Delhi - 110015
Phones : (011) 4172 2626, 98713 94815
e-mail : indology@dkprintworld.com
Web : www.dkprintworld.com

Foreword

In this engaging collection, Indian scholars steeped in knowledge of classical Indian materials, while also acutely aware of the developments in contemporary Western thought, seek to open up their cross-cultural reflections to a wider audience. Ranging across classical Indian systems, often in comparative dialogue with modern Western thinkers, the essays here offer a wide perspective on efforts in the Indian academy (all except one author being based at Indian universities) to globalize discussions not only conceptually but geographically.

When consciousness as a category of analysis became a focus in the emerging fields of neuro and cognitive science in the last quarter of the twentieth century, the scientistic presumptions that informed its study cohered well with a certain branch of Anglo-American philosophy that sought to treat philosophy as the handmaiden of the sciences. But from early on, even many trained in analytic philosophy raised fundamental questions about extending well-established techniques of objectification, experimentation and third-person analysis to consciousness. From this uneasy engagement arose a variety of theories about how to mediate between third-person and first-person analysis, with greater or lesser emphasis on the difficulty posed by the challenge of mediation. Meanwhile, the phenomenological tradition of European philosophy sought to figure out how it was to relate to these emerging sciences of consciousness, given the high phenomenological denial of the objectivity of consciousness ever since Husserl. It is only in recent decades that the elaborated theories of subjectivity in phenomenology have gradually come to inform the role of first-person analysis in the study of consciousness, especially in that strand of thought that resists the reductive presuppositions of the scientific study of consciousness.

Meanwhile, the cultural and institutional prejudices of the Western academy resulted in painfully unjustified ignorance of a welter of pre-modern traditions which had thematized consciousness in ways the Western philosophical traditions had not. But gradually, with Mahāyāna Buddhist thought in particular (still the dominant comparativist paradigm in consciousness studies in the West), recognition dawned that there existed other conceptual resources for thinking through afresh the by-now familiar questions of objectivity and subjectivity, the first- and third-person perspectives (even the second-personal), ontological and phenomenological approaches, the possibility of experiential experimentation, etc. Advaita Vedānta too, very slowly, joined in this cross-cultural and interdisciplinary exploration. I think it is now safe to say that only willful – even outright racist – prejudice can maintain that critical philosophical engagement with contemporary scientific claims about consciousness is best confined to Western philosophical traditions.

A structural–historical problem does beset this enterprise, beyond the mere institutional dominance of Western philosophy. It is that, because of the imperial history of the modern world, the very framework of global contemporary science, including of cognitive and neuroscience, arose from the language of early modern Western thought. Whether agonistic or collaborative – grappling with mind–body dualism, debating the definition of naturalism, critiquing or affirming physicalism or reductionism – the relationship between science as a global paradigm and Western philosophy is historically baked in. So, to bring other traditions of thought into the enterprise, on the basis that, if science is global so too must philosophy be, is a provocative and difficult undertaking. Why globalize the culture of thought other than as mere lip service to multicultural identity? Would other traditions contribute to a sharper understanding of how to frame the problems in the study of consciousness than is available through Western philosophy? This hostile question, even if not always articulated explicitly, has pervaded the efforts of scholars to bring Indian and other traditions into the contemporary conversation. It has also constrained such scholars, by making them accept the presuppositions of Western thought on consciousness and then trying to find new answers to questions that have already been asked. It is only gradually that specialists of Indian and other traditions have asked the more searching questions about consciousness that arise from these traditions themselves, even if they are sometimes met with bafflement by those assuming that the only legitimate questions are those that have arisen from the Western traditions (*Brahman* and *ālaya-vijñāna* are potent examples). Usually, it is left to the specialists of these non-Western traditions to rearticulate their questions and answers in a way that becomes comprehensible to the perspective of specialists of Western thought. And we are, of course, a very long away from mutual comprehensibility and engagement between various non-Western traditions of thought (including such complex cases as the Islamic, which at once shares Greek materials with the Western tradition and offers radically alternative ideas too). But patient engagement with each other is clearly the task of this century if we are to decentre the Westernist paradigms of the past two centuries and truly open up philosophy as a global inquiry.

Furthermore, there is also institutional decentring: global inquiry must be truly global. In this context, the undertaking by the Indian Knowledge Systems Centre of the University of Assam is really worthwhile and an exemplary step in contributing to the emerging global conversation on that central question of humanity, consciousness. I commend this collection of essays to the reader.

Ram-Prasad Chakravarthi
Fellow of the British Academy
Distinguished Professor of Comparative Philosophy and Religion
Department of Politics, Philosophy and Religion
Lancaster University, UK

Preface

An "ego" sense of I and Me is not denied by any philosopher. Ego accompanies all our activities in the waking, dreaming and deep-sleep states. An ethical Self is equally not denied by any thinker in the East or the West. "Affirming a reality, independent of what really is, is called the ego" (Swāmī Krishnananda). That works as the centre of personality. It is a myth, yet the whole life revolves around this mythical self. The "Anātmavāda" of the Buddha is meant to counter this mythical self, not the transcendent Self. *Vyāvahārika mithyātma* is equally denounced by the Upaniṣads. Something separate from the organic structure of this universe is what our personality is. Our belief that we are unique, that we are distinct from all that is outside of us. This is the cause of suffering and sorrow of the humans. This separateness from nature is created by the "ego". How to universalize our existence, which is the original status of all the *jīvas* is the primary concern of the Vedas. Contemporary times have seen a rise in the interest in the studies on subject, subjectivity, Self, etc. There are references to Buddhist texts, Vedānta and other schools of Indian philosophy. It is a good development indeed.

I have been contemplating for a long time on the ways in which Indian philosophy can be carried on. Indian philosophy, generally, is presented in the language of Kant, Hegel or Husserl. The challenge before us is: Can we reverse this model of doing Indian philosophy? Can we understand and present the Western philosophies in the language and conceptual framework of Indian traditions, may be that of the Nyāya or Vedānta? This does not mean distorting the philosophies of Kant or Husserl, but to creatively interpret them, and thereby improvise the domain of knowledge. Instantly, two names of Indian philosophers come to my mind. One is K.C. Bhattacharyya who appropriates Kant's philosophy and creatively interprets it using an Indian language, and also using terminology and concepts from Vedānta tradition. The second is Professor R. Balasubramanian who was rooted to Vedānta tradition and creatively interpreted Husserl.

It is very hard to convince European scholars that there existed consciousness studies for the last 4,000 years in India, and that several contemporary issues were discussed in detail which resulted in several schools of thought within Buddhism and Vedānta. There were other systems as well that contributed to consciousness studies in India. The chapters in this book are written with an aim to introduce the reader to contemporary problems in consciousness studies and the way they were handled by the thinkers from the East. Not resting at that, the objective is to further the research based on Indian methodologies, approaches and cultural contexts.

This book is a result of the project work undertaken at the "Centre for Indian Knowledge Systems", Assam University sponsored by the AICTE, Ministry of Education, New Delhi. The centre aims at revisiting traditional Indian knowledge systems and finding their contemporary relevance in addressing global concerns. The centre advances research in areas such as consciousness studies, agriculture, fermented foods, export potential in handlooms and handicrafts. All these themes have a special reference to north-east India.

I thank all the contributors of the chapters in this book from both the Eastern and Western world. My special thanks to Professor Ram-Prasad Chakravarthi, Professor of Comparative Philosophy and Religion, Department of Politics, Philosophy and Religion, Lancaster University, UK for writing the Foreword to this volume. Dr Munmun Chakraborthy has worked hard in bringing out this volume, she had contacted the authors often and got the chapters written, reviewed and edited. I thank her as well. Lastly,

D.K. Printworld needs a special mention, Shri Susheel Mittal has continuously reminded us to complete the work well within time, and I thank him for bringing the manuscript into readable form.

Jyeṣṭha, Kr̥ṣṇa Trayodaśī
2 June 2023
Bangkok

Nataraju Adarasupally
Professor, Centre for Philosophy
JNU, New Delhi

Contents

Introduction

THE quest for consciousness is not new, it has a long history. Modern science has shown its immense expertise in unfolding the nature of the external world, yet the inner world has remained a mysterious domain so far. It is only from the beginning of the twentieth century that Western philosophers, cognitive scientists, neuroscientists, psychologists, biologists and others have become anxious about studying this inner private world. However, for Indian thinkers, this is not a new affair as the quest started along with Upaniṣads. It would not be a mistake to argue that the nature of self or consciousness is the central theme in Upaniṣads. Even many times Upaniṣads declare that the study of consciousness or self-inquiry is not only essential but has more importance than any other study and thus conducted an extensive inquiry into our inner subjective world. Today, the problem of consciousness is the problem of explaining this subjective experience that is inner, private, imperceptible and inexpressible yet so self-evident that it is totally absurd to deny it.

The sole reason that makes the study of consciousness challenging is that consciousness is a subjective experience or first-person experience unlike the objects of our experience. There is an intrinsic sense of "I"ness associated with every conscious experience that cannot be apprehended or known like any material object of the world. There are many arguments against the ontological existence of such "I" or subjective experience but the problem is how to deny the sense of "I"ness or subjectivity we all essentially retain. This book would like to discuss and address the issues related to consciousness or subjective experience from Indian perspectives. The purpose is to understand how far these multiple approaches offered by these classical and contemporary Indian thinkers are still relevant in contemporary consciousness studies. There is no doubt that great thinkers of Vedānta, Tantra, Sāṁkhya and Buddhism have done enormous work which can be explored, examined and enhanced even today for a better comprehension of the subjectivity and conscious experience. It is quite interesting to note that some of the leading contemporary Western scholars like Jonardan Ganeri, Evan Thompson, Mark Siderits and many others have made a great effort to set a global platform by bringing ideas and examining theories of several non-Western traditions to discuss and resolve the problems of self, and the nature and structure of consciousness. They just did not open a door for a cross-cultural exchange of ideas and debate, but at the same time have expanded the scope of contemporary consciousness studies. The present work firmly upholds this novel attitude of these contemporary scholars and aims to see the modern problems of consciousness or subjectivity through the lens of Indian scholars.

Broadly, the study of consciousness can be classified into two categories. There are good number of philosophers, cognitive scientists and neurobiologists who hold that consciousness is nothing more than a natural phenomenon. They adopted a third-person scientific approach and explain consciousness in terms of physical phenomena or functions of the brain. Consciousness or mental states are biological phenomena and very much part of this natural world like photosynthesis or digestion (Searle 2004). Of course, neuroscientists still do not know how the brain produces this consciousness or why we have this subjective experience. But they contend that it would be possible to define consciousness in near future like the way they defined life processes. On the other hand, there is another popular Indian approach that considers consciousness as fundamental and universal. The non-dual philosophy of Vedānta that strongly supports this position refutes any materialistic interpretation of consciousness or theory of correlation or reductionism. This is a radical position that challenges the objectivistic attitude of modern philosophers and scientists. However, what draws our attention here is the revolutionary claim of well-known cognitive scientist David Chalmers who in the line of non-dualism suggests the necessity to admit consciousness either as universal or fundamental like time, space and mass (Chalmers' Ted Talk). He writes, "I would bet fairly confidently that experience is fundamental and weekly that experience is ubiquitous" (Chalmers 1996). There are many more philosophical perspectives similar to these two broad approaches which contemporary scholars uphold. This volume intends to provide a platform to explore and reflect on these various contrasting theories of consciousness and tries to understand and clarify the complex issues related to the nature of consciousness, self, mental states and subjective experience.

At the beginning of the *Kena Upaniṣad,* it is asked by a disciple – what is that because of which the mind, the vital force, the ears, the eyes and the speech become active? To put it in modern language, what is that inner subjective experience that makes me different from any material body or a sophisticated machine? Why do we have this subjective experience unlike a computer or a robot? The entire philosophy of Vedānta, which refers to the quintessential teachings of the Upaniṣads, has answered these questions in an extensive rational manner. It is not mere faith or imagination or assumption rather a rigorous rational inquiry and also a phenomenological study of our everyday experience, an insight deeply rooted into the nature of world phenomena. As stated in the *Kaṭha Upaniṣad*, the highest Truth, i.e. consciousness is realized when the intellect is sharper than the "edge of a razor" (1. 3.12). Like modern analytic thinkers and neuroscientists, Indian thinkers are also thoroughly logical and persistent in dealing with their methodologies to explore the nature of consciousness in terms of evaluating the three states of experiences (*Māṇḍūkya-Kārikā*) and in examining the *pañca-kośa* (five sheaths) of the body (*Taittirīya Upaniṣad*) through the rigorous technique of "seer" and "seen" distinction. The "hard problem" of consciousness is to describe the subjective inner experience that seems to emerge from the physical body or through our engagement with this material world yet so distinct from it. While the physical body is public, universal and can be explained or demonstrated, our subjective inner experience is uniquely private, inner and inexplicable. The important point is that *Upaniṣad* does not repudiate this subjective experience like the materialists or reductionists or illusionists. It firmly admits that an individual conscious being is more than this psychophysical complex. Unlike a machine or a robot that works many times more perfectly than a human being does, there is an inner subjective awareness that makes him different from the former. Precisely, the real hard problem is the problem of explaining this consciousness experience which is different from many other related problems of consciousness known as "easy problems". Neuroscientists and neurophysiologists have developed some mechanisms to explain the subtle functions of the brain and cognitive processes like integration, information processing, neural mechanism and behavioural activities. But, unfortunately, the hard problem is not about them, it keeps knocking even if we answer all other questions regarding human behaviour and cognitive functions. The question is: "why is there a subject experience or self-awareness in all neural, cognitive and behavioural activities?" Precisely, the hard problem takes us beyond the apparatus of mind, body and brain. It is about understanding the "explanatory gap" that persists between these physical functions and the subjective experience that cannot be answered by explaining how the body and the brain operate.

The essential point to note in this context is that for Vedānta and Sāṁkhya consciousness is not what we call thinking, remembering, reasoning, doubting, imagining, feeling and so on. But, it is something that makes all these possible. It is neither the thinking mind nor this physical body but the one that pervades them all. Thus, the *Kena Upaniṣad* again declares – "it is due to which the ears hear, the eyes can see, the mind can think, the life is possible"

(1.2). Consciousness is the energy that makes the mind think, the sense organs act and objects move yet it is not anything that can be associated with them. Therefore, the subjective experience of the inner life is not a product of the physical elements nor it is empty or mere thinking but the very awareness that manifests through the channels of cognition and action, it is the awareness that makes experience possible, yet it is detached from everything physical and mental.

Honestly, theorizing consciousness or subjective experience is a big challenge. As Husserl argues, the nature of consciousness escapes any effort to measure it like a natural phenomenon. It is the transcendental subject that confers meaning and value to every object. Yet, in itself, it is absolute, self-contained and reflexive. The uniqueness of Husserl's phenomenological approach is that he never seeks to grasp consciousness like an object. He has condemned all efforts of modern philosophers and scientists to objectify the subjectivity or conscious experience and revealed to us its transcendental or world-constituting role that is the basis of all cognitive processes. Further, the first-person approach that Husserl has adopted to study the nature of consciousness, its structure and intentional character is indubitably a distinct and radical method which many Indian thinkers have employed extensively to depict the nature of subjective experience, self and consciousness. Both classical and contemporary Vedānta thinkers have made use of different methodologies to unfold this inner subjective world and challenged the objectivistic approach of mainstream philosophers and neuroscientists.

The book makes an effort to discuss, examine and understand all these diverse approaches proposed by different schools and philosophers of Indian traditions and further aspires to enhance the discussion and investigation in consciousness studies. Consciousness being a multidimensional and interdisciplinary concept demands a cross-cultural exchange of thoughts and dialogues to address the problem. It is essential to have a critical attitude towards every approach before we endorse it as the ultimate way to define the subjective experience. Modern philosophers of mind, cognitive scientists, neuroscientists, phenomenologists and biologists have done enormous research in this area and uncovered many unknown facts about our conscious experience, brain functions and neuron activities. Many of them even claimed to solve the problem of consciousness. And many of them denied accepting any such problem. However, what is the nature of subjectivity or consciousness has remained a question even today. It is imperative, therefore, to explore Indian theories and perspectives to enrich and extend the contemporary debate on consciousness and subjectivity.

II

The above discussion provides just a glimpse of the problem related to consciousness and subjectivity, and does not include the explorations taken up in all these different chapters. The purpose of writing this Introduction is to offer a preliminary yet core idea of the problem of consciousness to a reader before approaching for a more specific problem considered in the chapters. The chapters of this present volume thoroughly explored and examined many classical Indian theories of consciousness along with cross-cultural perspectives. Keeping in view the objectives of this volume the contributors have made a very decent and effective effort to reflect critically on Indian theories to answer the contemporary problems of consciousness. There are chapters discussing and examining the standpoints of Indian thinkers like Abhinavagupta, Utpala, Śaṅkara, Rāmānuja, Swāmī Vidyāraṇya, Nāgārjuna, Gautama and many more. On the other hand, there are chapters engaged in reappraising the philosophical positions of Kant, Hegel, Sartre, Chalmers, Searle, Dennett and other contemporary thinkers. In brief, the articles of this volume have addressed the main theme from a wide-ranging stances and have also taken a step towards establishing a platform for an intense and critical study of Indian theories of consciousness.

In the first chapter of the volume, Sthaneswar Timalsina provides an extensive analysis of the concept of *aham*, subjectivity and ego in the philosophy of Abhinavagupta. The crux of his argument is that the concept *ahaṁ* (I-am) does not only refer to the Absolute I-consciousness but also comprehends the individualities within its cuddle. There is no categorical distinction between the embodied subject and the absolute subject. Consciousness is both *prakāśa* (self-aware) and *vimarśa* (manifest); the dynamism of the self cannot be separated from the subjective experience. The chapter is a real treat for the scholars interested in the philosophy of Śaivism and Abhinavagupta. It also offers the references of many Śākta commentaries.

R.C. Pradhan, in his paper "Two Ways of Understanding Consciousness", has developed a very strong critique of naturalism from a non-naturalist's perspective. He firmly argues that the non-naturalists have a better and more justified way to understand the nature of consciousness. The uniqueness of this approach is their ability to overcome the trap of naturalism, reductionism and epiphenomenalism. Naturalism fails the moment it tries to naturalize consciousness denying its autonomy. He goes on to argue that a transcendental theory of consciousness is a more appealing attitude to counter naturalism, positivism, reductionism and other materialistic positions. This chapter makes a genuine attempt to address contemporary problems of consciousness and shows the limitations of contemporary approaches in many ways.

Raghunath Ghosh, in his paper "The Concept of Ātman in Nyāya", offers a critical study of the concept of self from the Nyāya realists' perspective. He discusses why the knowledge of self or *ātman* is indispensable for a moral life and also has soteriological value. Following Gautama, he challenges the materialistic interpretations of self and affirms its prime role in all epistemic engagement. One important claim of the chapter is the essential and structural difference between mind and self which are ordinarily considered one or identical in contemporary Western traditions. The chapter presents a series of inferential arguments to prove the existence of the self, distinguishing it from the mind, body and consciousness.

R.P. Singh's paper "Notion of Absolute Consciousness" tries to expound on and examine the nature and status of the notion of Absolute Consciousness in the intellectual traditions of the East and the West. He proposes a dialectical dialogue between Śaṅkara, Kant and Hegel. On the other hand, the paper briefly assesses the positions of Śaṅkara and Kant on consciousness and again moves towards exhibiting a brief comparison between Śaṅkara and Hegel on the nature of Absolute. However, the paper goes far beyond these mere similarities and differences between these two traditions and presents many clarifications and observations necessary for a deeper understanding of the development of philosophical tradition.

In her very interesting paper, "Consciousness: What It Is and How It Is to Be Realized", Shakuntala Bora explores the possibilities of describing and knowing the nature of pure consciousness. She contends that pure consciousness is unknowable but it can be realized by the mind emptied of thought. Consciousness free from thought is called *samādhi* and it is distinct from sleep that involves duality. The paper further explains the nature of *samādhi*, the state of *nirvikalpa samādhi* and distinguishes it from *dhyāna*. The uniqueness of the *nirvikalpa samādhi* is that it discards the possibility of arising any further thought. However, it presupposes a theoretical knowledge, attention and contemplation.

Akoijam Thoibisana, in her paper, "On Sartre's Theory of Consciousness", ponders on Sartre's account of the phenomenology of consciousness. She shows how Sartre was influenced by Husserl's phenomenology of consciousness yet challenges Husserl's transcendental approach and the ego in the realm of consciousness. Consciousness, for Sartre, is object-directed, absolute, non-substantial and also nothingness. The paper examines Sartre's commitment to phenomenology and the application of the phenomenological method in questioning the transcendental ego.

Arup Jyoti Sharma in his paper takes up The Problem of Alienation and the process of overcoming alienation in Hegel's phenomenology of spirit. The concept of alienation plays a central role in Hegel's philosophy as self, being a social and historical being, manifests itself through alienation. Consciousness understands itself better when externalizes itself and overcomes the ontological opposition between itself and the object recognizing an organic spiritual unity.

In her paper, "Transcendence of Subjectivity", Sindhu Poudyal explores the development of Advaitic consciousness (both classical and contemporary) in several dimensions in the name of "transformed subjectivity" bearing a profoundly meaningful approach and rigour. Precisely, she tries to understand and analyse the epistemological and ethical aspects of a social self in the light of P.R. Sarkar's neo-humanism. The paper also investigates for an alternative theory of a social self which is relevant in this century.

Saumya Kanti Biswas, in his paper "The Idea of Self and Mahāyāna Buddhism", proposed a theoretic analysis of the psychology in Buddhism, particularly from the Mahāyāna perspective. The paper highlights Nāgārjuna's intensions in his methodological criticism against the categorical foundations of selfhood. It is affirmed that Nāgārjuna rejects the selfhood, but not the self.

Hari Shankar Prasad in his paper "The Problematic Mind, Meditation and the Deep Structure of Consciousness: A Buddhist Perspective" explains and interprets the three mutually related components – the mind, meditation and the deep structure of consciousness – in the process of the mental development in its culmination. Describing the deep structure of consciousness, he argues that it is a dynamic flow like a stream of water, the root-cause from where the faculty of memory arise and also the factor that maintains the link between death and rebirth.

In the next paper "Physical Brain's Self-awareness as Physical: A Case of Arthāntara", P. Milan Khangamcha seeks to investigate the unwitting affirmation of Śaṅkara's view of pure consciousness by the reductive scientific interpretations of consciousness. He argues that the latest view of Roger Penrose that human intelligence or understanding or consciousness cannot be reduced to a computational process points to this view of Śaṅkara. Swāmī Vidyāraṇya's example of "canvas of a painting" (*citra dīpa, Pañcadaśī*) "bare consciousness" (*cinmātra*) and the "light of theatre" (*nāṭaka dīpa*) had anticipated Penrose's favourable view.

The second last paper by Adarasupally Nataraju starts with a critique of what he calls "positive metaphysics" and goes on to discuss the method of Vedānta in understanding the Self. The paper titled "Dhyāna Bhāṣā or the Language of Meditative Reflection: Understanding the 'Existence' or 'Sat'" emphasizes on the necessity to adopt methods that are suitable for the study of the "Self". This is not a thing in nature, therefore, any approach that hinges on naturalism should be abandoned. The nature of the "Self" is unlike anything that is part of the nature, which we know through the combination of sensory data and categories of mind. The paper argues that most of the modern-day philosophers are reducing their studies on self to naturalism. Call them by any name – epiphenomenalism, panpsychism, reductionism or naturalism, they all exhibit a tendency to fall into the trap of naturalism, while dealing with a subject that is transcendent to nature, though its immanence cannot be overlooked. This paper initially focuses on a critique of metaphysics and then goes on to discuss meditative reflection techniques as presented in the Vedānta literature.

In the last paper, A. Nataraju and Munmun Chakraborty discuss and examine three profoundly correlated concepts – self, subjectivity and consciousness – in the light of a well-known text *Pañcadaśī* of Śrī Vidyāraṇya Swāmī. The paper tries to bring out the techniques used by the post-Śaṅkara Advaitin for investigating the nature of consciousness or self and, at the same time, explores the possibilities to decode its relevance in addressing the contemporary problems of consciousness.

This book is a result of the project undertaken under the "Centre for Indian Knowledge Systems" of Assam University. The project focuses on consciousness studies and the contemporary approaches. Are there answers to the present vexed problems in understanding consciousness from the Vedic literature? This question with some relevant objectives is the research area.

References

Chalmers, D., 1996, *The Conscious Mind: In Search of a Fundamental Theory*, New York: Oxford University Press.

Searle, J., 2004, *Mind: A Brief Introduction*, New York: Oxford University Press.

1

Ahaṁ, Subjectivity and the Ego

Engaging the Philosophy of Abhinavagupta

Sthaneshwar Timalsina

Abstract: This paper engages Abhinavagupta's philosophy of *ahaṁ*, "I" or "I-am", in a global philosophical platform. Abhinavagupta reads *ahaṁ* to ground speech in experiencing and expressing subjectivity.[1] *Ahaṁ*, in this background, has three distinctive topographies: *ahaṁ* as the ego of the empirical subject, *ahaṁ* as subject of experience that objectifies the ego and *ahaṁ* as the ego that embodies the totality.[2] While *ahaṁ* in its most exalted

1 For this identification, see *PTV*, pp. 4-5:

sā ca śaktiḥ lokānugrahavimarśamayī prathamataḥ parāmarśamayyā-paśyantyā āsūtrayiṣyamāṇānantaśaktiśatāvibhinnā prathamataraṁ paramahāmantramayyām adeśakālakalitāyāṁ saṁvidi nirūḍhā, tāvat paśyantyudbhaviṣyaduktipratyuktyavibhāgenaiva vartate ।

Read also Padoux 1990: 190, 380 and 386. For the analysis of phonetic expression in the light of triadic mysticism that becomes central to the analysis of *ahaṁ*; also see *Tantrāloka* (*TĀ*), chap. 3, vv. 66-234. For the expression of speech in accordance with the manifestation of *ahaṁ*, see *TĀ*, chap. 3, vv. 236-40.

2 It is generally problematic to assign any specific concept to a particular philosopher. For example, the all-embracing nature of *ahaṁ* is already found in Utpala's writings (Dyczkowski 1990: 11). Nemec (2011: 42) reiterates the fact that the concept of *pūrṇāhantā* →

sense relates to the absolute I-consciousness that embraces the totality, it immanently encloses all individualities within its embrace, enveloping all to find a singular identity through its transcendental gaze. *Ahaṁ* in this sense is the "I-am" in which all those within the parameters discover their individuality while also finding collectivity. It is the I-sense that determines or delimits the parameters of the body and in this sense *ahaṁ* also stands for the embodied self-experience.

Keywords: *Ahaṁ*, ego, subjectivity, *ānanda*, Abhinavagupta, finite element analysis.

Background

THE objective of this essay is to engage the concept of *ahaṁ*, "I" or "I-am", in Abhinavagupta's (eleventh century) philosophy in a broader perspective. My approach is mostly exegetical.[3] I read select examples from Utpaladeva (tenth century) and use other references only to buttress their arguments. My focus is on *ahaṁ*, acronymically read in triadic and dyadic forms. These philosophers read *ahaṁ* to ground speech in experiencing and expressing subjectivity. The *ahaṁ*, I argue, has three distinctive topographies: *ahaṁ* as the ego of the empirical subject, *ahaṁ* as the subject of experience that objectifies the ego and *ahaṁ* as the ego that embodies the totality. Again, the word totality here is not to be read in the Hegelian sense, as this *ahaṁ* retains its generative power,

← or the vocabulary to support this concept is absent in Somānanda. Besides Abhinava, I am incorporating later Śākta commentarial texts in this analysis. My justification for giving Abhinavagupta main credit is that he formally established this concept and later commentators primarily expanded upon his insights. See also Bäumer 2011: 101-24.

3 If explored historically, this concept of affirmative *ahaṁ* is not just an evolution of ideas within Śaiva/Śākta monism, but this is also a result of a sustained dialogue with the Buddhist philosophers. For the conversation of these ideas, see Eltschinger and Ratié 2007; For a comparative approach, see Ganeri 2011; MacKenzie 2011.

it embodies diversity within and in many regards is an assemblage of mutually exclusive–inclusive self-determining potentialities (*śakti/mātr̥kā*). While *ahaṁ* in its most exalted sense relates to the absolute I-consciousness that embraces the totality, it immanently encloses all individualities within its embrace, enveloping all to find a singular identity through its transcendental gaze. *Ahaṁ* in this sense is the "I-am" in which all those within the parameters discover their individuality while also finding collectivity. It is the I-sense that determines or delimits the parameters of the body and in this sense *ahaṁ* also stands for the embodied self-experience.

The more we read Utpala and Abhinava, the more we realize that the subject of experience in their system is plastic. Yogic practices are meticulously designed to reinforce the idea that one's own sense of "I-am" is subject to expansion or blossoming. At the basic level, there is no categorical difference between human and animal ego-sense, as this is determined by the body. This also means that our primary sense of self-consciousness relates to our bodily consciousness and bodily being. The plasticity of the ego comes into play when we engage the way these philosophers understand speech: not just that our self-awareness has semanticity, it is also flexible.[4] Mantric speech is utilized to reinforce the idea that one's own sense of "I-am" is in fact the object to be constructed by meticulous visualization. While at times this speech is depicted as mantric, meaning it has transformative power, most often this remains secular speech, or the mechanism of conceptualization that constitutes the foundational concepts of the Self and other. Reading *ahaṁ*, therefore, is not a project of taxonomy but of phenomenology.

From an Abhinavaguptian perspective, the Self has both transcendent and immanent domains. It can be expunged of horizon, or of the sense of interiority and exteriority, while

[4] I am deriving this on the basis of a gradual evolution of the ego in the Trika system. Starting from an individual ego (*sakala*) to the absolute, Parama-Śiva, this system provides seven stages for the surge of subjectivity.

retaining its dynamism. When consciousness is actualizing its own immanence, it is transcendent (*viśvottīrṇa*). This is because it is not expressing itself by means of the totality of the expressed entities. When consciousness transcends itself and encounters the other, it is explained in terms of immanence (*viśvamaya*) as this is where consciousness finds itself in the myriads of forms. This is not therefore contradictory for consciousness to manifest as expunged of conceptualization (*nirāśaṁsā*) while at the same time remain full (*pūrṇa*).[5]

From the perspective of Abhinavagupta, the evolution of the ego begins from the self-actualization of *ahaṁ* as full, as the totality. This experience of all-encompassing singularity of the Self is not in negation of the other; the other has not emerged from within. The *ahaṁ* then unfolds itself, giving rise to the manifold, by the primordial division of subject and object. The *ahaṁ*, however, is not a monadic singularity as the freedom embedded within it is defined in terms of its mirroring or assuming the manifold. When the *ahaṁ* is merely gazing within, the polarities of illumination (*prakāśa*) and reflexivity (*vimarśa*) are homogenized. In other words, reflexivity grasps the illuminating aspect of itself while the illuminating aspect illuminates its own reflexivity. When reflexivity is externalized, there is the first expression of "this" (*idam*) and the absolute ego experiences its singular presence, with it being divided in terms of a mere illumination and a mere reflexivity. That is, consciousness itself constitutes its horizons and gives sense of something being out there and subject as spatially located within.

On this backdrop, we can glean that the emergence of the embodied ego is a gradual process that begins with the absolute ego. While the absolute ego encompasses the totality, similar to the body determining its singular being, the individuated ego

---

5 Wenta (2016: 364-67) interprets *pūrṇa* in Utpala's writings in three distinctive senses of the fullness of sensory experience, the fullness of I-ness and the composite of the transmental (*unmanā*) with the mind (*samanā*).

determines itself within the epidermis, like an organ discovering its own vitality. Just as a person can define himself based on his individual or collective identity, so too does this *ahaṁ* express itself in collective as well as in individual forms. For Abhinavagupta, the real challenge is not of explaining or categorizing *ahaṁ* but in nurturing the *ahaṁ* from its fragmented actualization to the totalized realization. This totalization dawns with experiencing oneself as "I am this" (*so 'haṁ*) where that which is externalized and objectified becomes one and the subject and object interpenetrate and merge in a singular identity. The metaphor of sexual union to describe this homogenization further highlights that while the embrace gives the sense of oneness, this does not erase difference.[6]

Ahaṁ and the Lacanian Ego

Following Jacques Lacan, the jubilant moment of *aha* parallels virtual wholeness, but since this is experienced in the initial stage of mirroring, it is not possible for subjects to attain this wholeness again.[7] That is, we are biologically conditioned in such a way that this primordial experience is not possible to repeat. We can find parallel to this *aha* in Abhinavagupta's orgasmic expression of *āh*, as it is in this moaning (*śītkāra*)[8] that the wholeness reveals itself and the *m* added in the *āh* to compose *ahaṁ* or I-am is merely the

6 This is one of the central themes of the Yāmala Tantras. I have addressed the dialogical aspect of consciousness elsewhere (Timalsina 2014). For example: *rudrasya rudrāyāś ca yad yāmalaṁ saṅghaṭṭaḥ nirvibhāgapraśnottara-rūpasvarūpāmarśanaprasarād ārabhya yāvad bahir anantāparigaṇanīyasr̥ṣṭisaṁhārabhāsanaṁ yatrāntaḥ* । – *PTV*, p. 103, lines 2-4.

7 For basic Lacanian concepts, consult the entry by Adrian Jonston (2018), Jacques Lacan: https://plato.stanford.edu/entries/lacan/

Also read Fink 1995. Lawrence (2008: 47-48, 143, 152) made first attempt to read cosmic I-sense of *pūrṇāhantā* in light of Lacan.

8 For Abhinava's application of the term *śītkāra*, see *TĀ* 3.167, 5.112. For *saṅghaṭṭa*, see *TĀ* 28.47, 29.49, 29.53, 29.116, 29.136, 29.140, 29.144, 29.152, 32.56.

banging together (*saṅghaṭṭa*) of the two polarities of revealing and reflexivity. Subjectivity (*pramātratā*) is an aftermath of this experience. Just as *ahaṁ* swallows differences within, subjectivity designates the expunging of diversity. This subjectivity, for Abhinava, can have a course from the absolute *ahaṁ* to the embodied and spatio-temporally determined *ahaṁkāra*. The difference is the integral experience in innate and retraceable for Abhinava.

The freedom of consciousness, for Abhinava, lies in its capacity to remain in its own immanence even when it transcends itself and actualizes its horizons. The jubilant *aha* moment in Lacan or the orgasmic *aha* moment in Abhinavagupta are not different in phenomenology. The difference is, while the orgasmic *aha*, or the primordial state of totality is achievable, Lacanian *aha* is biologically determined and is accessible only as an infant. Abhinavagupta uses the embrace of the primordial couple, Śiva and Śakti, as a metaphor to depict the mingled and as if inseparable relation of the two domains of consciousness: *prakāśa* (illumination) and *vimarśa* (reflexivity). Furthermore, Abhinavaguptian analysis culminates with an actualization of "I am that" (*so 'haṁ*), as the moment of *āh* is not described merely in terms of rapture but as total awakening or the recognition of the Self as the totality.

When it comes to alienation and the discovery of *moi* or *ahaṁ*, I do find something that resonates with Lacan. Yet again, I am not reading "mirroring" as with a fixed temporal location. On the contrary, I read mirroring as an internal property of consciousness that can manifest as the external conditions emerge. Basically, mirroring is not a singular event. It is inherent to consciousness and it is the *ahaṁ* that mirrors or simulates, both as a unitary whole that can grasp the totality of subject and object, and also as the fragmented poles of subject and object. *Ahaṁ* therefore is constantly mirroring itself and this mirroring gives it diversity. For Abhinavagupta, this mirroring is an expression of the inherent potency of being the manifold. The example of mirroring comes oftentimes to demonstrate a simultaneous presence of the entities that have been externalized. There is, however, another dimension of mirroring: an inverse mirroring. Once the subject actualizes its mirror-like nature, it can trace the gaze back to its primordiality and rediscover its pristine form. The experience of "I am that" (*so 'haṁ*), for instance, describes this inverse mirroring where the subject takes control of the experience that is remote but not lost. The experience engendered in this process is therefore described in terms of "recognition" (*pratyabhijñā*) rather than fresh experience. That is, the experience of tracing back to this identity unfolds as being merged with recollection rather than in the form of pure experience.

In terms of the discovery of the ego, I do not read a line between the imaginary and symbolic, as does Lacan. As far as the real ego is concerned, it is always in flux, constantly interacting between the imaginary and symbolic. Nevertheless, the ego is the sum of all possibilities and a constantly modifiable plastic entity. Abhinavagupta uses this plasticity as an example for the potential of the ego for self-transcendence. Every new experience presents to the ego a new possibility and in every mode of transformation, the ego reconstitutes itself, discovering its new identity. Even though the transcendent Self, *nirāśaṁsā* (devoid of concepts), is hardly given any constitutive role, it is reasonable that every new constitution of the ego rests on this Self. It is because change implies difference and only the entity that transcends both the differing entities can be credited for maintaining the flow. It is the freedom inherent to consciousness that makes the shift in the ego as well as the transcendence of the ego possible.

What is unique to Abhinavagupta is, he does not conceive of consciousness expunged of the potentials that embody difference. There lies some form of speech in consciousness, even in its most pristine form and it is for this reason that the ego recognizes itself and differentiates among each other. There is, therefore, a subtle form of speech, even if merely in self-referential form, in the first initial gaze of the ego actualizing itself. This is where *ahaṁ* is expressed that is both "I am" and "I". As "I am" it already has a semantic structure. If a line were to be drawn between Lacan and Abhinavagupta with regard to their understanding of what constitutes "real", that which is actually real for Abhinavagupta is the pre-given, or pre-presented, pre-objectified Self. What Lacan calls "real", in contrast, is a product of the imagination in collaboration with the symbolic to generate the sense of real ego. For both, phenomenal ego endures for a longer period of time, or at least maintains the illusion of being continuously identical, with similar ego-selves constantly modifying themselves and preserving homogeneity that is then translated into identity.

Along these lines, the "recognition" in the initial stage that Lacan calls mirror stage is not "mis-recognition" in Abhinavaguptian terminology. The initial stage of fullness is "recognition" only in the sense that the *nirāśaṁsā* recognizes itself in terms of fullness, but it is not a real recognition because this is the first emergence of *ahaṁ;* the first encountering of the absolute ego, the first experience. It is therefore noteworthy that "mirroring" for Lacan and Abhinavagupta is not the same. Mirroring, for Abhinava, is both the simulation of the ego as well as all that is externalized. It is in the externalized world that consciousness mirrors. For Abhinava, everything that can be objectified is objectified, including the very ego. Even the encountering of the ego, objectifying "I-am" is itself a mirror image. Abhinava's use of the mirror metaphor is not an analysis of the ego per se. On the contrary, it is to explain teleology. It is to re-educate what he calls the aspectival (*sakala*) ego for the possibility of re-blossoming or regaining fullness. This is where the philosophy of recognition comes into play.

There is yet another dimension of the ego that Lacan does not address, i.e. the role of *saṁskāras*. This ego is not merely "extimité" or internal externally, crystallizing the desire of the other.[9] For Abhinava, it primarily crystallizes its own desires from deep-seated memories and is on this basis that Abhinavagupta acknowledges the chain of memory to transcend a particular embodiment. In other words, memory goes beyond a particular individuation. The *moi* of Abhinavagupta is therefore both the finite ego that determines its extension within the body and the *ahaṁ* that circumscribes the totality. Moreover, the other in Abhinava's philosophy is not the ultimate or absolute other. The parameters that determine the Self and the other are not just negotiable but can also be subsumed within the overarching *ahaṁ*. This also is not the case that the ego is just the mirror of the other. The dialogical other is often the mirror of the ego, a mutual exchange of subjectivity that makes recognition of other egos possible even in the unrecognized state. But fundamentally, what Lacan would call the "absolute other", God, is the very Self for Abhinava. In the full blossoming of the ego, the other is felt within the domain of the Self. One can argue that this position threatens the privacy of the other, as in the recognized state, the domain of the other and that of the Self are one and the same. In this sense, the transcendent absolute other is fully revealed not when it is exposed as the other but in the fullness of the ego. Even if the other is subsumed within the absolute ego, making it a room without walls, the potency for individuation is not erased.

The same applies to desire. Desire in Abhinavagupta goes much deeper, as it lays the foundation for the emergence of subjectivity. The reflexivity that transforms into active agency, allowing the embodied ego to interact both intersubjectively and with objects and things, for Abhinava, is inherent to consciousness, or the Self that goes beyond the discovery of subjectivity. It is in the blueprint of consciousness that desire is imprinted. In other words, it is not possible to expunge desire from consciousness, only that the

---

9 The word *icchā* has a wide range of applications. For instance, volition, will and desire. While I have read *icchā* in this paper as "desire", this is just to engage psychoanalytical theories.

directionality of desire can be altered. Desire, in this account, is fundamental to reflexivity. Externality and objectivation are embedded within reflexivity, as what constitutes *vimarśa* is not just in being aware of itself, it is in discovering the other. In contrast to Lacan, Abhinavaguptian desire is not something determined by our need and demand. It is the desire that even desires the needs. Moreover, desire is not necessarily a relationship with other. In other words, desire is not constituted in reaction to other as even the very constitution of the other, the mirroring requires desire. Without denying the constructive nature of desire and also of the ego, this is to affirm that the ego and the desire that constitutes the ego are both dynamic but their possibility is pre-given in the very formation of the ego, which is then expressed in interaction with other subjects/objects.

Abhinavagupta is interested in developing a soteriology that makes it possible for the ego to rediscover itself, to rescue itself from being a simulation and actualize its fullness, reclaiming the absolute ego. When we discuss the authentic Self in Abhinava, this is what it implies. It is the foundation wherein the ego is constituted and is constantly being remodified. This is where we can compare *jouissance* with *ānanda*, because just like Lacanian *jouissance*,[10] orgasmic bliss for Abhinavagupta is beyond the pleasure principle and is therefore not to be confused with mere sensory satisfaction. To extend further, *ānanda* retains the embodied *āhā* moment that is explained in terms of the orgasmic embrace. This is also where we can compare the ways transgression has been accommodated by both Abhinavagupta and Lacan. Nevertheless, Abhinava's *ānanda* is not to be conflated with the *jouissance*. To begin with, *jouissance* that is beyond the pleasure principle is not "more pleasure", not the surge of *ānanda* that expands and encompasses the totality the way Abhinavagupta would have, but instead pain. Both Lacan and Abhinavagupta consider that there is a limit to which subjects can

---

[10] See Laplanche and Pontalis 1988; Iversen 2007 for discussion on *jouissance*.

experience pleasure. However, Abhinavagupta creates a hierarchy of subjects, successively transcending the horizons of each in their capacity to experience *ānanda* and their ability to expand and encompass the totality. For Lacan, the result of transgressing pleasure is pain. There is no growth, no expansion in the subject's horizon of experience, but simply subject succumbs to pain at the apex of pleasure. This is why Lacan links *jouissance* to aggression of the death drive.

For Abhinavagupta, all drives are the drives to recognize the absolute ego (*ahaṁ*). Even abnegation of subjectivity results in this account of the discovery of foundational, overarching being, complete with bliss and awareness. It is therefore not to be conflated with an actual death drive. In every account of self-negation, what is confirmed is a foreground, some foundation, upon which subjectivity has exercised its freedom of self-annihilation. The fundamental *telos* of the individuated ego is therefore to "recognize" (*pratyabhijñā*) the oneness of the "I" and "this", expressed in terms of "I am that" (*so 'haṁ*).

I Am That: So 'haṁ

To say that the teleology for the ego is to discover itself as the absolute ego is to argue that every instance of consciousness is directed towards recognizing itself in terms of "I am that" (*so 'haṁ*). There is no categorical epistemic difference in the ego discovering objectivity and it recognizing itself as the totality. This is where Utpala's phenomenology encounters his teleology:

> The reposing in its own essential nature or the reflexivity in the form of "I am that" is the fulfilment of the finite reflexivity, [expressed] as "this".[11]

"This", or objectivity, according to Utpala, is a finite reflexivity, as consciousness discovers its own finiteness when manifesting

[11] *idam ity asya vicchinnavimarśasya kr̥tārthatā* ।
yā svasvarūpe viśrāntir vimarśaḥ so 'haṁ ity ayayam ॥
– *Ajaḍapramātratāsiddhi* (APS) 15

the other. Utpala consistently describes objectivation in terms of being non-sentient (*jaḍa*). In other words, when consciousness constitutes something as its own other, it also determines that entity as non-sentient. This is why even the determination of another subjectivity relies upon either affirming it as an extension and expression of the very Self, or ascertaining it in terms of an object. Following Bhartṛhari's treatment of the second person,[12] Abhinavagupta expands on this issue and addresses that the "you", or second person, is a mingling of "I am" and "this". It has both subjective and objective domains. The state of consciousness that recognizes "you" is distinct from the recognition of "I am that" (*so 'haṁ*), since in the latter recognition, what was objectivated before becomes one with the subject. Whereas, in the recognition of "you", there is a recognition of something both as object and subject. Utpala explains this recognition further, saying,

> *so 'yam ahaṁ eva tattadbhāvavaicitryātmanā prakāśe iti* ।
>
> – *APS Vṛtti*, v. 15

> that which manifests as this is myself, [as I] is manifest in the forms of every single entity.

When I and this become one, that is, in the phenomenology of the manifestation of an object when there is an intermingling of subject and object, the reflexivity inherent to consciousness is bestowed upon object for its self-recognition.[13]

Utpala lays the foundation for two tiers of the ego in the following lines:

---

12 If compared closely, Abhinavagupta's treatment of three persons clearly follows the way Bhartṛhari analyses the grammatical persons in the chapter Puruṣasamuddeśa of the *Vākyapadīya*.

13 As Utpala adds further:
caitanyaprakāśatādātmyād ahaṁpratyavamarśātmā jīvitasthānīyo yadāśrayāj jaḍam api vastu vimraṣṭṛsvabhāvapramātraikyād ahaṁbhāvaviśrānter ajaḍatvam āyāti । – *Vṛtti* upon *APS* 15. (I have read *vimarṣṭṛ* here instead of *vimarśṣṭṭ* as it appears in the print.)

> This Self is twofold, finite and infinite. One restricted by the life-force, etc. is finite and the absolute Self is infinite. The resting ground of both [the egos] and also of the consciousness of all objects is singular, as is confirmed by synthesis. No other [foundational ground] is established.[14]

My analysis of the hierarchy of the ego rests on above-mentioned parameters. Even with regard to the premise of the analysis of *ahaṁ*, it is not possible to exhaust the entire Abhinavaguptian literature in a single essay. I therefore focus primarily on the *Parātrīśikā-vivaraṇa* (*PTV*). Even in this, I am primarily analysing the two-tier structure of the ego with a particular focus on the semantic and speech domains of *ahaṁ*. Preliminarily speaking, *ahaṁ* stands for both "I" and "I am" and as Abhinavagupta explains, this also functions as an acronym for Sanskrit phonemes, /*a*/-/*h*/. This is to say that there is a verb expressing dynamism infused within the ego. In other words, ego is constantly in motion. Both the phenomenology and soteriology of ego in Abhinavagupta follows the parameters laid out by Utpala. While this is a monistic picture, it is not a passive singularity. Neither is there negation of dichotomies. This actually is the singularity of contrasting and commingling potentialities, particularly epitomized by equating the ego with *mātṛkā*s (phonemes).

Ahaṁ is presented here in various ways: it is a singular indivisible entity as I; it represents the dyad of *a* and *ha* representing the primordial couple and also explaining two properties of consciousness; and it also has a triadic structure explained in terms of /*a*/-/*h*/-/*m*/. Besides these, the term also resonates an orgasmic expression of *ah*, stressing bliss as foundational to self-awareness. Even the analysis of *ahaṁ* in dyadic terms grounds its singularity

---

14 *dvidhā sa eṣa evātmā mito 'parimitas tathā* ।
prāṇādinā niruddho 'ṇuḥ paramātmā tv akhaṇḍitaḥ ॥ – APS 16

ubhayo 'py eṣa paryantabhūmiḥ sarvārthasaṁvidām ।
eka evānusandhānād ato 'nyo nopapaddyate ॥ – APS 17

since "I" is singular, albeit expressed in terms of the dyad of subject and object, illumination (*prakāśa*) and reflexivity (*vimarśa*). If equated with the foundational triad of body, mind and speech, the ego we encounter here, with *ahaṁ*, is radically different from the Cartesian ego, as this embodies both speech and the body. I have already argued for its plasticity. Now we encounter the ego as embodied. If "I" acronymically stands for all the phonemes and they in turn stand for all the potentialities of consciousness, we also encounter this "I" as synthetic. At the same time, it is the ego without a nucleus, as "I am" is identified with "I", which in turn is a composite of all the potentialities. Manifold, in other words, is splashing within the ego to overflow, objectivity and manifold as its inherent nature. In essence, the ego in Abhinavaguptian paradigm is original.

Abhinavagupta correlates the three phonemes */a/-/h/-/m/* with the triadic deities of Parā, Parāparā and Aparā, where the first and the last terms stand for the transcendent and immanent, while the middle term stands for their union. A problem with these anthropomorphized philosophical categories is that it becomes easier to engage theology but we miss phenomenology entirely. The ego that we encounter in light of this triad is the ego that is both transcendent and immanent, but also has a distinctive category of the fusion of both. This also explains the modes of consciousness that engage in a triadic parameter of inside–outside–middle and also suggests full transcendence. The ego in this depiction not only transcends the manifold, it also is very much the manifold and the epistemic means to bridge the inside and the outside. This presents us with the ego both as the manifold and also as transcendence of the manifold, both as ontology and also as function. The subjectivity that is subsumed under this ego, therefore, is "dynamic subjectivity" or "subjectivity in the flux".

By borrowing Bhartṛhari's analysis of three grammatical persons, Abhinavagupta explains that these three persons are phenomenologically given in terms of subject, object and the fusion of both. In other words, the ego (*ahaṁ*) is a fusion of all, is an expression of the totality, and therefore is not just in its transcendent form but also in its most objectifiable form of the embodied ego. Abhinavagupta explains this by alluding to *mātr̥kā*, the matrices, that represent the cosmic forces depicted in terms of the Sanskrit phonemes with initial *a* and the final *ha*. It is in this articulation of *ahaṁ* that the creative forces identified collectively in terms of *mātr̥kā* are expressed. It is thus in the very encounter of the ego (*ahaṁ*) that the totality is exposed in seminal form. In Abhinava's terms:

> In this context {*tatra*}, that which is located exclusively in the Self, that is yoked with the property of insentience and is therefore of the form of *nara*, just as "the pot stays". What is left is, this is the object of the first-person subject. On the other hand, that which is being manifest as "this" and that which is being summoned has the form of *śakti* in the sense that this is described by the term "you", as in, "being this" circumscribed by the sense of "being I", corresponding to the speaker. This is the meaning of you in the example of "you stay", in addition to being summoned. That is, just as "I stay", this stays the same way. [The subject] summons that with respect to having the form circumscribed by the form of I which is the relishing or the wonder of subjectivity [expressed as] freedom, as in the form of uninterrupted relishing of subjectivity. This is the all-surpassing luminosity {*bhagavatī*} of Parāparā.
>
> There then emerges the majestic Parā with the reflexive awareness of subjectivity that is not contingent upon anything else [as it is of the character of] uninterrupted relishing/wonder, as in "I stay". This is where the transcendentality (*uttamatva*) of the *puruṣa* lies. ... Even while being of the character of Śiva, one enters the bodies as characterized by *nara* and *śakti*, as if having consciousness expunged. In the examples such as "who am I?", "I am this", "Oh! Me", "shame on me", "bravo to myself", for instance, freedom [that characterizes the Self] is subordinated

while what manifests as primary is "thisness" as being finite, wherein arises the all-surpassing luminosity {*bhagavatī*} Aparā.[15]

The passage above needs further unpacking. First, it is easy to miss the phenomenological arguments in the thicket of Tāntric esotericism. Also, Abhinavagupta does not like to repeat things that he has said elsewhere and we need to read this passage in light of the entire text. First of all, it is evident that *ahaṁ* is not merely the first person but the totality of subjectivity discovered in the subjective I and the objectified "him" as well as in "you", the fusion of both. While these three are separate egos, *ahaṁ* as a singular ego also stands for the collection of all three. The first person, in this account, is identified with the transcendent ego, as it is linked with Parā. Aparā, or "not-transcendent", is likewise equated with the third person. Parāparā, referring to the state that stands for both the transcendent and immanent, is equated with the second person.

As I have outlined earlier, the transcendence recognized in the state of Parā actually denotes the immanence of consciousness as it is in this stage that the gaze of consciousness reflexively

---

15 *tatra yat kevalaṁ svātmany avasthitaṁ tat kevalaṁ jaḍarūpa-yogi mukhyatayā narātmakaṁ ghaṭas tiṣṭhati itivad eṣa eva prathamapuruṣaviṣayaḥ śeṣaḥ* । *yat punar idam ityapi bhāsamānaṁ yad āmantryamāṇatayā āmantrakāhaṁbhāvasamācchādita-tadbhinnedaṁbhāvaṁ yuṣmacchabdavyapadeśyaṁ tacchāktaṁ rūpam, tvaṁ tiṣṭhasi it yatra hi eṣa eva yuṣmacchabdārthaḥ, āmantraṇatattvaṁ ca* । *tathā hi yathā ahaṁ tiṣṭhāmi tathaivāyam api iti* । *tasyāpi asmadrūpāvacchinnāhaṁbhāvacamatkārasvātantryam avicchinnāhaṁcamatkāreṇaiva abhimanvāna āmantrayate, yathārthena madhyamapuruṣeṇa vyapadiśati, seyaṁ hi bhagavatī parāparā* । *sarvathā punar avicchinnacamatkāranirapekṣasvātantryāhaṁvimarśe'haṁ tiṣṭhāmīti parābhaṭṭārikodayaḥ, yatra uttamatvaṁ puruṣasya* । ... *śivasvarūpam api cojjhitacidrūpam iva naraśaktyātmakaṁ vapur āviśaty eva* । *ko 'haṁ, eṣo 'haṁ, aho ahaṁ, dhiṅ māṁ, aho mahyaṁ ityādau hi ahaṁ iti guṇīkṛtyāvicchinnaṁ svātantryaṁ, mukhyatayā tu vicchinnaiva idantā pratīyate yatra bhagavatyā aparāyā udayaḥ* । – *PTV*, pp. 25-27 (commentary upon vv. 3-4)

returns to itself. The same applies to Aparā, as the immanence of Aparā is that of consciousness transcending itself and reaching out by both objectivating and objectifying. If we return to *ahaṁ*, this is where the ego transcends itself and objectifies the other egos. These three stages are the modes of consciousness or the powers inherent in consciousness, expressed in terms of three different forms of subjects. This anthropomorphism now assists us in grounding embodied subjectivity which anticipates objectivity, and is determined in dialogue with objectivity. Parā, in this sense, is reflexively given and therefore immanent, but is transcendent as far as sensory perception is concerned. What constitutes the ego (*ahaṁ*) is not precisely in its transcendence nor immanence but in the totality of its expression since it is the very ego that assumes both these modalities. It is because it is not just Parā but also the other two, including Aparā, that is integral to the ego (*ahaṁ*). Borrowing from Bhartṛhari, the scope of Parāparā assumes the middle ground, a compromise, between subject and object, between exteriority and interiority, between transcendent and immanent. Once again, these three modes are expressions of the inherent potencies of consciousness (*citi*), anthropomorphized in terms of the triadic deities.

The ego (*ahaṁ*) presented by Abhinavagupta is therefore not to be reduced to how ego is analysed by other philosophers.[16] Most importantly, it is not in its subjectivity nor immediacy that the ego is constituted. It is not even in it being self-present or in sentience, as the other, the outside, is as much an integral part of *ahaṁ* as the inside, the subject. Additionally, he makes semantics inextricably essential to the ego. That is, "I am" presents itself as a subject and a predicate, and as immanent and transcendent. It is in this "I am" that the threefold grammatical persons are imprinted.

---

16 In particular, this is not the Cartesian or Husserlian ego. While Freud's analysis of the unconscious subverts the Cartesian ego as it rejects the equation among subject, ego and consciousness, this also is not the Abhinavaguptian *ahaṁ*.

Every experience in which the ego is confirmed has then two horizons of subject and object. That is, it is in being in the world or in directionality that the *ahaṁ* expresses or actualizes itself.

What the first-person subject that has been objectified and treated as the third person lacks is reflexivity, the essential precondition for being a subject. On the other hand, if semantics bestow reflexivity upon inanimate objects, they relish subjectivity, i.e. the experience of *so 'haṁ* or "I am that". This is to say that when the other enters the periphery of self-awareness, it also borrows its subjectivity: the outside becomes the inside. But it is also where the inside becomes the outside, or it objectifies itself in the midst of the myriad of things. The discovery of the absolute ego, therefore, is not in finding transcendental subjectivity – which does not exist, but in a dialogue that infuses the inside with the outside. The second person "you" presents a unique case as this is not pure objectivity, it is not pure externality, but neither is this the subject in its immanence. The dialogical expression of consciousness grounds the second person "you", as it is in this person that both horizons merge. When the "you" is objectified, there is already a semantic structure, as it is the subject of the speech act that makes the other subject as its object, calling him "you", bringing the sheer invisible subject to its visibility, making it objectifiable.

The plasticity that we find in consciousness expresses itself by means of *pratibhā* (creativity). This stands for inherent creativity and is a foreground for the emergence of the ego (*ahaṁ*). The triad explained above, both in deified form and in the triadic structure of grammatical persons, is this very *pratibhā,* the potential of self-expression. Here again, we have to separate the esoteric discourse and the anthropomorphized form of *pratibhā* for any philosophical conversation. What we glean yet again from this is that externality and internality or being an object and a subject are thus modes of the same ego (*ahaṁ*) and it is this euphoric expression of the ego that is what we call the manifold. Grasping of this manifold is possible when the consciousness manifests in the triadic form of subject, object and their meeting ground, a state being interpenetrated by both, a chiasm. Aparā literally translates as the "other". Noteworthy here is, Aparā is as much an integral mode of consciousness as Parā and she enjoys as much subjectivity as Parā does. It therefore makes sense to explain Aparā as the other subject, the subject that has been objectified. Rather than this being a state of materiality that has expunged consciousness from within, this is the subjectivity that has accomplished its process of externalizing itself and discovering its objectivity.

What makes objectivity possible, then, is the very externalized subjectivity and it is in the absolute ego that all the opposite poles are subsumed. The second person, you, which the Sanskrit grammarians call the "middle person" (*madhyama-puruṣa*), is where both subjectivity and objectivity are merged. And it is in you, the chiasm, that the fluidity of these two poles is epitomized. Consciousness, accordingly, is the foundation, with the potential of *pratibhā* (creativity) that makes the "resting within" as well as "expressing" possible. Therein the self-expression of consciousness first manifests as the absolute ego and then in the triadic form, gradually objectifying itself. Since *ahaṁ* is not an expression of difference, there is no categorical difference when it comes to consciousness that can be constituted as subject and object. In other words, subjectivity is not a precondition for consciousness and objectivity is not outside of its periphery. Just as both constitute two poles of the same ego, the very expression of the ego is a condition determined by the freedom inherent to consciousness. The experience of "I am", therefore, is not a mere phenomenology, as the ego (*ahaṁ*) is both ontology and semantics. It embodies not just the transcendent pole of experience but also that what is experienced. At the same time, this experience is not bereft of speech, as *ahaṁ* or "I am" is given as semantically structured in the first encountering of the ego.

There is no categorical difference between *ātman* (Self), which also describes "inherent nature" and *ahaṁ* (absolute ego). When a contrast is made, it is in relation to the embodied ego that determines self-experience within the epidermis. Abhinavagupta says with regard to the Self that:

> The Self is the life, the essence, devoid of any limitation, a unique form of experiencing within. This is the reflexive awareness in the form of "I" that has the character of resting on freedom that is characterized as not relying on anyone else.[17]

Noteworthy here is, the experience of ego is not described in terms of *bodha* or *jñāna* or other similar terms to mean "awareness". It is rather explained in terms of *parāmarśa*. This term, along with others like *pratyavamarśa* are synonymous to *vimarśa*, reflexive awareness. In the case of *parāmarśa*, there are both the parameters of without and within (*para* + *ā*(*ṅ*)+ √*mṛś*) and therefore the consciousness identified in terms of *parāmarśa* encapsulates both the immanent and transcendent forms of experiences, the reflexivity that circumscribes itself in its exteriority and discovers itself within. There is a subtle form of recognition, a judgemental consciousness, on the foundation of *parāmarśa*.

"I am that" (*so 'haṁ*), in this account, is the real *parāmarśa*, or reflexively being aware of one's own ego. Consciousness in essence manifests as a loop in which there are not just objective and subjective poles but a dialogical middle ground where the ego is externalized and the object is subjectified. This is the triadic account of the ego.

The Dyadic Structure of the Ego

The above conversation has brought to light that the ego is an integral state of the triadic expression that accounts for the "middle

---

[17] *ātmā jīvitabhūtaḥ sārasvabhāvo vicchedaśūnyo 'ntarabhyupagamakalpo 'nanyamukhapre-sitatvasvātantryaviśrāntirūpo 'haṁ iti parāmarśaḥ* ।
– *IPV*, vol. 1, pp. 302-03

ground" besides the two poles of subjectivity and objectivity. Sanskrit terminology of *madhyama-puruṣa* (middle person) explains this better than the term second-person, as according to this depiction, "you" refers both to subject and object. Following this account, "you" is not just an objectivation of the other ego, it is also an acknowledgement of subjectivity. This triadic depiction is both a taxonomy as well as the functionalist account of the ego. As for its ontology, the dyadic structure explains it better.

A superficial reading of the dyad is that /*a*/ and /*a*/ stand for the first and the last phonemes and again acronymically the word *ahaṁ* stands for the totality that is expressed by means of *prakāśa* (illumination) and *vimarśa* (reflexivity). Extending the earlier conversation further, this dyad stands for intersubjectivity between two dialogical subjects but it does not circumscribe that which has been expunged from the scope of the ego. The dyadic structure is therefore expressed before externality arises within the realm of consciousness. If this is a dialogue, it is between two coextensive subjects, between two subjects without boundaries. What is buried underneath the metaphor of two polarities is that /*a*/ and /*h*/ are not two ontologically distinctive categories and that the primary *ahaṁ* antecedes the dyadic analysis of consciousness in terms of *prakāśa* and *vimarśa*. That is, the separation is merely an analytical device, a conceptual framework for analysing properties of a single event, similar to breaking a word into prefix and the base and suffix. Just as in the triadic expression of the ego, there is no ontological division in this dyad that is collectively expressed in *ahaṁ*. Abhinavagupta credits Somānanda for this dyadic interpretation when he cites a passage that identifies /*a*/ with Śiva.[18] What goes without saying is that the second phoneme /*h*/ stands for Śakti. Abhinava's contribution here is in the equation of the primordial dyad with two functions of consciousness. Abhinavagupta explains *ahaṁ* by adopting this paradigm in the following lines:

---

[18] *tad uktaṁ śrīsomānandapādair nijavivṛttau – a-bījaṁ śuddhaśivarūpam* ।
– *PTV*, p. 20: 1-2

> The reflexive consciousness (*parāmarśa*) when it is full (*nirbhara*) within the non-dual nature of Śiva and Śakti, having the character of the absolute [referring to the phoneme /*a*/] and the reflexive consciousness [referring to the phoneme /*h*/], is called "I am".[19]

Even terms such as *samarasa* (mingling of the fluids) and *yāmala* (pair), are not meant to establish an ontological divide. On the contrary, these tropes are there to reject fundamental dualism of what is phenomenologically presented in two poles of subject and object, or as illumination and reflexivity. Just as reflexive awareness is not a second-order consciousness, or a higher gaze, objectivity is also not distinct from subjectivity: these two poles are constituted within the ego (*ahaṁ*) and they appear as opposites only in the post-experiential analytical mode of consciousness. This is to reject that pure phenomenology supports dualism.

I have compared above the fragmenting of the ego in terms of the dyad and triad with grammatical analysis. This is to say that pure phenomenology reveals the absolute ego effulgent in its totality and what is given to us in dyadic and triadic structures are post-experiential, analytical states, similar to what the Sanskrit grammarians call *prakriyā daśā* or a "state of analysis", a hypothesized state of morphing words where words are broken into prefix, base and suffix, and where separate meanings are derived from each part. Even then, grammarians maintain that meaning is integral. It is the same consciousness that manifests and also reflexively grasps its own act of being manifest and these two functions of consciousness inherently reveal dynamism. Once we acknowledge the ego with its own syntactic structure, we can easily derive the primacy of operation or the primacy of action because Sanskrit semantics confirm the primacy of the verb in a sentence. The ego is understood in this sense as an integral state

---

19 *anuttaravimarśātmaśivaśaktyadvayātmani* ।
parāmarśo nirbharatvād ahaṁ ity ucyate tadā ॥ – *TĀ* 3.203

tasya pratyavamarśo yaḥ paripūrṇo 'hamātmakaḥ ।
sa svātmani svatantratvād vibhāgam avabhāsayet ॥ – Ibid. 3.235

that embodies both modes of consciousness. Along the same lines, subjectivity is subsumed within the absolute ego, maintaining that *pramātratā* (subjectivity) as well as *prameyatā* (objectivity) are circumscribed within *ahaṁ*. In this dyadic presentation, the phoneme /*m*/ depicts the seminal drop, the centre (*bindu*) which in essence is the confluence of these two polarities. If this *bindu* is the centre of a *maṇḍala*, this is not in addition to the polarities when we unpack the metaphor of the genesis of the drop. In a maṇḍalic depiction, the drop stands for the subject with its periphery being compared to the body. Yet again, this neither gives primacy to the drop nor poses any form of dichotomy.

The Morphology of the Ego

As evident in the above conversations, Tāntric texts excavate deeper into the meaning of the ego by means of the morphology of *ahaṁ*. Most scholars fail to read the philosophical framework for such an analysis, as the depiction is rich with technical terminology and infused with Tāntric esotericism. With an intent to uncover philosophy buried under Tāntric esotericism, I read the following passage from the *Saṅketapaddhati*:[20]

> [The phoneme] /*a*/ is the first among all the phonemes and is luminosity and the supreme Śiva. /*h*/ or the last [phoneme] is of the character of Śakti [or *kalā*], which is known in terms of reflexivity. ... The head of the first part [or the phoneme /*a*/] is identified as Raudrī, the face as Vāmā, arms as Ambikā and Jyeṣṭhā relates to the tip of the nails. [With regard to the last phoneme /*h*/] desire (*icchā*) constitutes the head, action (*kriyā*) the torso and cognition (*jñāna*) constitutes the feet. The resting energy (*śāntā*) [or the last aspect of /*h*/] is located in the middle of the heart.[21]

---

20 This text is not currently available and I am using the passages based on citations.

21 *akāraḥ sarvavarṇāgryaḥ prakāśaḥ paramaḥ śivaḥ* ।
hakāro 'ntyaḥ kalārūpo vimarśākhyaḥ prakīrtitaḥ ॥

→

If we ignore technical terms and anthropomorphized concepts, we derive the first phoneme /*a*/ and the last /*h*/ as integral wholes on their own that can be analysed in four parts each. *Ahaṁ* therefore is the eleventh, if we consider this as yet another integral whole.[22] Or, the ego is an emergent structure that has within it at first instance, illumination and reflexivity. Accordingly, both illumination and reflexivity have four aspects, expressed in terms of distinctive dynamic potencies.

If we analyse the eight constituent potentialities that are morphed into the absolute ego, we derive a unique perspective. Ambikā, the last of the aspects within /*a*/ relates to seeing or actualizing the expression of the world and this is also identified as absolute speech that has not been objectified (*parā vāc*).[23] Vāmā, the first of the aspects embedded within /*a*/, is defined as the force that emits or releases (metaphorically "vomits") the world out from within the belly of consciousness.[24] This is also the stage where the speech reflexively actualizes itself, or comes to the stage of *paśyantī vāc* or the speech that has not been separated from within consciousness. Two additional states of Jyeṣṭhā and Raudrī relate to the further expressed forms of speech, *madhyamā* (middle) and *vaikharī* (expressed) speech.[25]

← ... *ādāv asya śiro raudrī vaktraṁ vāmā prakīrtitā* ।
ambikā bāhur ity uktā jyeṣṭhā caiva nakhāgragā ॥

icchā śiraḥpradeśasthā kriyā ca tadadhogatā ।
jñānā pādagatā hy asya śāntā hṛnmadhyagā bhavet ॥ – *Saṅketapaddhati*

Cited in the *Artharatnāvalī* commentary upon the *Nityāṣoḍaśikārṇava*, p. 35

22 For the elevenfold analysis of *ahaṁ*, see Vidyānanda's *Artharatnāvalī*, *Nityāṣoḍaśikārṇava*, p. 35.

23 *ātmanaḥ sphuraṇaṁ paśyed yadā sā paramā kalā* ।
ambikārūpam āpannā parā vāk samudīritā ॥ – *YH* I.36

24 *vāmāviśvasyavamanādaṅkuśākāratāṁgatā* ॥ – Ibid. I.37

25 *jñānaśaktis tathā jyeṣṭhā madhyamā vāg udīritā* ॥ – Ibid. I.38
... *kriyāśaktis tu raudrīyaṁ vaikharī viśvavigrahā* ॥ – Ibid. I.40

Just as the aspects of /*a*/ are linked with speech, the aspects of /*h*/ explicitly relate to desire/volition (*icchā*), cognition (*jñāna*) and dynamism or action (*kriyā*). *Ahaṁ*, in this account, is both the speech in immanent and transcendent forms as well as the articulation of consciousness in terms of volition, emergence of consciousness with its directionality and the dynamism where it incorporates physicality. *Ahaṁ* therefore is not just the consciousness directed towards the physical object, it also is physicality, as epitomized in embodiment. If we bracket all the technical terms, what we derive is that there is no ego in this paradigm in isolation from speech, desire and action. Ego, therefore, is the dynamic force that expresses itself or expunges from its transcendence towards objectivity. Desire is its integral form, as there is no ontology of the ego in isolation of desire. The potencies within the ego are called as such, following *Yoginīhṛdaya* I.41 because they "manifest the world within itself and also without".[26] The ego, then, is the totality and it is within the ego that subjectivity and objectivity are carved. Even then, exteriority is first constituted within the ego, before the fragmentation or before being determined as the centre and the periphery.

When we reflect upon common-sense experience, we immediately encounter the bifurcation of subjectivity and objectivity. And this is what the division between /*a*/ and /*h*/ relates to. The above passage dilutes even the distinction between *prakāśa* and *vimarśa* wherein externality is attributed to reflexive consciousness. It is because the two primary modes of the surge for externality both relate to the first phoneme /*a*/, also identified as *prakāśa* (illumination). These are:

1. Seeing or actualizing the blossoming of oneself as the world, identified as Ambikā.
2. The externalization of the world that first manifests within ego, identified as Vāmā.

---

26 *bhāsanādviśvarūpasyasvarūpebāhyato 'pi ca* ।
etāścatasraśaktyastu. . . . ॥ – *YH* I.41

Accordingly, illumination or *prakāśa* is a synthetic unity of four distinctive functions and this is the same case with reflexivity or *vimarśa*. What is lost in this exposition is that *ahaṁ* antecedes this bifurcation and all we can say is the analysis of the potentialities is similar to doing morphology for deriving a terminal meaning.

Ego Embodies Speech (Vāc)

As we peel off layers from the text cited above, what we encounter is that *ahaṁ* (ego) is the will that "sees" its own externalization or blossoming and that actualizes its othering by means of discovering a cognitive horizon and by exerting action that requires corporeality. This at the same time is an integral form of the speech that gradually morphs into the expressed words, starting from its absolute state of Parā that is identical to pure consciousness to its articulated form of *vaikharī* where corporeality and physical action are central. The body, mind and speech, are thus already interwoven within the very fabric of the absolute ego. Rather than it being a transcendent subjective pole, this is the potency that encloses within itself all the dichotomies. Ego, therefore, is both the potency and its expression, as this embodies both the speech and volition wherein corporeality is explained in terms of the morphing of volition.

Parā, the latency identified in terms of speech, embodies both the signifier and the signified, and is therefore the foreground for the speech to manifest. It is this foundation that has the zeal towards effulgence, a dynamism that finds its completion with externalization. The drive for differentiation is embedded within this seminal speech, as this is the first amongst the ripples within the absolute ego that emits the world outside, or more literally, vomits externality, making it possible for consciousness to constitute the other. This emergence of externality or the first mirroring of consciousness is identified with speech *paśyantī*, as this is where what has been externalized is being gazed upon. It is in this stage of speech that the expression and the expressed are inseparable.

It is where sense and reference are not split apart. Moreover, it is where the self-seeing consciousness and its articulation in terms of speech are not separated. However, it is also the stage where the inside and outside are conceived upon. This also is the foundation where volition (*icchā*) emanates.

The next stage of speech identified as *madhyamā* conceptually resonates the grammarian's "middle person" (*madhyama-puruṣa*) where subjective and objective commingle. It is because this "intermediate" speech retains its subjective character, its interiority, its immanence, as well as its exteriority, as this is fully objectified by the subject. This is also the stage of *jñāna*, cognition, of judgemental consciousness or of propositional knowledge. This is where conceptualization becomes manifest. Or, the subject can distinguish a concept as a concept and a reference as a reference. Finally, the most externalized form of speech is *vaikharī* which also is the articulation of the potencies for action. The fundamental divide between the signifier and the signified is thus subsumed within the absolute ego *ahaṁ* that embodies the potentialities constituting the fundamental divide of /*a*/ and /*h*/ which blossom in the form of articulated speech on the one hand and dynamism and materiality on the other.

Speech, in this paradigm, is not a vessel to carry meaning, as the objective world penetrates the very being of the speech. We cannot conceive of *paśyantī* without having the reference intermingled with the sign. There is no truth that transcends the absolute ego and there is no objectivity that is beyond the scope of speech. Both the propositions, that language is meaningful only in conveying the truth that escapes its grasp, or that there is no truth for language to describe since language is self-referential, fail to recognize the embedded creative thrust that the *vāc* embodies. This is not about it referring itself or about signifying something else but it is in actively and agentively creating something that transcends the parameters of speech that the novelty of speech lies.

Accordingly, the emergence of volition and speech are simultaneous. Volition, just like *paśyantī*, retains double intentionality, with it being directed towards objects while at the same time revealing itself to consciousness, which is its very inner fabric. The approach to exfoliate desire from consciousness, to trace back to pure consciousness, is futile in this paradigm, as desire is what constitutes consciousness; it is one of its inherent potentialities. There is always some form of intentionality, even in consciousness objectifying itself within this paradigm. Therefore, even to expunge consciousness of its intentionality is not possible.

A question emerges, what is *nirāśaṁsā*, free of conceptualization then? I read this as identical to what Abhinavagupta identifies as the state of Bhairava wherein the paradoxes reside not as paradoxes but subsumed under the gaze of Bhairava. This is a fully blossomed active subjectivity that not only circumscribes the totality but also transcends the totality: it is both transcendent and immanent.

This state is metaphorically described as empty (*rikta*) and full (*pūrṇa*). The gaze of Bhairava describes this state with his bulging eyes glaring outside while the gaze remains inward. The paradox intended here is that consciousness is simultaneously expressed in terms of the totality but is still retaining its pure phenomenology. Both speech and desire are inherent within the "I-am", or consciousness affirming itself, depicted as Bhairava. Purity of consciousness is not therefore a lack of potentials, as all the horizons of consciousness merge in this inward gaze that circumscribes the totality and expresses itself as "I-am". Just as *paśyantī* expresses the reflexive aspect of speech that is still object-directed, desire fulfils itself by means of intentionality or its object-directedness without being expunged of the foundational consciousness in the very fabric of being. This is to say that desire is expressed in a stage that is in-between subjectivity and objectivity, a reflexive flash that grasps itself being objectified. There is no materialized desire that is expunged of reflexivity in this paradigm. This is because desire is the articulation of this very reflexivity.

If speech is the means by which subjectivity is actualized, what is affirmed in this recognition is not something expunged of speech: this is the speech, knowing itself, that confirms subjectivity. *Madhyamā*, therefore, is not just a stage of speech manifest in the conceptual form, it is also the subject discovering its objectivation. It is in the concept or in the realm of immanence that the subject first encounters itself. With regard to the gazing subject, *madhyamā* is fully objectified, is external to the subject or is phenomenologically given in its objectified form. However, *madhyamā* does not transcend itself by means of self-objectivation; it is still contained within the mind–body complex. This resonates the stage of subjectivity that has been objectified but not expressed outside.

The objectivity that finds its first expression in *paśyantī* is fully blossomed in this "intermediate" ground while still being circumscribed within the periphery of subjectivity. The bodily subject confines the objectified consciousness in the form of concepts even though this has been ejected outside of the horizon of the subject, with the subject splitting itself from the body, pulling as if outside and accessing the body as if from outside. The subject that was not separated from what was there to unfold as object under the state of *paśyantī* is now completely separated in this intermediate zone, creating for the first time an immanent horizon. While in *paśyantī* the very gaze is the speech and this is both subject and object, here in the intermediate zone, objectification has been accomplished, having the conscious gaze expunged from what now has been externalized.

In all accounts, the inherent dynamism of consciousness is central to the analysis of the absolute ego. If we look for the defining terms to explain this state, what we encounter are the terms such as "throbbing" (*sphurattā*), "splendour" (*ullāsa*), "spreading" (*vistāra*), "wave" (*ūrmi*) or "blossoming" (*vikāsa*), each expressing some form of dynamism. Even in its singularity, the absolute ego is therefore teeming with the potentials of the manifold. This therefore is not the totality that absolves differences, but rather, this is the holographic singularity with each possibility replicating within. The manifold, in this account, is the *ahaṁ* actualizing itself: just as it regains its absolute ego by the recognition in terms of "I am that" (*so 'haṁ*), it actualizes its potentials, or better put, the potentials recognize their being within the manifold. If we describe pure phenomenology as the absolute ego recognizing itself, the world is the *śakti*s or the potentials recognizing themselves. In other words, there is no state that is encompassed by the two modes of consciousness described in terms of illumination (*prakāśa*) and reflexivity (*vimarśa*).

Creation or the expression of the inherent latencies is therefore to be understood as the "surplus" in the mode of transformation. *Pariṇāma* is not merely an alteration of the structure; there are new emergent properties that are additional to the potentials embedded within the cause. The point is, these properties do not exceed the latencies that are determined within the singularity of the absolute ego. *Pariṇāma*, therefore, is not merely a reassembly of the forms but of gaining something new. The metaphoric blossoming explains the fact that creation is not a mere alteration of the structure. There are no flowers in the seed but only potentials. Creation discovers newness in a way that every emergent structure is unique but at the same time there resides some form of homogeneity, identity between cause and effect. What constitutes one as cause and the other as effect is not the diametric opposition, but it is the surplus that effect makes in being different. There never is a state in which *ahaṁ* is bereft of these powers. Nor is consciousness expunged of its power to express by means of speech. It is in this effulgence that the *ahaṁ* discovers its fullness.

The Dynamism of the Ego

What I need to reiterate before finishing this conversation is that both the aspects that constitute the ego are described in terms of potentialities and this is the case with the potentialities that they do not rest in passivity. The *ahaṁ* (ego), then, is not an object among objects, nor a pole against the other, an object. It is the constantly unfolding dynamism that is pre-given in the poles of subjectivity and objectivity. If we cannot conceive of *ahaṁ* without *vimarśa*, we cannot likewise conceive of *vimarśa* as passive. *Ahaṁ*, then, is dynamic, that the absolute ego is constantly unfolding itself and as it unfolds, the totality of being becomes equated with the totality of things. The essential fabric that constitutes the *ahaṁ* is its immanence and so there is no moment when it manifests as fragmented. Even in it "splitting itself" and discovering the transcendental object, it retains to some extent the sense of fullness. The dynamic nature of *ahaṁ* does not preclude it from assuming spatio-temporality, neither does this mean that this is spatio-temporally finite. On the contrary, this dynamism as an inherent dimension of *ahaṁ* makes spatio-temporality possible, allowing directionality for consciousness. *Ahaṁ*, along these lines, is not a mere *vimarśa*, a mere reflexive mode, it is also *parāmarśa*, a consciousness that epitomizes an inverse gaze. It is in this bi-directional effulgence of consciousness that the concept of *mantra* is conceived in Tantrism. Accordingly, just as speech expresses itself and divides itself as the signifier and the signified, it can trace itself back to its pristine state and this is what *mantras* are for. Speech, therefore, assumes both poles of uncovering the absolute ego by means of inward flow as well as projecting the external and being identified with it. Because every articulation has the same Parā as the foundation, the absolute ego is inscribed in every mode of expression. Since the absolute speech of Parā antecedes every instance of subjectivity, the *vāc* underscored here is not a mere vessel for meaning but an articulation of the absolute ego to express its manifold.

The metaphors of the mirror image or simulation miss the point of the absolute ego confining itself within the body and turning into an embodied ego. A more suitable metaphor would be that of a hologram, for each and every ego retains every single potential, albeit in seminal form, of the absolute ego. Therefore, the embodied *ahaṁ* is not categorically distinct from the absolute *ahaṁ*. Just as being embodied and actualizing the manifold is an expression of the intrinsic potentials of the absolute *ahaṁ*, so also is the transformation or the evolution of the ego in different stages. Every single potential within the *ahaṁ* depicted above comes in iconic form; every aspect retains the potentials to be fully embodied. Returning to *vāc*, it is the very life that pulsates first in terms of speech and it is in this living that the being discovers the rapture of being: a circle completed in the act of self-recognition. If "I am" incorporates both life and speech, living and self-expression that incorporate speech are not two distinctive modes of being.

It is the very being that expresses itself through vitality and speech and these aspects are integral to the absolute ego. Therefore, it is while in the body that the ego discovers its felt and tangible domains and self-recognition is possible. It is not that embodied ego needs to be liberated from bodily bondage. If embodiment is one extreme of the expression of the being, reversing the gaze to the immanent, then absolute ego is the other. It is in materiality that the potentials are expressed and it is in this lived moment that the recognition of the self-embeddedness of the totality becomes possible. Every form of objectivity, every dust particle in a sense, is teeming with life in its potential form and when it is expressed, *vimarśa* actualizes itself. Furthermore, there is no subjective experience removed from the dynamism expressed in the dichotomous yet complementary terms of *prakāśa* and *vimarśa*. When we synthesize all these aspects, we come to the conclusion that the Self is inherently dynamic – *saspandam ātmatattvam* – rather than resting and expunged of creativity.

Every mode of actualizing subjectivity implies recognizing this inherent dynamism within. Furthermore, experiencing the self-nature or encountering one's own subjectivity equates with experiencing freedom, the freedom that demands its totalization, its enveloping all that is there, with it assuming externality and grasping that what has been externalized. Every instance of experiencing subjectivity is thus the expression of the powers inherent to consciousness and this expression includes actualization not just of the Self as the Self but also of what has been expunged from within the periphery of the ego; the world that manifests as something other is now recognized within the domains of the own expressive powers of the reflexively gazing Self. Recognition of the Self, in this reading, is not about negating subjectivity and one's embodied being. On the contrary, it is experiencing the absolute ego within the embodied ego; it is allowing the totality to manifest while in the body. Therefore, to experience oneself as the pulsating heart in the dyadic form of Śiva and Śakti is diametrically different from the approach of expunging the Self from within experience.

The model of causality that explains the manifold while retaining the singularity of the absolute ego in this platform is that of expression (*abhivyakti*) combined with transformation (*pariṇāma*). While the second category in this explains effect without making the cause irrecoverable, the first explains the emergence of the potentials that are latent in the cause but are not accessible without their expression in the form of effect. Accordingly, the two poles of subjectivity and objectivity and their mingling in embodiment are an expression or blossoming of the ego, *ahaṁ*, that has all potentials in seminal form. Amr̥tānanda, therefore, explains:

> *atrotpādanaṁ nāma kāraṇe sata eva kāryasya sphuṭīkaraṇa* ।
>
> – *Dīpikā* on *YH* I.40
>
> Emergence here means the vivification of the effect that is already there in the cause.

This understanding of the world or externality embedded within the ego is further confirmed in Amr̥tānanda's statement:

> *garbhabhāvenātmodaragatasya viśvasya bahir vamanād vāmā* ।
>
> – Ibid.
>
> *Vāmā* is called as such for expunging out the world that resides in her womb in an embryonic form.

To sum up, the inextricable connection between volition and speech, as is manifest in the reflexive mode of speech called *paśyantī* and its emergence, either in the form of cognition and action or in the form of the intermediate and articulated forms of speech, lies at the heart of the ego that is in constant dynamism. Just as the expressed form of speech is inherently embodied within consciousness, so too is action (*kriyā*), identified as the force embedded within *ahaṁ*. Just as recognition (*pratyabhijñā*) implies a reflexive gaze upon the absolute ego, it also stands for the recognition of one's own embodiment. When "I-am" manifests as "I-am-that" this is not a recognition of something other at the cost of the Self but the fusion of two horizons of immanence and transcendence.

References

Bäumer, Bettina, 2011, *Abhinavagupta's Hermeneutics of the Absolute: Anuttaraprakriyā: An Interpretation of His Parātrīśikā Vivaraṇa*, New Delhi: D.K. Printworld.

Bruce, Fink, 1995, *The Lacanian Subject: Between Language and Jouissance*, Princeton, NJ: Princeton University Press.

Dyczkowski, Mark, 1990, *Self-awareness, Own Awareness, and Egoity*, Varanasi: Ratna Printing Works.

Eltschinger, Vincent and Isabelle Ratié, 2007, *Self, No-Self, and Salvation: Dharmakīrti's Critique of the Notions of Self and Person*, Wien: Verlag der Österreischischen Akademie der Wissenschaften.

Ganeri, Jonardan, 2011, "Subjectivity, Selfhood and the Use of the Word "I", in *Self, No Self?: Perspectives from Analytical, Phenomenological, and Indian Traditions*, ed. Mark Siderits, Evan Thomson and Dan Zahavi, New York: Oxford University Press.

Īśvarapratyabhijñā, With the Vimarśinī of Abhinavagupta, ed. K.A.S. Iyer and K.C. Pandey, Delhi: Motilal Banarsidass, 1986.

Iversen, Margaret, 2007, *Beyond Pleasure: Freud, Lacan, Barthes (Refiguring Modernism)*, Pennsylvania: Pennsylvania State University Press.

Jonston, A., 2018, "Jacques Lacan", in *The Stanford Encyclopaedia of Philosophy*, ed. E.N. Zalta, https://plato.stanford.edu/archives/fall2018/entries/lacan/

Laplanche, Jean and Jean-Bertrand Pontalis, 1988 [1973], "Pleasure

Principle, *The Language of Psycho-analysis,* pp. 322-25", London: Karnac Books.

Lawrence, David Peter, 2008, *The Teachings of the Odd-eyed One: A Study and Translation of the Virūpākṣapañcāśikā,* with the Commentary of Vidyācakravartin. Albany, NY: State University of New York Press.

MacKenzie, Matthew, 2011, "Enacting the Self: Buddhist and Enactivist Approaches to the Emergence of the Self", in *Self, No Self?: Perspectives from Analytical, Phenomenological, and Indian Traditions,* ed. Mark Siderits, Evan Thomson and Dan Zahavi, New York: Oxford University Press.

Nemec, John, 2011, *The Ubiquitous Śiva: Somānanda's Śivadṛṣṭi and His Tantric Interlocutors,* New York: Oxford University Press.

Nityāṣoḍaśikārṇava, With the Commentaries Ṛjuvimarśinī of Śivānanda and Artharatnāvalī of Vidyānanda, ed. Vrajavallabhava Dviveda. Varanasi: Sampurnanand Sanskrit University, 1984.

Padoux, André, 1990, *Vāc: The Concept of the Word in Selected Hindu Tantras,* tr. Jacques Gontier, Delhi: Sri Satguru Publications.

PTV = Parātrīśikāvivaraṇa of Abhinavagupta: The Secret of Tantric Mysticism, tr. Jaideva Singh, Delhi: Motilal Banarsidass, 2005.

TĀ = Tantrāloka of Abhinavagupta, With the Commentary Viveka of Jayaratha, ed. R.C. Dwivedi and Navajivan Rastogi, Delhi: Motilal Banarsidass, 1987.

Ratié, Isabelle, 2007, "Otherness in the Pratyabhijñā Philosophy", *Journal of Indian Philosophy,* 35: 313-70.

Siddhitrayī of Rājānaka Utpaladeva, With Hindi Translation by Surya Prakash Vyas, Varanasi: Chaukhambha Sanskrit Sansthan, 1989.

Timalsina, Sthaneshwar, 2014, "The Dialogical Manifestation of Reality in Āgamas", *The Journal of Hindu Studies,* 7: 6-24.

Vākyapadīya of Bhartṛhari, Chapter III, Part II, ed. K.A. Iyer, with English translation and exegetical notes, Delhi: Motilal Banarsidass, 1974. For Puruṣasamuddeśa, see pp. 91-94.

Wenta, Aleksandra, 2016, *Utpaladeva: Philosophy of Recognition,* ed. Raffaele Torella and Bettina Bäumer, New Delhi: D.K. Printworld.

YH = Yoginīhṛdaya, With the Commentaries Dīpikā of Amṛtānanda and Setubandha of Bhāskararāya, ed. Gopinath Kaviraj, Varanasi: Sampurnanand Sanskrit University, 1979.

2

Two Ways of Understanding Consciousness

Naturalism vs Non-Naturalism

Ramesh C. Pradhan

Abstract: This essay explores the two prominent ways in which the nature of consciousness can be understood. One of the ways which is mostly adopted by naturalistically inclined philosophers is that of the cognitive scientists, neuroscientists and the natural scientists in general. The other way is the way the non-naturalist metaphysical thinkers adopt to make consciousness intelligible. For both, the problem is how to make sense of our being consciousness. While the naturalist way of making sense of consciousness is not committed to the idea of the absolute fact of consciousness, the non-naturalists presuppose that consciousness is an irreducible and absolute fact about the universe.

In this essay, I intend to show that the non-naturalists have a better way of understanding consciousness as they do not fall into the trap of naturalist reductionism thus retrieving consciousness from a near-slide into the materialist nihilism. The non-naturalist anti-reductionist metaphysicians go to the extent of claiming that there is an absolute fact of consciousness which has a non-material nature such that no amount of naturalist posturing can minimize and ultimately eliminate consciousness from the cosmos.

Keywords: Advaita Vedānta, Absolute Consciousness, naturalism, transcendental dualism, non-dualism, reductionism

Two Hypotheses about Consciousness

THERE are two dominant hypotheses about consciousness which need to be examined: they are the one which the naturalists in general provide about the natural origin of consciousness in the universe, and the other making the claim that consciousness has no natural causal origin in the universe, it being a permanent feature of the cosmos. While some naturalists (Dennett 1991; Kim 2010; Tye 1989) go the reductionist way to make their point that consciousness is a material phenomenon which does not have an independent existence. However, the anti-reductionist naturalists like Searle (1992), Chalmers (1996) and Nagel (2012) have a broader framework for accommodating consciousness within the cosmos making the claim that consciousness, though irreducible, is yet a natural phenomenon.

In defence of reductive naturalism, the prevailing argument is that in no way can consciousness be irreducible because the conscious states, in fact, are none other than the brain states as the brain alone is the causal source of consciousness and that an understanding of the brain activities can explain how the conscious states arise at all (Churchland 2002; Dennett 1991; Tye 1989). But the argument for reductive materialism and naturalism does not prove effective because the problem of the subjective nature of consciousness keeps open the possibility of the hard problem[1] of consciousness (Chalmers 1996) and the problem of explanatory gap[2] (Levine 1983). The anti-reductionists among the naturalists do

[1] David Chalmers (1996) has introduced the idea of "hard problem" of consciousness which raises the hard question about how subjective consciousness is possible in the material world. It is different from the "easy problem of consciousness" which provides solution to the problem of consciousness in terms of the cognitive functions of the mind and brain.

[2] Joseph Levine (1983) has introduced the idea of "the explanatory →

show that consciousness cannot be reduced to the brain activities because of the subjective ontology of consciousness (Searle 1992) and because there is something irreducibly fundamental about consciousness in the universe (Chalmers 1996). The anti-reductionists have a better method of explaining consciousness without succumbing to the reductionist strategy of the naturalists.

It is the anti-naturalists (Husserl 1960; Kant 1929; Śaṅkara 1972; Sri Aurobindo 1973) who have a robust metaphysical approach to the problem of consciousness which avoids the naturalist dilemmas regarding consciousness. They not only make the problem of reduction of the conscious states irrelevant but also put aside the problem of the material origin of consciousness. For them, consciousness is an absolute cosmic fact which needs to be explained in its own terms rather than in terms of matter or brain, and that consciousness has primacy over matter or the brain. The metaphysical approach to consciousness makes consciousness not only an absolute reality but also a transcendental reality beyond the boundaries of nature thus making room for a non-materialist and non-naturalist theory of consciousness.

Why Naturalism Fails?

Naturalism as a theory of consciousness fails to explain consciousness for a number of reasons. First, it naturalizes consciousness, mind and all the functions that the mind carries on thus bringing the entire domain of conscious life within the ambit of the material world. It therefore makes consciousness by default a material phenomenon.

Second, though the liberal naturalists admit the subjectivity of consciousness and its first-person character thus admitting an explanatory gap between the first-person and the third-person

← gap" between the first-person approach to consciousness and its third-person counterpart. This suggests an irreducible gap between the subjective and objective methods of explanations of mind and consciousness.

points of view, the overall framework remains naturalistic and materialistic in character as a result of which the subjectivity so admitted remains largely vestigial. That is, the so-called subjective ontology of consciousness remains supervenient on a materialist ontology.

Third, the emergentism[3] that is admitted by some naturalists does not allow full autonomy to consciousness thus allowing for the primacy of the material phenomena over the conscious phenomena.

Fourth, as the naturalists accept the idea of the materially closed universe, there is little scope for the conscious mind to have autonomy in this universe.

Lastly, within the naturalist framework, there can hardly be any scope for admitting the evolutionary possibilities of consciousness to transcend its own limits and ascend to a higher state than its own lower states.

As regards the first point regarding naturalization of consciousness, it should be noted that the wholesale naturalization and hence materialization of consciousness is not possible, because consciousness is not a by-product, epiphenomenal or otherwise, of the material forces. If we press forward the naturalization process, we may reach a dead-end where consciousness is to be admitted as an irreducible absolute fact which is non-material in nature. Second, the naturalist admission of subjectivity of consciousness (Chalmers 1996; Nagel 1974; Searle 1992) may turn out to be a lip-service to the first-person approach to consciousness because the overriding presence of the third-person perspective within naturalism makes the first-personal consciousness a miracle or mystery within the material world. The miraculous nature of the subjective consciousness is further reinforced by the emergentist account of consciousness within the material world because there is no way we can show the conscious mind to emerge from the

[3] The emergentist hypothesis was suggested by Samuel Alexander (1920) regarding the evolution of the mind in the universe.

unconscious matter. Emergentism (Alexander 1920; Searle 1992) is handicapped by the fact that consciousness cannot emerge from matter unless it is admitted to be pre-existent in matter itself which the naturalists cannot allow.

The greatest difficulty with naturalism is that it is committed to the principle of physical closure of the universe which does not allow for the cosmic presence of consciousness as a trans-individual phenomenon thus making it impossible to imagine the cosmos as a manifestation of consciousness rather than imagining the cosmos as giving rise to consciousness within its physical boundaries. The naturalists have, therefore, never been open to any kind of evolution of consciousness except the Darwinian one (Nagel 2012) that promises the evolution of the conscious mind within the limited materialist trajectory of the universe.

Liberal naturalism as a full-scale metaphysical theory is bound to view consciousness as a reality co-present with matter admitting dualism as a cosmic necessity thus making consciousness have ontic presence covariant with the ever-present material phenomena (Chalmers 1996). This is hardly a solace for the non-naturalists who view consciousness as an ever-present cosmic reality with the material world as its manifestation (Sri Aurobindo 1973). Non-naturalist metaphysics makes room for the ascending consciousness to embrace all the cosmic phenomena within its creative ambit without denying the reality of the cosmic matter but by making the latter a fragment of the cosmic reality of consciousness.

The Non-Naturalist Metaphysics of Consciousness

The non-naturalist metaphysics of consciousness provides not only a negative critique of the naturalist theory of consciousness but also a positive metaphysical account of consciousness and its multiple functions. In its negative account, it exposes the limitations of any naturalist theory by showing that it fails to account for consciousness as a fundamental reality. It is this aspect of the non-naturalist account that we must examine.

The process of naturalization and by default materialization of consciousness can never succeed because consciousness remains irreducibly fundamental thus exposing the limitations of the method of naturalization. The naturalist theories explain consciousness either in terms of the brain functions (Dennett 1991) or in terms of the computations of the mechanical mind (Fodor 1975) or in terms of biological nature of the mental activities (Searle 1992). All these models of explanation fail to arrive at consciousness as a fundamental reality.

The very idea of the first-personal consciousness which the liberal naturalists accept (Chalmers 1996; Nagel 1974) does not do away with the third-person approach of the natural sciences which dominates consciousness research because the first-person approach cannot resist the over dominance of the third-person objective approach to consciousness (Dennett 1991; Tye 1989). The subjectivity of consciousness remains accidental in a predominantly material universe.

The naturalist theory is committed metaphysically to the primacy of the material world (Flanagan 2007; Searle 1992) which makes materialism the core metaphysical theory. This is the legacy of the pre-Kantian and the pre-Hegelian materialist metaphysics which has spelt doom for any non-materialist metaphysics of consciousness. Unless the primacy of consciousness is admitted, there can be no proper account of consciousness in its true nature.

The subject–object or the self–world duality which is central to the naturalist theories of consciousness leads to the idea of the world being opposed to the mind and consciousness thus reviving the old dualism which was overcome by the post-Cartesian thinkers by making the mind a fundamental reality. The mind–matter dualism itself stands largely discredited because of its own contradictions which were exposed by the monist metaphysicians like Hegel, Husserl and many other anti-dualist metaphysicians.

The monist approach, if deepened further, can make the mind

the absolute reality and the world a manifestation of consciousness (Hegel 1977; Sri Aurobindo 1973). This can lead to the disappearance of the subject–object duality and make room for a form of non-dualism with consciousness as the sole reality (Śaṅkara 1972; Sri Aurobindo 1973).

The Cosmic Consciousness as One and Infinite

One of the strongest arguments of the non-naturalist metaphysics of consciousness is that consciousness in itself is one and infinite in the sense that it is universal and unlimited in nature. It is called the universal spirit[4] (Hegel 1977) or *Brahman*,[5] Saccidānanda (Śaṅkara 1972; Sri Aurobindo 1973). The argument for the universal and infinite consciousness is that consciousness cannot be divided into "my consciousness" or "your consciousness" in the narrow individual sense of the term. According to this argument, consciousness can in no way be divided because it cannot be measured like the physical objects, nor can it be divided into parts like the physical objects. By nature, consciousness is one and indivisible so that we cannot make any sense of there being many consciousnesses.

Individual consciousness arises only when the one consciousness manifests itself in many individual beings. In this sense only we can talk of "my consciousness" as a limited form of consciousness. However, I cannot call "my consciousness" a primary reality; it is at best a limited form of the universal consciousness. The Advaita Vedāntins[6] amongst the non-naturalist metaphysicians calls the ego or individual consciousness a limited reflection of the universal

---

4 Hegel (1977) is well known for the introduction of the idea of the spirit or absolute consciousness in his explanation of the nature of the mind and the world.

5 *Brahman* is the Vedāntic idea of the absolute reality of consciousness which has a predominantly Upaniṣadic origin.

6 Advaita Vedānta founded by Śaṅkara (1972) is the most dominant system of Vedāntic philosophy that holds a monistic theory of consciousness.

consciousness. This makes the duality between individual ego-consciousness and the universal consciousness ultimately dissolved. This also rejects as absurd any idea of universal consciousness as a summation of the individual consciousness, as consciousness by nature is one and infinite. Any finite appearance of consciousness is ephemeral and contingent.

Since by nature consciousness is infinite, it cannot allow for any finite consciousness being absolutely real. That is, the ego-consciousness which is finite and contingent cannot be absolutely real. For that reason, as the Advaitins maintain, the infinite consciousness is alone absolutely real. Consequently, they do not find any valid argument in favour of the materialist theory that consciousness has to be always finite and conditioned. It is only the anti-Vedāntins and the anti-Hegelians who see merit in the hypothesis that consciousness is limited to the material body and the brain and so cannot claim any universality.

For the Vedāntins and the anti-materialists, consciousness is not limited to the body because though it is located in the body, it is really non-local in character. That is, consciousness being universal and infinite cannot be located in any finite body and so it cannot originate in any material body at all. If consciousness originates in the brain and the body, it can be limited to the body and cannot be universal and unlimited. The infinite consciousness transcends the material body and the brain.

The Absolute Consciousness as Transcendental

That the infinite cosmic consciousness is absolute cannot be denied because there is nothing that makes it relative to any human body or any material system. Even the material universe is not its causal source. It is *sui generis* and therefore absolute as the ultimate ground of everything as the Upaniṣads[7] declare (Śaṅkara 2001, 2002). This

[7] The Upaniṣads constitute the philosophical part of the Vedas which teach the philosophy of *Brahman* or *Ātman* as the absolute transcendental consciousness.

hypothesis of the Upaniṣadic thinkers makes sense because we cannot conceive of anything including the universe in the absence of the absolute consciousness called *Ātman* or *Brahman*. The absolute consciousness is thus made the source of the material universe in the sense that it is one and non-dual having nothing else to be contrasted with.

The absolute non-dual consciousness is supposed to outstrip the limits of the material universe and by default the limits of the human brain and body. So, it is transcendental in nature as we cannot limit it to the universe itself. It is the consciousness-force that makes the world its manifestation in space and time (Sri Aurobindo 1973). The position of the world in the Advaitic metaphysics is that of a secondary reality that cannot claim absolute reality. Keeping this in mind the Advaitins like Śaṅkara call it *māyā*[8] not meaning any sort of illusion for that matter, but of a derived reality that is at best a manifestation of consciousness. There is no reason to suppose that the material world is unreal in the empirical sense of the term, but from the transcendental point of view it remains a secondary reality.

The absolute consciousness being outside the limits of the material world cannot but be transcendent to the ordinary forms of expressions in language. This has been the main contention of the Upaniṣads (Śaṅkara 2001, 2002) that the absolute consciousness defies our language and mind for its expression and therefore is considered beyond language and its myriad words and concepts. This inexpressibility in language of course does not amount to some kind of unintelligibility because consciousness is self-manifesting or self-revealing. This marks the highest point of the Vedāntic idea of the absolute consciousness or *Brahman* as the transcendental reality which is beyond the reach of language and mind notwithstanding its self-revealing character.

---

8 *Māyā* is the term used by Advaita Vedānta to indicate the secondary and relative existence of the world. It does not literally mean illusion.

The idea of transcendental self or *Ātman* as the absolute consciousness, which is the fundamental contribution of Vedānta to the world thought, emerges as the potential concept which can resolve the difficulties we face regarding the nature of the self, mind and consciousness in contemporary times. The search for the self as a transcendental reality and as the locus of absolute consciousness culminates in the discovery of the absolute ground of the material world. The world is no more a reality that gives rise to consciousness as it is but a reflection of the latter. Had consciousness been a product of the world-process we would have no clue as what makes the world intelligible at all. Consciousness as outside the limits of the world makes the world intelligible as something empirically knowable. Thus, the transcendental self as the absolute consciousness is the source of meanings and values which the world embodies. The sense of the world must be traced back to the transcendental self itself (Husserl 1960).

The metaphysics of the transcendental self and consciousness makes itself worthwhile to study because it solves many of the old worries about the origin of the world and its relation to the self and consciousness. The materialist metaphysicians have left the problem unsolved because it started from the wrong end by supposing the world to be the source of the self and consciousness. But transcendental metaphysics of consciousness puts the whole materialist ontology upside down by making the self and consciousness the absolute ground of the world.

The Really Hard Problem of Consciousness

The really hard problem of consciousness as Chalmers (1996) suggests does not lie in how there is subjective first-person experience in a material world, nor does it lie in what Flanagan (2007) suggests how meaning is possible in a material world, but it really lies in how the material world is possible at all when consciousness is absolutely the only reality. Thus, there is a shift of the hard problem from the possibility of consciousness to the possibility of the material world. That is the really hard problem because it is not easily understandable how there can be a material world at all when reality is consciousness itself. This problem bothered the Vedāntins, the Hegelians and all those who accepted the absolute reality of consciousness. This is the question which is faced by all the idealist thinkers who make the conscious mind the absolute reality.

The contemporary philosophers of mind have followed a false lead in making the hard problem turn around the possibility of consciousness as if its existence were a miracle in the universe as the material universe might not have allowed the possibility of the conscious experience under some other conditions excepting those which allowed this possibility. This is the self-doubt which Descartes faced at the beginning of modern philosophy. Surprisingly, he came to the *cogito* thesis which affirmed one's own existence in a material universe. This self-assertion was the fulcrum of much of modern philosophy till the so-called hard problem was raised to question the Cartesian assertion about one's own self. The real problem should be the other way round: Can the material world exist without the conscious mind?

The transcendental metaphysician is not worried about what the scientifically-minded philosophers say about the new turn of the hard problem in philosophy of mind. It is because the question is not whether anyone accepts it or not, but if it is intelligible at all. The new form of the hard problem takes us back to the old question about the existence of the world if we take Plato's Forms as absolutely real, or if we take Spinoza's absolute Substance as God, or if we take Śaṅkara's absolute reality as *Brahman*. In all these cases, the existence of the world is in question. One has to struggle to explain the existence of the world through any number of metaphysical theories from the imitation theory to the theory of *māyā*. The intelligibility of the world ultimately depends on consciousness or mind or reason as the case may be. The new twist to the hard problem ultimately turns to consciousness to explain the existence of the world.

The possible solution to the really hard problem is that the world is dependent on consciousness for its existence. That is, it is the absolute consciousness which is transcendentally real that makes the world its manifestation or expression such that the more we explore the essence of the world, the more we miss the materiality of the world and in its place find a form of consciousness however rudimentary it may be. We are thus bound to discover the conscious mind in the material world so as to make the material world ultimately one with the absolute consciousness or the spirit or *Brahman* (Hegel 1977; Sri Aurobindo 1973). This solution is as surprising as the earlier solution which Chalmers or Flanagan suggested but with less self-doubt and less mystery-mongering.

The Mystery Laid to Rest

The mystery regarding consciousness which is considered by Dennett (1991) as the last mystery in philosophy can be removed not by eliminating consciousness or declaring it as never knowable by our mind (McGinn 1999). The best way of solving the mystery of consciousness is by reaffirming its existence and also by making it the most fundamental and the absolute reality. This solution, of course, takes away the challenge facing any explanation by the methods of science and scientific philosophy since it does the impossible either by eliminating consciousness altogether (Churchland 2002) or pushing it beyond the cognitive capacity of the human mind (McGinn 1998).

The eliminative theories have gone wrong in placing consciousness in the company of the physical processes in the brain and have therefore missed its existence as an independent reality. That is the way they easily solved the mystery of consciousness not by confronting it but by explaining away the very reality of consciousness. Had they taken consciousness seriously as Chalmers (1996) and Searle (1992) do, the eliminativists would not have dismissed the mystery of consciousness so easily. The reality of consciousness is admitted to be fundamental for the reason that the dismissal of consciousness out of existence reinforces its existence. Consciousness is all the way down in the very process of its denial.

The argument, that we can never understand the deeper structure of consciousness as claimed by the theory of the unknowability of consciousness, cannot solve the mystery because it pushes it further into the limbo of ignorance. The denial of knowledge of consciousness, but not of consciousness as a reality, cannot be accepted because our very notion of not knowing consciousness is itself a form of knowledge of consciousness. Besides, since consciousness is so immediately given to us and since it reveals itself, it will be wrong to say that consciousness can never be known by the human mind. Though our concepts and thoughts are limited, it cannot be the case that they will always remain the same; the frontiers of our knowledge of consciousness can be pushed further in course of time. Though it can be admitted that consciousness in the absolute sense is beyond language and thought as admitted by many thinkers (Śaṅkara 2001, 2002; Sri Aurobindo 1973), it cannot be the case that the absolute consciousness does not reveal itself to our mind and consciousness since consciousness itself gives rise to the idea of absolute consciousness.

The absolute consciousness as claimed by the transcendental metaphysicians transcends our thought and language but it yet makes itself manifest in all our mental and conscious activities. The self-manifesting reality of the transcendental consciousness is affirmed by the theory that consciousness is not an unknowable reality but that it is the ground of every form of knowledge. The so-called unknowable consciousness is the ever-manifesting consciousness that can be grasped by the human consciousness which is part of the absolute consciousness. Our limited thoughts and conscious states are part of the all-pervading and all-manifesting consciousness.

Thus, the mystery of consciousness can be laid to rest if we take consciousness as absolutely real and as the source of all reality including the reality of the material world. In that case, there is no ultimate mystery about consciousness, though to our finite and limited mind, it will always appear to be a mystery. If we can transcend the limits of our mind, we can see the reality of consciousness directly and realize its absolute presence.

Ascent to the Supermind

Since the ordinary mind of ours is limited and so incapable of knowing the absolute consciousness, it has been suggested by Sri Aurobindo (1973) that the supermind equipped with supramental powers can unfold the secret of the absolute reality, *Brahman*. Such a suggestion has enormous implications for the present structure of the human mind but also for the evolutionary possibilities of the supermind. The questions about such possibilities are not easy to answer unless we revise the prevailing notions of mind and consciousness.

The first point to be noted in this suggestion is that the supermind can evolve out of the present mind, that is, out of the mind that has been struggling to overcome its own limitations by the evolutionary force underlying the entire history of the universe. Such an evolutionary view of the universe and mind has to be accepted as a metaphysical hypothesis so that we can place the present mind and consciousness at the apex of the evolutionary pyramid of which the base is the material world that implicitly involves the mind and consciousness. As Sri Aurobindo (1973) suggests, the material base is not the matter as science has let us know but the matter of the Vedāntins which is an implicit form of consciousness that because of the evolutionary impetus gives rise to life, mind and overmind, and subsequently the supermind.[9]

[9] Sri Aurobindo (1973) has introduced the idea of supermind to indicate the next highest stage of the evolution of the consciousness. The supermind stands for the highest form of consciousness that can be attained though evolution.

The supermind can comprehend the absolute reality with its supramental powers.

The supermind is not to be handicapped by its limited powers of the present mind which is circumscribed by ignorance of the ultimate reality. It can go beyond the present mind, which, however capable, it might have been in unravelling the nature of the material universe and life in it, has not yet unfolded the nature of the consciousness. The vast realm of consciousness, its non-dual unity, its complexity and creative expansiveness have remained beyond the realm of the present state of the human mind. That is why philosophers have lamented the fact that our mind which is rooted in the world has not liberated itself completely from its material and biological rootedness. The supermind can accomplish this liberation from matter by leaping into the supramental consciousness.

The evolutionary possibility of the supermind and supramental consciousness has been written into the history of the universe because in this universe has evolved a mind that has got enormous powers to map the universe in science and philosophy, created forms of beauty in art and literature and has made enormous strides to make the universe a place for a better living by changing some of the material conditions of life. There can be no denial of the fact that human mind has unimaginable powers of mathematical computations, scientific precision and literary creativity. But what is demanded from the mind is the knowledge of the ultimate reality which has slipped from its horizon. The supermind may succeed in the endeavour to understand the ultimate nature of the absolute consciousness.

Transformed Consciousness, Transformed Humanity

The supramental consciousness is what is expected to be the next higher stage of consciousness. The consciousness that we possess at this stage of the human evolution is one that has transformed the consciousness of the past humanity. But for the next stage of humanity, another level of transformed consciousness is needed.

Philosophers have always imagined a higher form of consciousness (Sri Aurobindo 1973) that can emerge out of the present stage which has fallen short of the ideal spiritual consciousness.

That the present stage of humanity has not come out of the shadow of materialism since the materialist world view has led to the fall of the spiritual and moral ideals of a better world governed by unity and harmony. This fall is more due to the limitations of our consciousness than to the ideals so far pursued. Human civilization itself is stunted because of the absence of a higher consciousness to match the higher ideas of morality and spirituality. The transformed consciousness will be a fully developed moral consciousness which is the first stage towards a fully developed spiritual or divine consciousness.

It is not difficult to think of transformation of consciousness because it is evident in the way our moral consciousness has emerged out of the primitive consciousness of the savage state of humanity. The savage past has not been completely overcome by the present humanity because of the presence of violence, bloodshed and colossal destruction of life which is part of the present civilization. This can be changed only when we as a human race rise above our present consciousness.

If we continue to deny the possibility of the evolution of consciousness, we can never progress beyond the present stunted humanity and we will be left hanging between the brutal past of the human history and the promised land of universal peace and harmony. The thinkers of the present times have to choose between a purely materialist world view and a world view of spiritualized humanity.[10]

Concluding Remarks

The quest for consciousness does not seem to cease too soon as there is no way we can claim in philosophy that we have seen the

---

10 The spiritual goal of the evolution of the human race lies in realizing the higher ideals of unity and harmony.

light at the end of the tunnel. Since consciousness has multiple faces to explore, there will always be new discoveries about the real nature of consciousness.

This essay has explored the nature of consciousness from a transcendental metaphysical perspective with the hope that such a perspective can counter some of the misleading pictures of consciousness based on the findings of the natural sciences. The scientific findings have not satisfied the metaphysical curiosities we entertain from time immemorial about mind and consciousness.

This is a modest attempt to present the non-naturalist way of understanding, especially from the Vedāntic perspective, of how consciousness has a still unexplored transcendental aspect which can pose a counter to the naturalist perspective of the contemporary times.

References

Alexander, Samuel, 1920, *Space, Time, and Deity*, Ann Arbor, MI: University of Michigan Library.

Aurobindo, Sri, 1973, *The Life Divine*, Pondicherry: Sri Aurobindo Ashrama.

Chalmers, D.J., 1996, *The Conscious Mind: In Search of a Fundamental Theory,* Oxford: Oxford University Press.

Churchland, P.M., 2002, "Eliminative materialism and the Propositional Attitude", in *Philosophy of Mind: Classical and Contemporary readings*, ed. David, J. Chalmers, Oxford: Oxford University Press.

Dennett, D.C., 1991, *Consciousness Explained*, Boston, MA: Little Brown.

Flanagan, Owen, 2007, *The Really Hard Problem: Meaning in a Material World*, Cambridge, MA: MIT Press.

Fodor, Jerry, 1975, *The Language of Thought*, New York: Crowell.

Hegel, 1977, *The Encyclopaedia of the Philosophical Sciences: An Outline,* tr. M.J. Petry, Dordrecht and Boston: D. Reidel Publishing Company.

Hegel, G.W.F., 1977, *Phenomenology of Spirit*, tr. A.V. Miller, Oxford: Oxford University Press.

Husserl, Edmund, 1960, *Cartesian Meditations: An Introduction to Phenomenology*, The Hague: Martinus Nijhoff.

Kant, I, 1929, *Critique of Pure Reason*, tr. N.K. Smith, London: Macmillan.

Kim, Jaegwon, 2010, *Essays in the Metaphysics of Mind*, Oxford: Oxford University Press.

Levine, J., 1983, "Materialism and Qualia: The Explanatory Gap", *Pacific Philosophical Quarterly* 64: 354-61.

McGinn, Colin, 1999, *The Mysterious Flame: Conscious Minds in a Material World*, New York: Basic Books.

Nagel, T., 1974, "What Is It Like to Be a Bat?", *Philosophical Review*, 83:435-56.

Nagel, Thomas, 2012, *Mind and Cosmos: Why the Materialist Neo-Darwinian Conception of Nature Is Almost Certainly False*, Oxford, NY: Oxford University Press.

Śaṅkara, 2002, *Eight Upanishads*, vol. I, tr. Swami Gambhirananda, Kolkata: Adviata Ashrama.

Śaṅkara, 2001, *Eight Upanishads*, vol. II, tr. Swami Gambhirananda, Kolkata: Advaita Ashrama.

Śaṅkara, 1972, *Brahmasūtrabhāṣya*, tr. Swami Gambhirananda, Calcutta: Advaita Ashrama.

Searle, J.R., 1992, *The Rediscovery of the Mind*, Cambridge, MA: MIT Press.

Tye, Michael, 1989, *The Metaphysics of Mind*, Cambridge: Cambridge University Press.

3

The Concept of Ātman in Nyāya-Vaiśeṣika

Raghunath Ghosh

Abstract: *Ātman* is admitted as one of the *prameyas* in Nyāya-Vaiśeṣika. If someone knows self, he refrains from doing some false activities which ultimately bring liberation in his life free from suffering and rebirth. It is tantamount to the attainment of salvation. In fact, there is a chain connection from suffering to the release of the same which is called *apavarga*. Normally, self is admitted as the locus of cognition or consciousness (*jñānādhikaraṇamātmā*). This self is of two types – individual self (*jīvātman*) and Supreme Self (*Paramātman*). *Paramātman* is God and one in number. *Jīvātman*, which is many in number, can be explained in the following manner. Self is the locus of the qualities like desire, aversion, motivation, pleasure, suffering and cognition. Hence, it can be said that self is an inherent cause of the qualities like pleasure and pain. Without consciousness, material objects remain inactive. If body were admitted as identical to self, self would have been destroyed after the destruction of body. After having a visual perception of an object, one remembers the taste of it and, subsequently, there is a change within mouth due to water accumulated in it. Just as a single object is seen through different windows, a single agent is to be assumed for knowing two objects, i.e. colour and taste, which is self. On the basis of another argument, it can be said that sense organs are not self. For, it is a well-known fact that after the destruction of any organ the phenomenon of recognition is possible.

Keywords: *Pravṛtti, iṣṭa-sādhanatā-jñāna, apavarga, yugapajjñāna.*

I

A QUESTION may be raised: why are our sense organ, etc. directed to the respective objects even without our intention? In the *Kenopaniṣad* such questions are asked by the disciple to his preceptor (*keneṣitaṁ patati preṣitam manaḥ*, etc.). Ultimately the preceptor gives his answer that the conscious entity called *ātman* is the impeller of sense organ, body, etc. Gautama, the founder of Nyāya philosophy, has substantiated the same opinion in his *Nyāyasūtra*.

In Gautama's list of categories, *pramāṇa* comes first, the reason of which is that through *pramāṇa* alone all objects are to be proved. If *pramāṇa* is taken as one of the categories, *prameya* is to be taken as the same. Otherwise, *pramāṇa* is to be taken as a meaningless entity. For this reason, a list of *prameya* is admitted which consists of *ātmā* (self), *śarīra* (body), *indriya* (sense organ), *artha* (object), *buddhi* (intellect), *manas* (mind), *pravṛtti* (inclination), *doṣa* (fault), *pretyabhāva* (rebirth), *phala* (fruit), *duḥkha* (pain or suffering) and *apavarga* (salvation):

> *ātmā-śarīrendriyārtha-buddhi-manaḥ-pravṛtti-doṣa-pretyabhāva-phala-duḥkhāpavargāstu prameyam* । – *Nyāyasūtra* 1.1.9

In fact, if someone knows self, he refrains from doing some false activities which ultimately brings liberation in his life free from suffering and rebirth. It is tantamount to the attainment of salvation. In fact, there is a chain connection from suffering to the release of the same which is called *apavarga*. The successive destruction of pain (*duḥkha*), birth (*janma*), activity (*pravṛtti*), fault (*doṣa*) and wrong cognition (*mithyā-jñāna*) in the reverse order gives rise to liberation or *apavarga:*

duḥkha-janma-pravṛtti-doṣa-mithyājñānāmuttarottarāpāye-tadantarāyāpāyadapavargaḥ । – *Nyāyasūtra* 1.1.2

That is, liberation (*apavarga*) is nothing but self's getting rid of the world which is possible through the removal of wrong cognition (*mithyā-jñāna*). Due to the removal of wrong cognition, his faults (*doṣas*), i.e. affection, etc. disappear. If these are not there, there will be no subject of activity (*pravṛtti*) and as a consequence he is free from rebirth and pain or suffering. In this way, he is conjoined with liberation which is taken as Supreme Good (*niḥśreyasa*). The last step for having liberation is the cognition of self. Let us see the characteristic features and importance of self as conceived by the Nyāya–Vaiśeṣika system.

Self (*ātman*) is one of the nine substances accepted by Vaiśeṣika system of philosophy and it is included in the list of six *prameyas*. Normally, self is admitted as the locus of cognition or consciousness (*jñānādhikaraṇamātmā*). This self is of two types – individual self (*jīvātman*) and Supreme Self (*Paramātman*). *Paramātman* is God and one in number. *Jīvātman*, which is many in number, can be explained in the following manner. Self is the locus of the qualities like desire, aversion, motivation, pleasure, suffering and cognition. Hence, it can be said that self is an inherent cause of the qualities like pleasure and pain. Without consciousness, material objects remain inactive. Our body being a material thing cannot act without the help of any consciousness. It is known from our ordinary experience that self is nothing but the locus of consciousness, because human body cannot do anything if it is not associated with self. When we are aware of something, we describe it as "aware of something" and hence awareness and to be conscious of anything is the same object which is possible through the existence of self.

II

The qualities like desire, etc. of an individual self (*jīva*) are not possible without the previous knowledge or recollection of an object. Self perceives an object and attains happiness or misery by having the object. When self perceives an object of similar kind, it again wants to get or avoid that for availing the same sort of pleasure and misery. This previous knowledge is nothing but an internal perception which is again the proof for the existence of self. As self cannot be perceived through our sense organs due to their subtle nature, it is inferred with the instrumentality of ear, etc. which are again inferred through the perception of sound, etc.

> *tasya saukṣmyādapratyakṣatve satikaraṇaiḥ śabdādyupalabdhy-anumitaiḥ śrotrādibhiḥ samādhigamaḥ kriyate* ।
>
> – *Praśastapādabhāṣya*, p. 167

In this context, the term *saukṣmya* (subtleness) means "the absence of capability of knowing through perception" (*pratyakṣopalabdhi-yogyatā-virahaḥ* – *Nyāyakandalī*, p. 168).

Praśastapāda had raised the view of the Pūrvapakṣin that when someone says – "I am a man", etc. this "I" or "man" indicates the body, but not self and hence there is no existence of self. The Cārvākas have endorsed this view that self and body is identical. Body is created by four elements such as earth and water. After the creation of body, there arises consciousness. So, according to Cārvākas, the body, which is united with consciousness, is called self. Praśastapāda had refuted this view of the Cārvākas in the following way. To him, if body is taken as equal to self, one cannot recollect the knowledge of childhood in his old age. Again, if body is taken as equal to self, then there should not be any change in body according to different age, because self is permanent and unchangeable. As we know, it is absurd, it is proved that self is not identical with body. Moreover, if body were admitted as identical with self, the self would have been destroyed after the destruction of body (*śarīradāhe pātakābhāvāt* – *Nyāyasūtra* 3.1.4). But, it is a well-known fact that self is not capable of being destroyed. Body which is the combination of various limbs will be destroyed if one limb is spoiled. If it is so, one cannot recollect his previous knowledge which he had attained before the destruction of the limb. Actually, it is not possible, because it is our common experience that we can recollect our previous knowledge though body is affected by the destruction of any limb. Hence, it follows that body is not self.

It is generally found that we feel inclination to what is conducive to our desired object (*iṣṭa-sādhanatā-jñāna*) and the absence of it to what is conducive to the undesired (*aniṣṭa-sādhanatā-jñāna*). If an inanimate body is self, such type of desire, aversion, etc. will not be possible. Without being guided by any conscious agent, body cannot do anything. From the movement of a chariot, for example, a charioteer is inferred. In the like manner, we have to admit a conscious agent different from body, which is nothing but self:

> *śarīra-samavāyībhyāñca hitāhitaprāpti-parihāra-yogyābhyāṁ pravr̥tti-nivr̥ttibhyāṁ rathakarmaṇā sārathivat prayatnavān vigrahasyādhiṣṭhātānumīyate* । – *Praśastapādabhāṣya*, p. 199

From the phenomenon of inclination and refraining someone having effort is inferred as existing in a body. Creeper, etc. have got inclination towards certain direction. In order to exclude such inclination, the term *śarīra-samavāyinībhyām* (inclination, etc. inhered in a body) has been inserted here. In order to exclude inclination and refraining in a dead body fallen in the current of water the term *hitāhita-prāpti-parihāra-yogyābhyām* (capability of getting happiness and of avoiding suffering (ibid., p. 200)) has been inserted as adjuncts of inclination and refraining. In this context, "a conscious effort" (*buddhi-pūrvaka-ceṣṭā* - ibid., pp. 199-200) has to be taken for availing happiness and avoiding suffering which is not found in the case of dead body fallen in water-current:

> *latādi-pravr̥tti-vyavacchedārthaṁ śarīra-samavāyibhyāmi-tyuktam śrota-patita-mr̥ta-śarīra-pravr̥tti-nivr̥tti-vyavacchedārthañca hitāhita-prāpti-parihāra-yogyābhyāmiti.* – *Nyāyakandalī*, p. 200

Volition, capable of providing happiness and removing suffering by way of accepting the means of happiness and avoiding the causes of suffering, presupposes some effort, as it is a specific action, just like action found in a chariot. An individual associated with effort must exist in a body, because it has a specific action just as chariot has got

> *sādhanopādāna-paribarjana-dvāreṇa hitāhita-prāpti-parihāra-samarthā ceṣṭā prayatna-pūrvikā viśiṣṭa-kriyātvāt rathakriyāvat* ।
> *śarīraṁ vā prayatnavadadhiṣṭhitaṁ viśiṣṭa-kriyātvāt rathavat* ।
> – *Nyāyakandalī*, p. 201

It is further said that through the activities of vital forces, an agent having effort is to be inferred:

> *prāṇādibhiśca prayatnavānadhiṣṭhātānumīyate* ।
> – *Nyāyakandalī*, p. 200

In fact, air always moves in a zigzag way, but vital airs remaining in body sometimes move upward and sometimes downward, which must be induced by something having effort called self, just as an inducer is always admitted behind the operation of a blower:

> *... prāṇādibhiśceti* । *katham? śarīra-parigṛhītevāyau vikṛta-karma-darśanād bhastrādhyāpayiteva* । – *Praśastapādabhāṣya*, pp. 199-200

Again, self can be known as differentiated from body when it is inferred as an agent of the normal twinkling and opening of the eyes in an unconscious body. Just as the existence of a conscious agent is inferred from the movement of the machine covered by wood and just as the existence of the owner of a house which is unconscious in nature is inferred through its reconstruction and repairing, self is inferred as a conscious agent of the unconscious body after observing the effort existing in the body and recovery of the strength therein. When a boy plays a ball and throws it in another corner of a room staying in some part of the room, he is described as an agent of the action, the cause for the movement of the ball:

> *... nimeṣonmeṣa-karmaṇā niyatena dāruyantra-prayokteva, dehasya buddhi-kṣata-bhagna-saṁrohaṇādi-nimittatvāt gṛhapatiriva ... gṛhakoṇeṣu pelaka-preraka iva dārakaḥ* ।
> – *Praśatapādabhāṣya*, pp. 200-202

Sometimes the twinkling and opening of the eyes of a wooden toy may be possible through passing of wind. In order to exclude this, the term *niyatena* (regularly) has been inserted in the theory. Through this, the twinkling, etc. are to be taken as actions performed out of the agent's own intention, but not through accidental passing of wind:

> *vāyuvaśenāpi dāruyantrasya nimeṣonmeṣau syātāṁ tannivr̥ttyarthaṁ niyateneti anenecchādhīnatvaṁ kathayati* । - *Nyāyakandalī*, p. 201

Hence, body is associated with someone having an effort, as it has a contact of the parts associated with twinkling and opening of the eyes caused by will, just as there is the same relationship with the wooden toy:

> *śarīraṁ prayatnavadadhiṣṭhitamicchādhīna-nimeṣonmeṣavadayava-yogitvād dāruyantravat* । - *Nyāyakandalī*, p. 201

In the same way, self is inferred as the conscious agent of the psychological action, which is the cause of the contact of the eye with a particular desired object:

> *abhimata-viṣaya-grāhaka-karaṇa-sambandha-nimittenamanaḥ-karmaṇā* । - *Praśastapādabhāṣya*, p. 202

After having a visual perception of an object, one remembers the taste of it and subsequently there is a change within mouth due to water accumulated in it. Just as a single object is seen through different windows, a single agent is to be assumed for knowing two objects, i.e. colour and taste, which is self:

> *nayanā-viṣayālocanānantaraṁ rasānusmr̥tikrameṇa rasana-vikriyā-darśanādaneka-gavākṣāntargata-prekṣakavadubhayadarśī, kaścideko vijñāyate* । - *Praśastapādabhāṣya*, p. 202

Lastly, self is inferred as a possessor of qualities like pleasure, pain, attachment, aversion and effort:

> *sukha-duḥkhecchā-dveṣa-prayatnaiśca guṇairguṇyanumīyate* । - *Praśatapādabhāṣya*, p. 202

Self is the substratum of knowledge which cannot exist in a body. As body is originated from five elements like earth, etc. it cannot be taken as a conscious object. That which is an effect of element cannot be conscious just as a jar. As body is an effect of material element, it is to be taken as unconscious:

> *yadbhūtakāryaṁ na taccetanaṁ, yathā ghaṭaḥ, bhūtakāryañca śarīram* । *tasmādetadapyacetanam* । – *Nyāyakandalī*, pp. 171-72

Moreover, it is known to us that in a dead body there is no consciousness even if the body remains unchanged. Had body been taken as self, knowledge would exist even in the dead body leading to the non-difference between a living and dead body. As it is not possible, it can be concluded that body is not the self:

> *na śarīrasya caitanyaṁghaṭādivadbhūtakāryatvāt, mr̥te cāsambhavāt* ।
> – *Praśastapādabhāṣya*, p. 171

One might argue that when it is said – "I am happy", "I feel pain", etc. – it seems that the body feels pleasure, pain, etc. But actually, body cannot be identified with self. Though axe is taken as the instrument for cutting wood, it does not have any power to cut wood without the help of any conscious agent. Without the help of consciousness, knowledge of something cannot be attained by anyone. Due to not having consciousness at the stage of deep sleep (*suṣupti*) there is a lack of knowledge. Hence, the locus of cognition is self:

> *jñānaṁ kvacidāśritaṁ kriyātvāt chidikriyāvat* । – *Nyāyakandalī*, p. 199

Similarly, without the inspiration of the conscious being an instrument cannot act in any sphere:

> *kuṭhārādīnāṁ chidādikaraṇānāṁ kartāramantareṇa phalānupadhānam dr̥ṣṭaṁ, evaṁ cakṣurādināṁ jñānakaraṇānāmapi phalopadhānaṁ kartāramantareṇa nopapādyata ityatirikta kartā kalpyate* । – *Siddhāntamuktāvalī* on v. 48

III

Self cannot be taken as identical with sense organ due to the following problems. It is found that after perceiving the colour of an object, i.e. mango, one can infer its smell and taste of the same. In the same way, one can infer some other properties existing in a mango after having the cognition of smell and taste. If sense organ is admitted as self, we can have only one type of cognition at a time due to its impossibility of having various types of cognition at a time. From this, we have to admit a conscious agent which can apprehend all types of cognition. This conscious agent must be regarded as self:

> *na cendriya-caitanye viṣaya-caitanye ca rūpamadrākṣaṁ rasamanvabhavaṁ sparśaṁ sparśāmi gandhaṁ ghrāsyāmīti rūpādi-pratyanāmekaika-rūpatva-pratipatti-sambhavaḥ, rūpādīnāṁ cakṣurādīnāñca bhedāt* । – *Nyāyakandalī*, p. 173

Again, if a sense organ is admitted as self, then we can have only perceptual cognition, but not the testimonial cognition. But in practical world, such types of cognition attained through both perception and verbal testimony are possible. For this, we have to admit a single and conscious entity by which such cognition can be attained. This conscious entity is self (*Vātsyāyanabhāṣya* on 3.1.3).

The sense organs are taken as inanimate objects just like a wooden chariot. As a wooden chariot cannot move without being guided by a conscious agent like horse, etc. our sense organs which are inanimate in character cannot act without being guided by a conscious agent, which is self. The existence of self can thus be inferred as the impeller of the sense organs. As ear, eye, etc. are not conscious by themselves, they cannot see or hear by themselves without the help of a conscious principle which is self:

> *Indriyānyacetanāni karaṇatvāddaṇḍavat* । – *Nyāyakandalī*, p. 172

On the basis of another argument, it can be said that sense organs are not self. For, it is a well-known fact that after the destruction of any organ the phenomenon of recognition is possible. A person might have a perceptual cognition of something when his visual sense organ was in order, but he can recollect the same afterwards if he loses the same organ. Had the organs like the eye and ear been regarded as conscious agents, it would have been destroyed along with the destruction of the sense organs. But it is not possible on account of the fact that the recollection of the same object is possible though organs are destroyed:

> *upahateṣu viṣaya-sānnidhye cānusmr̥ti-darśanāt* ।
> – *Praśastapādabhāṣya*, p. 172

> *vinaṣṭeṣvapīndriyayeṣu pūrvānubhūto 'rthaḥ smaryate, na cānu-bhavitari vinaṣṭe smaraṇaṁ yuktaṁ, tasmānnendriyaguṇo jñānam* ।
> – *Nyāyakandalī*, p. 173

IV

Mind cannot be equated with self, because mind is accepted as an internal sense organ acting as an instrument for the attainment of knowledge. If it is admitted as a conscious agent, there arises the possibility of simultaneous cognition (*yugapajjñāna*), which is not possible. Without being inspired by a conscious agent, an instrument cannot act and hence a conscious agent different from mind is to be accepted:

> *nāpi manasaḥ, karaṇāntarānapekṣitve yugapadālocana-smr̥ti-prasaṅgāt, svayaṁ karaṇabhāvācca* । – *Praśastapādabhāṣya*, p. 173

Mind is admitted as having atomic dimension (*aṇuparimāṇa*). Self is admitted as the locus of the qualities like desire, aversion, effort, pleasure and pain, which are the objects of perception. Something which is perceived cannot be of atomic dimension. If mind having atomic dimension were identified with self, how could it be the locus of those attributes which are, of course, not having any atomic dimension? Simply, as mind cannot be the locus of such attributes, it cannot be taken as self:

> *karaṇāntarapekṣāyāṁ tu tasyāṇutve sarvendriye-ṣusānnidhyābhāva dyugapadālocanānupattiḥ* ।
> – *Nyāyakandalī*, p. 174

By virtue of the fact that cognition is an effect of some inherent cause, it cannot exist in body, sense organ and mind, and hence cognition can be taken as an effect of self through the method of residues

> *jñānaṁ tāvat kāryyatvāt kasyacit samavāyikāraṇasya kāryyaṁ, śarīrendriyamanasāñca tadāśrayatvaṁ pratiṣiddham ... ataḥ pariśeṣādātmakāryyaṁ jñānam* ।
> – *Nyāyakandalī*, p. 175

V

From the discussions made above, the following comments can be made. First, it has been admitted by the Vaiśeṣikas that self is to be inferred as the locus of desire, aversion, etc. It should be borne in mind that such qualities are to be taken as accidental properties (*āgantuka dharma*) of consciousness, but not the permanent one. So long as consciousness is associated with the body, it can be admitted as the locus of desire, aversion, etc. Self cannot be the locus of such qualities, had there been no body.

Second, one could raise the question of whether self is eternal or not. From the fact of a newborn baby's inclination to suck mother's breast and the law of *karma*, the eternity of self can be admitted. When a newborn baby inclines to suck its mother's breast, it is the result of the memory of its previous birth about its conduciveness. In this way, the baby feels such inclination towards the desired object due to the existence of knowledge of its conduciveness in the previous birth. From this, it is inferred that there is some conscious agent (i.e. self) which is eternal in character. In the same way, it can be said that the law of *karma* would fail, leading to the fallacies like *kṛtahāna* and *akṛtābhyāgama,* had there been no locus of the record of *karma* done by an individual being. Hence, an eternal agent called self must be accepted.

Third, though the Vaiśeṣikas have given a series of inferential arguments in favour of the existence of self, it is true that self cannot act without its association with body and sense organ. But in the empirical world, it seems that we are doing everything with the help of body and sense organ as if without taking any help of self just as it seems that *ayo dahati* (i.e. iron burns), though actually the fire remaining in iron burns. In our everyday life, we use this due to certain kinds of superimposition, which is not properly understood by the materialists like Cārvākas.

Lastly, one could raise the problem which runs as follows. It is shown earlier that self is eternal. Though it exists in human body, it is not mentioned where self exists just after the destruction of our body. It is not clear to us whether self takes another body immediately after the destruction of the present one or it remains bodyless for a certain period of time. If the former, it is not mentioned how it goes to another body. Such a state of transition from one body to another is described in the *Bṛhadāraṇykopaniṣad* with the metaphor of *jalaukā* (leech), but no such discussion is found in the Vaiśeṣika texts. If the latter, it cannot be taken as a substratum of *karma* done by a particular individual for a certain period of time due to not having body. If this individual self is *jīvanmukta*, it may be merged with *Paramātman* (God).

References

Praśastapādabhāṣya with *Nyāyakandalī*, ed. Durgadhar Jha, Varanasiya Sanskrit Visvavidyalaya, Varanasi, 1963.

Siddhāntamuktāvalī, Bengali translation and elucidation by Gopal Chandra Tarkatirtha, Burdwan University, Burdwan, 1980.

Vātsyāyanabhāṣya, ed. Phanibhushan Tarkavagisha, West Bengal Book Board, Kolkata, 1989.

4

Notion of Absolute Consciousness

(Whatever is *is of* the as well as *in* the Absolute) Śankara, Kant and Hegel

Raghwendra Pratap Singh

Abstract: The intellectual expedition in the realm of consciousness is extremely complex and multifaceted. In the extensive field of philosophy, we come across consciousness as an ontological/ metaphysical being, an epistemological subject, a moral agent, an aesthetic being, a psychological being in psychiatry, psychoanalysis, Yoga and so forth. It has moved the philosophical insight so persistently that the combined study of the East and the West has not solved the problem of consciousness. Socrates, who shifted philosophic problems from physics to ethics, expressed it in the form of a command "Know Thyself" at Delphi, and the ancient Hindu saints, sages and seers expressed the problem in the form of a forceful interrogation *ko 'haṁ*? Obviously, there is deep philosophical unrest, anxiety and apprehension concerning consciousness.

In this paper, I will try to expound and examine the nature and status of the notion of Absolute Consciousness in the intellectual traditions of the East and the West specifically in the Advaita Vedānta of Śaṅkara and the absolute idealism of G.W.F. Hegel. One of the fundamental reasons for comparing Śaṅkara with Hegel is that both are philosophers of One Thought besides the fact that Hegel was fully aware of the Hindu religion and the Advaita Vedānta of Śaṅkara. In my attempt to defend the Advaita Vedāntin position and thereby to supplement Hegel's Absolute, I would like to present some clarifications, annotations and summations which may be useful for the limited end of an acquaintance with the Absolute in Śaṅkara on the one hand and that of Hegel on the other. In order to organize my discussion, I wish to divide my paper into two parts: in Part I, I will analyse the nature and status of the Absolute in Advaita Vedānta and give a brief comparison between Śaṅkara and Kant on consciousness; in Part II, I will discuss Hegel's notion of the Absolute and its dialectical appreciation by the thinking consciousness. Herein I will bring Kant's transcendental consciousness and the distinction between reason, understanding and sensibility. I will also give a short comparison between Śaṅkara and Hegel on the notion of the Absolute.

I will propose a dialectical dialogue between Śaṅkara, Kant and Hegel. However, I am proposing a dialectical dialogue, which will not simply be dia-logued but multi-logued in order to appreciate the plurality of ethnic identity, cultural identity, linguistic identity, etc. Dialectical dialogue could further be used as a method to facilitate a dialogue between persons, identities, ethnicities, communities, cultures and civilizations. The subject matter for such a dialogue will centre on the notion of Absolute between two cultural contexts, i.e. the East and the West. This comparison does not only imply detecting similarity and distinction, and cataloguing the resemblances between Śaṅkara and Hegel, but also paving the way for the arguments of one philosopher to pass into those of the other and thus helping the growth of the philosophical heritage.

Keywords: Monism, dualism, pluralism, dialectical dialogue, multi-logued, culture.

Part I

Nature and Status of the Absolute in Advaita Vedānta Comparison between Śaṅkara and Kant on Consciousness

ŚAṄKARA was a philosopher of One Thought and the same could be the claims of the Vedāntins like Rāmānuja and some others too. If I could bring, by way of illustrations only, two thinkers from the West, they are Hegel and Heidegger who have been regarded as philosophers of One Thought, i.e. Spirit (*Geist*) and Being respectively. Therefore, the first thing is that Śaṅkara is a philosopher of One Thought, i.e. Brahmavādī. I would like to explain the term *Brahman* before I go to elaborate the issues in and around it. The term *Brahman* has been derived from the root word *bṛh*, which means "to grow". It means that wherever we have growth or development, we have *Brahman.* There are several examples like *annam brahma*, *śabdam brahma* and *rasam brahma.* Wherever there is orderliness, purposiveness, motion or creation of some specific form, there is the hidden presence of *Brahman.* The awareness of the growth and the purposiveness, etc. involves the existence of a conscious being (*ātman*). Growth and the awareness of the growth cannot be separated. Hence, *ātman* and *Brahman* are in perpetual unity. This has been the prime concern of Śaṅkara. I may go against the often-repeated contention that Śaṅkara was a Māyāvādī. I would argue that the central doctrine of Śaṅkara is *Brahman* and *ātman. Māyā* and *advidyā* come only in the course of philosophical investigation that Śaṅkara undertakes.

Śaṅkara has certainly been inspired by Gauḍapāda, his *parama guru*, and the traditional method invoked by him. Śaṅkara makes use of that method. The method is known as *adhyāropa* (projection) and *apavāda* (refutation).[1] This is known to Vedāntins even before Gauḍapāda. Maṇḍana Miśra in his *Naiṣkarmyasiddhi* has referred

---

[1] *adhyāropapavādabhyāmniṣprapañcam prapañcyate* । – Śaṅkara 1970: 1. Also I am grateful to R. Balasubramanian's lectures on Advaita Vedānta on 26 May 2000 at India International Centre organized by Centre for Studies in Civilizations.

to this method. *Adhyāropa* is the natural propensity of man to formulate a view of that which is observed. It precedes observation, because observation is not possible without *adhyāropa*. Śaṅkara calls it by the name of *adhyāsa* and explains it in terms of being natural, beginningless and firmly established in common sense. What is Śaṅkara's prime interest in philosophy? Though Śaṅkara is a Brahmavādī, he is primarily interested in *jīva*, its existential problems and of the worldly life (*lokavyavahāra*). It is to find out what human being is, what he thinks and experiences as an agent of action involved in the day-to-day life and activity. Therefore, Śaṅkara looks at the Vedānta text in order to identify the causes of human problems and to make the way out to resolve human problems. Unlike other Vedāntins who started their thought with the interpretation of first *sūtra*, i.e. *athāto brahmajijñāsā*, Śaṅkara does not go to this *sūtra* to start with. He begins with an introduction to the *sūtra* and his introduction is known as *adhyāsa-vākya*. To understand Śaṅkara's Advaita is to understand the problem of *adhyāsa*. *Adhyāsa* provides a foundation to Śaṅkara's *Sūtrabhāṣya*, *Upaniṣadbhāṣya* and *Gītābhāṣya*.

How does Śaṅkara begin with the doctrine of *adhyāsa*? The theory of *adhyāsa* begins with day-to-day life and experience, a kind of naiveté of outlooks containing certain elements of truths and untruths. This is a kind of power of discrimination. Every proposition contains a truth content and a falsity content. So it is natural for every seeker of truth to undertake the work with critical evaluation. When he finds a view which contains more untruths than truth, he rejects it and accepts another view, which has a greater degree of truth than the previous one. This rejection is known as *apavāda*, which literally means discordant view and that it does not accord with the reality any more. Advaita Vedānta maintains that there are views, which accord with the reality more adequately than others. Śaṅkara, for example, prefers Sāṁkhya to Vaiśeṣika and some of his later followers prefer Śāktism to Śaivism.

Since Śaṅkara's prime concern is to understand *ātman* and its relation to *Brahman*, let us dwell on this issue. Let us take chapter VI of the *Chāndogya Upaniṣad*, which discusses the most basic problems of Śaṅkara's metaphysics – the problem of *Brahman* and that of *ātman* – which is the widest, the deepest and the most fundamental problem. All other problems can be derived from this basic problem. We have a dialogue between Sage Uddālaka and his son Śvetaketu. The Upaniṣad conceives the problem systematically. It makes a promissory statement and it is followed by certain examples drawn from the empirical life and then it formulates the grand thesis. Śvetaketu returns home after having a formal education for nearly about twenty-one years. Then his father Uddālaka puts this question to Śvetaketu – Have you known that after knowing which everything else is known? This is traditionally known as "from the knowledge of one to the knowledge of all", *ekavijñanatu sarvavijñāna.* This is the promissory statement that the Upaniṣad gives to us through the teacher Uddālaka. Śvetaketu says that he does not know that. He even goes to the extent of saying that perhaps his teacher did not know, because if he had known, he would have definitely told him (Śvetaketu). Then the illustrations are given from *empirical life.* Even the *Brahmasūtra* begins with this. It begins with the need for an enquiry and it goes into causes of the world. So, there is an empirical example. The person, who knows clay, knows that everything is made of clay, is known to him, because clay is the *upādāna kāraṇa* (material cause). The forms may change, the names may change, but what remains in all the objects made of clay is the clayness. All the modifications have certain names, certain forms, but in all these cases what is real is the cause. Then a grand thesis is formulated that the supreme reality that is the cause of the world is ONE – *ekamevādvitīyam.* For Śaṅkara, it is enough to build up a metaphysical system out of this *grand thesis.* Śaṅkara's Advaita can be identified by four doctrines – there is the theory of *Nirguṇa-Brahman,* there is the theory of *vivarta,* there is the theory of *anirvacanīya khyāti* and finally there is the doctrine of *jīvan mukti.* One can go from the first to the second, from both to the third and finally to the fourth. There is consistency in Śaṅkara's writings. There is coherence and comprehensiveness in Śaṅkara's Advaita. Śaṅkara begins his philosophy with the inquiry into the *pramāṇas*, *pramāṇa-vicāra* to establish the metaphysical system. Śaṅkara says that existence and non-existence of a thing can only be established by means of *pramāṇa.* How do we know that something exists here or that something does not exist here? We know it only through *pramāṇa.* Śaṅkara starts with the world given in day-to-day life. To start with, Śaṅkara does not talk of the illusoriness of the world. In the *sūtras*, Śaṅkara asks how do we decide that something is and something is not. If the world is proved by all the *pramāṇas*, we cannot say that it does not exist. But there is a *pramāṇa-vyavasthā*, every *pramāṇa* operates in a particular area, it has its own subject matter. What one *pramāṇa* comprehends, another *pramāṇa* cannot, just as what one sense organ comprehends another sense organ cannot. On the basis of *pramāṇa-vyavasthā*, Śaṅkara repeatedly points out in his writings that there is absolutely no conflict between a scripture on the one hand and other *pramāṇas* on the other. If *pratyakṣa* has validity so far as empirical world is concerned, scripture has validity to what is transcendental. Śaṅkara says that an object which has got certain quality (*guṇa*), generic feature (*jāti*) is involved in action (*karma*), has some kind of relation with something else (*sambandha*) or which has name and form (*nāma–rūpa*). That is all about empirical world. There is a complete breakdown of language in the case of supreme reality because it does not have *jāti, guṇa,* etc. It does not even have a name. These are simply the contextual forms that are required to convey what ordinarily cannot be conveyed. The *Śārīrakabhāṣya* says that wherever there is orderliness, purposiveness, motion or creation of some specific form, there is hidden presence of *Brahman.* This can be explained only by *śruti,* other *pramāṇas* cannot explain it.

The first condition for objective knowledge, according to Śaṅkara, is:

a. that an object should possess a generic unity with specific differences –

evam hi tat jñānambhavatiyadanyebhyonirdha item
– Mukherjee 1943: 154 (comm. on *TaitUp* II.1)

An object can be known only when it is differentiated from things other than itself.

We can identify an object only under the conditions in which we can differentiate the object from the rest of the objects. We can know a table, its size, its colour, etc. only if we distinguish it from the rest of the things.

yadā hi tadaviśeṣaṇasyārthavattvam । – Ibid.: 154-55

The category of substance-attribute, therefore, implies for its application a plurality of things that should at the same time belong to the same genus.

b. The characteristics of an object, such as generic unity, specific qualities and actions, it is urged elsewhere, are the conditions of intelligible discourse:

tat anyasamaiupadestumsakyam jāti-guṇa-kriyā-viśeṣaṇaiḥ ।
– Comm. on *KenUp* I.3

Śaṅkara has also said:

Every word employed to denote a thing can do so only insofar as it is associated with certain *genus*, or a certain *act*, or a certain quality, or a certain mode of *relation*. The cow and horse imply genera, teacher and cook imply acts, white and black imply qualities, wealthy and cattle-owner imply possession.
– Comm. on *Gītā* XIII.12; Mukherjee 1943: 155

In this case, if one thing is distinguished by the other and therefore it is necessarily limited by the other, it must be remembered that both must belong to one class, they must be *ekajātiyāni*, as Śaṅkara puts it. This is true for Śaṅkara as it is true for Descartes. The Cartesian distinction between the *cogito* and the unthought, though distinct as far as their attributes are concerned, yet somehow they are conceived under the common concept of "substance". Even Immanuel Kant could also formulate it in the form of judgement, under relation, specifically in the disjunctive relation – "Earth exists either through a blind chance, or through an inner necessity, or through an external cause". These three possibilities mutually exclude each other but jointly somehow they give us complete knowledge. It is the category of "community", which is operative here. Apart from this community, they could not be defined in antithetical and mutually conflicting terms. Vācaspati Miśra has very clearly explained that all differences and conflicts would be impossible if there had been differences at their foundation. The judgement "intellect is non-eternal", for instance, cannot conflict with the judgement, "the soul is eternal" (*na cābhinnasrayaviruddhaḥ* । – Mukherjee 1943: 156; Shastri 1933: 821). Hence, conflicts can neither be foundationless (*anāśraya*) nor can they exist when there is difference at the very basis of the conflicting ideas or judgements (*bhinnāśraya*). This requires an elaborate analysis of the nature and status of consciousness. Let me begin with consciousness.

The doctrine of consciousness has been discussed by the Upaniṣadic seers, not only in the *Māṇḍūkya Upaniṣad* but also in the *Bṛhadāraṇyaka Upaniṣad*, in the famous dialogue between Yājñavalkya and King Janaka. There is also an in-depth study of consciousness in the commentaries by Gauḍapāda, Śaṅkara and others, down to Vivekananda and Sri Aurobindo. The discussion that we come across in the *Māṇḍūkya Upaniṣad* is very much complemented by all succeeding works of the kind. Here, I will be basically concerned with Śaṅkara's analysis of consciousness. For Śaṅkara, to get into the problem of consciousness is to begin with the three states of consciousness – the *avasthātraya* – in the Vedāntic tradition. Whenever we come across the problem of consciousness, we not only have a reference to human being alone but also to *Brahman* which is *sat, cit* and *ānanda* – particularly the *citsvarūpa* of *Brahman*.

To being with the consciousness of the human being, we have to begin with the human body, i.e. the vital force, the senses, the *antaḥkaraṇa* – the internal organ, popularly known as mind, endowed with *buddhi,* of intellect, with *ahaṁkāra* – the "I". Deeper than *ahaṁkāra,* the Vedāntins have an entity, i.e. consciousness, *cit, caitanya, saṁvṛta* or the self. In the German idealist tradition, there is no such distinction between the ego, mind, spirit, self or consciousness. These terms have similar meanings. However, Husserl has drawn a distinction between ego, *cogito* and *cogiteta.* These are tripartite stages involved in Husserl's phenomenology – descriptive stage, transcendental stage and egological stage. In the descriptive stage, issues are raised, everything around us is an object of consciousness. It is because of consciousness that we are aware of the objects or ideas and so on. What is so fundamental at this stage is that a distinction has been drawn between consciousness and the objects of consciousness. Husserl assigns several functions to consciousness such as consciousness objectivates, identifies, supplements and unifies. Husserl has made a distinction between pure ego and empirical ego, between transcendental ego and the psychological ego. But there remains a fundamental difficulty, i.e. the distinction between consciousness, ego, mind, etc. has not been clearly defined in the German idealism including Husserl's phenomenology. But this problem no longer exists in Vedānta. The functions that Husserl assigns to consciousness like objectifying and unifying are all the functions of *antaḥkaraṇa* under the witnessing act of consciousness in the Vedānta tradition. The *antaḥkaraṇa* is a material and it requires the witnessing act of spiritual force, i.e. consciousness. The sense organs can work properly under the close relationship with the *antaḥkaraṇa*, which in turn has to be guided by the consciousness. In his commentary on the *Brahmasūtra,* Śaṅkara refers to the I/Thou problem in the *adhyāsabhāsa,* i.e. *asmat/yuṣmat* problem, *asmat* is the self and *yuṣmat* is other than the self in which comes the mind, senses, body and things of the world. Any claim regarding affirmation or negation made for anything in the world presupposes evidence provided by the consciousness by means of the *pramāṇa*. Not only that even the ultimate presupposition of all *pramāṇas* – perception, inference, verbal testimony, is provided by consciousness. Given the consciousness, all *pramāṇas* operate, absence of consciousness, no *pramāṇas* can operate.

To understand *antaḥkaraṇa*, we have to go into the details of the three stages of consciousness – *jāgrat, svapna* and *suṣupti.* Related with these three stages of consciousness, there is the problem of *intentionality* and self-consciousness. One of the Vedāntins, Rāmānuja, for instance, regards these three states as double intentional: on the one hand, it is intentional towards the subject; on the other, it is intentional towards the objects. But the other Vedāntins including Śaṅkara believe that consciousness by its nature is not intentional, but it becomes intentional because of its association with the mind. In the *Māṇḍūkya Upaniṣad*, at waking state, consciousness is intentional; it is in relation to several objects and their mechanisms and operations. These objects in their properties and relationships act on our senses and the mind. Thus, our consciousness becomes aware of the things. What is true of waking level is equally true at the dream level because in dream experience, consciousness encounters the objects. The *Māṇḍūkya Upaniṣad* brings the association of consciousness with the mind, senses, body and things at the waking level; and the association of consciousness at the two levels, i.e. waking and the dreaming states. This also involves the knowledge situation, i.e. the *tripuṭī-jñāna* – the subject, the object and the means of knowledge. At waking level, there is knowledge-situation *prajñā*, which is outward, but at the dream level, the similar knowledge-situation is there but not the same knowledge-situation. Consciousness at waking level is called *viśva,* at dream level it is called *taijasa* and at deep-sleep level or *suṣupti* it is called *prajñā.* These are three different terms used for consciousness depending on its three involvements. At the level of deep sleep, we are not aware of the objects of the outside world, or anything internal, because mind as mind is not functioning at this level. At this level, we do not have a knowledge-situation, we are free from all desires is what the fifth *mantra* of the *Māṇḍūkya Upaniṣad* declares. Consciousness is uniformly present in all the three stages of experience. The body and the senses are present at the waking level, but these are absent at the dream level, even the mind is absent at the deep-sleep level, but consciousness is present at all the three levels of experience. Consciousness is the witness of all the three episodes. But consciousness as such cannot be known under the knowledge-situation just as tongue cannot taste itself. This is the fourth state, the nameless, i.e. *turīya*. It is the state where consciousness is left to itself, trans-empirical, trans-rational, trans-linguistic. At the most, we can describe it negatively. There is no other than anything outside, no other than anything inside, is the way that *turīya* state is described in the seventh *mantra* of the *Māṇḍūkya Upaniṣad*. Then the question arises: how does *turīya* state differ from the *suṣupti* state? *Turīya* state could be a mystical state, through meditation, etc. which if one has it, one has it, one does not have it, one does not have it. It is *adṛṣṭam*, *avyavahāryam*, *agrāhyam*, *alakṣaṇam*, *acintam*, *śāntam*, *śivam*, *advaitam*, etc. It is at this stage that *ātman* is to be entirely identified with *Brahman*. In other words, if I am the *ātman* and the *ātman* is the Absolute, then it follows syllogistically, that I am the Absolute. I am *Brahman*: *aham brahmāsmi*.

So far as the knowledge of self is concerned, there is an astonishing similarity between Śaṅkara and Kant. Kant has criticized Aristotle's formulation of categories like this: "he simply picked them up as they came in his way". Kant gives a systematic formulation of the categories. The common structure of consciousness, Kant designates as "transcendental unity of self-consciousness" (Kant 1973: A97). It consists of "forms of intuition" (space and time) and "forms of understanding" (the categories), which are not static forms but forms of operation that exist only in the act of apprehending and comprehending sensibility. The "forms of intuition" synthesize the manifold of sensibility into spatio-temporal order and by virtue of the categories, they are brought to universal and necessary relations of cause and effect, substance, reciprocity and so on – "receptivity is thus combined with spontaneity" (Kant 1973: A97, p. 130). This entire complex is unified in the transcendental apperception, which relates all experience to the "thinking ego" (Kant 1973: 143). This is what Kant calls as beginningless, transcendental, original, synthetic unity of apperception. In the synthetic unity of apperception, according to Kant, I am conscious of myself not as I appear to myself, not as I am in myself, but only that I am. The "I think" must be, Kant insists, capable of accompanying all my presentations. But the "I think" always remains unknown and unknowable by means of the categories because it cannot as such be given in representation. If we try to apply the categories to the "I think", such categories as "substance", "existence", "person", etc. we come across a series of paralogisms (ibid.: 327).

This view of the self, developed by Kant, is very close to the Advaitic doctrine of *ātman* developed by Śaṅkara. Kant has worked on the same position which had inspired Śaṅkara from the Upaniṣads "How can you know that which is the knower of everything". The categories of understanding can be applied to objects given in sensible intuitions. Generic unity, specific difference, act, quality, relation, etc. are supposed by Śaṅkara to be the ultimate conditions of knowledge. To these, he sometimes adds space, time, causality and non-contradiction (*deśa-kāla-nimitta-sampattiravadhaśca – Śāṅkarabhāṣya* III.2-3). Śaṅkara emphasizes that the categories are not applicable to the witnessing self. It was for the first time in European philosophy that a view of the self approximating to the Advaitic doctrine of the self was so clearly formulated. It goes to the credit of Kant to have conceived so clearly that the self is not to be identified with the individual self involved in the subject–object dualism, the self is the universal principle of the consciousness or thought which is the pure or the transcendental subject as distinguished from the empirical subject and that this subject cannot itself be known as an object of knowledge. Here, the Kantian doctrine of self looks like Upaniṣadic view expressed in the words "How can you know that which is the knower of everything". The self cannot be dislodged from its pivotal position as a knower. It can never be shifted from the centre to the periphery, because in every attempt to do so, we shall be compelled to put it back again into the centre under the force of logical necessity. The upshot is that it will remain there in the centre and it can never be the knower and the known simultaneously. That which we must presuppose as the precondition of all knowledge cannot itself become an object of knowledge. This is as much true for Śaṅkara as it is with Kant. The basic purpose of Kant's critical philosophy is to present an effective solution to Hume's scepticism. The first *Critique* with the transcendental deduction of categories tries to "justify the claims of science philosophically" or "to provide a philosophical basis for physical science". As opposed to this, the primary motive of Śaṅkara's philosophy is to emphasize the self-shining character of the pure *cit* and consequently placing it far beyond the ambit of inference and reasoning. Kant appears to be more interested in the organization of the experience than in the agency that organizes it. But Śaṅkara shows much more interest in the revelatory consciousness than in the objects that are revealed.

Part II

Hegel's Notion of the Absolute and Dialectics Critique of Kant's Transcendental Consciousness: Reformulation of Reason, Understanding and Sensibility

In the Preface to the *Phenomenology of Spirit*, Hegel has this to say:

> The True is the whole. But the whole is nothing other than the essence consummating itself through its development. Of the absolute it must be said that it is essentially a result, that only in the end is it what it truly is; and that precisely in this consists its nature, viz. to be actual subject, the spontaneous becoming of itself. – 1973: 11

And in his *Lectures on the Philosophy of Religion,* Hegel adds:

> Philosophy is itself, in fact, worship (*Die philosophieist der selbst*

> *Gottesdienst*); it is religion, for in the same way it renounces subjective notions and opinions in order to occupy itself with God. ... The object of religion as well as of philosophy is eternal truth in its objectivity, God and nothing but God and the explication of God. ... In philosophy; religion gets justification from thinking consciousness. – 1895, vol. III: 353

This position of Hegel is in sharp reaction to what Kant has to say in the Preface to the First Edition of *Critique of Pure Reason*:

> Human reason has this peculiar fate that in one species of its knowledge it is burdened by questions which, as prescribed by the very nature of reason itself, it is not able to ignore, but which, as transcending all its powers, it is also not able to answer. – 1973: 7

The central claim of Hegel's philosophy as against Kant is that we cannot speak of the Absolute without at the same time speaking of self-consciousness of human mind, nor fruitfully pursue that interrogation itself unless we conceive our activity in doing so as one sustained and made possible by the Absolute. This is perhaps the best part of Hegel's philosophy responsible for the origin and sustenance of the Absolute Spirit and its epistemological justification by the subjective spirit or the thinking consciousness. At the same time, there is no part of Hegel's philosophy except this, which the post-Hegelians, including the present-day postmodern and critical theory Hegel scholars, are less willing to accept on its own terms.

Hegel's spirit is, above all, a doctrine about the relationship between thought and objective reality. Hegel means by speaking Spirit the mediation or middle point between the idea (the categories and the notion which are also known as the truth in the most absolute and objective form) and nature (the sphere of external existence which the truth is "about"). By the term "idea" Hegel designates to the absolute truth. Nature is the term, which Hegel gives to that truth as we find it in the outward existence of the world. Spirit, however, is the mode of existence of the whole in which everything, which is known, is embodied in being. Idea and nature are dialectical opposites, but spirit is the unity between them. Hegel's contention is that there is something, which is identical neither with the sphere of our thought nor with the objects of our thought. It is the *Geist* that imparts an intelligible form of both these spheres. Spirit is the active synthesis of our consciousness of the world and what we are conscious of. This is Hegel's epistemological quest too. In epistemology, then, we are concerned with the object which we have with our consciousness of it. But this is of such a nature that the distinction between what exists *for us* and what exists *in itself* is not a distinction between what is available to us in consciousness and what is not. Both sides of distinction fall within the grasp of consciousness. In other words, the Kantian distinction between phenomena and thing-in-itself is not acceptable to Hegel. The basic question, for Hegel, is how in consciousness we are related to our objects, and when our object is our own consciousness, it is clear that there is no danger that our consciousness should have an existence *in itself* which is in principle hidden from us and separates from that consciousness as it exists *for us.*

In formulating his own position, Hegel applauds Kant's discovery of the "transcendental consciousness" as the ultimate source of conceptual synthesis. He approves Kant's criticism that consciousness cannot be an object of sensibility and hence categories cannot be applied to it. But this is not, Hegel contends, because categories overstep their legitimate limits, but because soul is a living and active being, just as complex as it is self identically simple. In fact, its simplicity is just as an indivisible whole that is constituted solely by the cohesion and inseparability of its diverse traits, aspects and activities. Kant's objections, according to Hegel, are valid but his reasons are wrong ones.

Hegel elucidates two aspects of spirit: first that spirit requires the distinction of subject and object, and second that spirit overcomes the supposed distinction between subject and object. The first is the moment of estrangement and the second is its transcendence or enlargement. Spirit is, thus, the locus of both estrangement and enlargement.

Hegel takes over the doctrine from Kant that consciousness is necessarily bipolar and it is part of Hegel's general espousal of the view that

> ... rational awareness requires separation. Consciousness is only possible when the subject is set over against an object.
>
> – Taylor 1979: 26

First of all, we should recall that Hegel's *Encyclopedia of the Philosophical Sciences*, his most general presentation of the philosophic system, is divided into three parts:

I. *Logic*: The science of the idea in and for itself.

II. *The Philosophy of Nature*: The science of the idea in its otherness.

III. *The Philosophy of Spirit*: The science of the idea comes back to itself out of that otherness (Hegel 1977: section 18).

Since the philosophy of spirit is followed by logic and the philosophy of nature, the philosophy of spirit is concerned to show *that* and *how* spirit "frees itself from nature, from its otherness". All three moments of this "movement" – anthropology, phenomenology and psychology – are concerned with this "notion of freeing itself" (Hegel 1977: 91), but only the moment of psychology shows the *reality* of reason: the anthropological moment of subjective spirit shows reason to be the goal of nature, and the phenomenological moment shows reason to be the goal of consciousness. But the goal of the psychological investigation of spirit is to show that reason is the element of subjective spirit, that reason is the active power of spirit. To develop Hegel's psychological investigation of spirit, we have to discuss three sources of knowledge–sense certainty, understanding and reason along with dialectic – with its features of contradiction and sublation operating in it.

The opening arguments of the *Phenomenology of Spirit* are good illustrations of the procedure Hegel adopts. The notion of spirit with which Hegel begins is our ordinary consciousness of things and from there he takes us to the true perspective of spirit. The work is called "phenomenology" because it deals with the way things appear for consciousness, or with the forms of consciousness. But "appearance" here is not to be contrasted with "reality" – which is most real, the absolute, is essentially self-appearance. Phenomenology is not a science of lesser things, which can be left behind but one way of ascending to absolute knowledge of making the absolute apparent.

The method Hegel adopts to appreciate the Absolute Truth is to start with "ordinary consciousness" of things and does not introduce at this moment anything from the activity of mind whatsoever. From this ordinary experience of things, Hegel proceeds through the stage of "understanding" and finally comes to "reason", which is no longer a prey to contradiction and holds it reconciled within itself.

Hegel accepts and further develops the distinction manifested in Kant's philosophy between "understanding" and "reason". In Kant, "reason" is never in immediate relation to an object. It is "understanding", that holds sway in his epistemology. By "understanding", Hegel means, the capacity of reflective interpretation, a capacity which unrelentingly separates identity from difference, particular from universal, one from many, form from content and so on, and allows neither to contaminate the other. The "understanding", however, restricts itself to the finite, and its thinking is always finite thinking. Hegel often calls it "finite reason". Hegel also uses the expression "isolated reflection" to the numberless polarities, which emerges out of the operation of "understanding". The distinction and precise determination of things in terms of identity and difference, characteristic of "understanding", depends upon negation. A thing is what it is just because and so far as it is not another thing. What it determines is what it excludes, and what it excludes defines what it is.

For Hegel, that which is negated issues itself in a result, brings with itself and carries in itself that from which it has emerged, "sublated and preserved within it; although it is also cancelled in its original finite formulation". This state is higher than the original finite one and it holds within itself both the finite and its negation. The result is thus more concrete, more complete and comprehensive than the first abstract, finite and limited one. Hegel here brings "reason" to unify that which the "understanding" has divided. "Reason" shows that the function of "understanding" – to define things in terms of their isolation–constitutes a process of abstraction. The function of "reason" is to make manifest the "concrete" relation in which an idea, concept or thing subsists. In the process of unifying the opposites, "reason" negates the finite and its negation and binds them together in mutual dependence so that they are revealed as moments of more inclusive whole. This wholeness in which the antagonisms are resolved, Hegel terms "the Absolute", "the Truth" of which I have mentioned at the beginning of the paper. The mutual exclusion of finite and its negative are complimentary so that they are revealed as moments of a more inclusive whole. The whole, which is thus achieved, is rational through and through, because it is systematically ordered.

With this interpretation of sense-certainty, understanding and reason, Hegel gives strikingly new interpretation of logic. Novelty consists in Hegel's attempt to incorporate dialectic into logic. It requires two lines of argument: the first showing that a given category is indispensable; the second showing that it leads us to a characterization of reality, which is somehow contradictory. Hegel, in fact, fuses these together. This makes Hegel's logic fundamentally different from Kantian–Aristotelian tradition. The categories, in Kant's formulation, are valid if they were correctly formed and if their use was in conformity with the laws of thought and the rules of syllogism – no matter what the content to which they were applied.

Contrary to this procedure, Hegel's *logic* and with it his dialectic are always dynamic and express dynamics of objective reality as well.

The negative or contradictory character of the categories basically motivates Hegel's dialectic. As stated, Hegel's categories denote and deal with the reality, so the dialectical operation in reality is basically the dialectic operating in the formulation of the categories. There are two terms, which are operative in Hegel's dialectic. These are: (i) contradiction, and (ii) sublation or *aufheben*. In fact, these are not two separate terms but are mutually interdependent and under certain circumstances they pass into each other. Let me first explain Hegel's position on contradiction. In the *Science of Logic*, Hegel emphasizes by saying:

> ... everything is inherently contradictory and in the sense that this law in contrast to other expresses rather the truth and the essential nature of things. It is one of the fundamental prejudices of logic as hitherto understood and of ordinary thinking, that contradiction is not so characteristically essential and immanent a determination as identity. Nevertheless, if it were a question of grading the two determinations and they had to be kept separate, then contradiction would have to be taken as the profounder determination and more characteristic of essence. For, as against contradiction, identity is merely the determination of the simple immediate, of dead being; but contradiction is the root of all movement and vitality; it is only insofar as something has a contradiction within it that it moves, has an urge and activity.
>
> – Hegel 1909: 439

Contradiction, for Hegel, is internal to each term. That is why every term, whether a concept or a reality, develops. Hegel continues,

> ... internal self-movement proper, instinctive urge in general ... is nothing else but the fact that something is, in one and the same respect, self-contained and deficient, the negative of itself. Abstract self-identity is not as yet a livingness, but the positive, being in its own self a negativity, goes outside itself and undergoes alteration. Something is therefore alive only insofar as it contains

> contradiction within it and moreover is this power to hold and endure the contradiction within it. – Ibid.: 439-40

Hegel concludes near the end of the *Logic* that there is nothing, whether in actuality or in thought that is as simple and abstract as is commonly imagined.

> Nothing exists as just brutally given and simply possessing one or two fully positive characteristics. Nothing exists that is just first and primary and on which other things depend, but they cannot really succeed in doing so unless they stay on the level of imaginative pictures. Imagining that such things exist is possible only as long as we are ignorant of what is actually present. What appears at first simple and immediate is actually complex and mediated. – Kolb 1986: 46

Mediation (*vermittlung*) and mediated (*vermittlet*), and the opposites, immediacy (*unvermittlung*) and immediate (*unvermittelt*) are key terms through which Hegel explains not only contradiction but also sublation and dialectic. Let me clarify these terms.

To "mediate" is to be in the middle, to connect two extremes. Everything, Hegel states, is mediated that nothing exists as "immediate" first. In the *Logic*, "mediation" will involve the gradual development of categories to a point where there is nothing that is posited as first and independent. In Hegel's dialectic, the thesis is always regarded as "immediate" or as characterized by "immediacy'. The second term, the anti-thesis, is "mediate" or "mediation'. The third term, the synthesis, is the merging of "mediation" and emerging as a new "immediacy'. And this process goes on.

The synthesis of a triad both abolishes and preserves the differences of the thesis and the anti-thesis. Hegel expresses this activity of the synthesis as *aufheben* (sublation), which is the other operative term of Hegel's dialectic. It may be seen as manifesting three distinct but mutually interrelated moments.

> First, it has the moment of "transcendence", in which it goes beyond a "limit" or "boundary"; second, it is "negation" of this first negation, this "limit", in which it is overcome or removed; and third, it is the moment of "preservation", in which what has been "gone beyond" or transcended is brought again into a new relation.
> – George 1984: 123

These three moments of sublation, though distinct, form a unitary process of *Logic,* which is differentiated into its various components only for the purpose of helping as "understanding" of the process itself. The very process by which a category is formulated and is intimately related to another is, at one and the same logical moment, the process by which it transcends its limited abstract self-identity, "negates" that identity and emerges into a connected unity or nexus, in which it is preserved as an intrinsic part of some greater whole. The differences between the first and the second member of each triad are sublated by the third. This, however, requires sufficient explanation and necessary substantiation. For this purpose, I shall take up the categories of Being, Nothing and Becoming, and bring out the various ways in which dialectic is operating in the formulation of the categories of Being and Nothing, and their sublation in the category of Becoming. Herein operate two fundamental principles of Hegel's dialectic, viz. *unity and struggle of opposites* and *negation of negation.* The same process is applicable to the rest of the Hegelian categories.

As a matter of fact, the more general and more abstract concept is always prior to the less general and less abstract. And this principle not only decides for Hegel that the first category is being, but also determines the order of the subsequent categories. Moreover, every logical deduction is essentially based on the principle that the subsequent must be contained in the antecedent. The breach of this principle of formal logic is what is called the fallacy of *illicit* process. There cannot be anything present in the conclusion, which is not present in the premises. This is really the old principle *ex nihilo nihil fit*. I will try to show that this is just as true of the Hegelian logic as of the humble formal logic. The exclusion is not absolute, what is absolute is the mutual supplementation. The result of the supplementation is a growth, a development. This is a principle of Hegel's dialectic known as "*the negation of negation*". Just as Being is implicitly Becoming, so Becoming is implicitly the next synthesis. In the next synthesis, we find that Becoming expresses itself in the moment of a "determinate being", which is further expressed as below:

i. As determinateness, such as quality.
ii. As determinateness transcended: quantity.
iii. As quantity qualitatively determined: measure.

Quality, for Hegel, is the internal self-determination, which is identical with the being, which it determines. Quantity is a determination, which is external to what it determines. The combination of quality and quantity is found in what Hegel calls as measure. Quality, when fully developed through repulsion and attraction, passes into quantity and vice versa. Hegel calls this unity as measure. It is the synthesis of the spheres of quality and quantity as the thesis and the antithesis respectively. With this synthesis, we arrive at another principle of Hegel's dialectic known as "the transition from quantitative changes to qualitative changes and vice versa".

We have so far explicated three laws of Hegel's dialectic, viz.:

i. unity and struggle of opposites,
ii. negation of the negation, and
iii. transition from quality to quantity, and vice versa.

These three laws of dialectic are operating not only in the whole process of Hegel's deduction of categories, but also in the appreciation of the Absolute.

If, therefore, we understand by Hegel's dialectic as a gradual explication and development of the "connectedness" of the categories of logic, then dialectic is operating in our thought alone. But such a dialectical nexus of concepts is not itself sufficient to account for our knowledge of the objective reality. Dialectic must come out of thought and confront the world, which is given. That is to say, it must have a relation to the objective world of matter into which man daily finds himself thrown.

Hegel very clearly recognizes this fact and in the subheading 81 of the *Encyclopedia of the Philosophical Sciences.* He writes:

> Everything that surrounds us may be viewed as an instance of Dialectic. We are aware that everything finite, instead of being stable and ultimate, is rather changeable and transient; and this is exactly what we mean by that Dialectic of the finite, by which the finite, as that which in itself is other than itself, is forced beyond its own immediate or natural being to turn suddenly into its opposite. ... All things, we say – that is, the finite world as such – are doomed; and in saying so, we have a vision of Dialectic as the universal and irresistible power before which nothing can stay however secure and stable it may deem itself. We find traces of its (Dialectic's) presence in each of the particular provinces and phases of the natural and the spiritual world. This moment the planet stands in this spot, but implicitly it is the possibility of being otherwise the planet brings into existences dialectical. ... It is the same dynamic that lies at the root of every other natural process and as it were forces nature beyond itself. – 1892: 150

The above passage sufficiently demonstrates that the laws of dialectic are not only operating in our thought but are also the fundamental features of the change and development taking place in the material reality. So, the dialectic has this dual function to perform, viz. to show that dialectic is operating in human thought and that simultaneously it is operating in the objective reality. But as an absolute idealist, Hegel regards the dialectic of thought as primary and the dialectic of reality as secondary, as an externalization of the dialectic of thought. This is evident from the fact that Hegel first formulates the principles of dialectic in the sphere of logic – the concepts and categories – and then introduces those laws of dialectic to the world outside. The laws of dialectic are the "externalization" of the spirit. This is another illustration of what Derrida calls Hegel's "idealizing mastery" because it is spirit that gives rise to the laws of dialectic.

With the above exposition of Hegel's doctrine of spirit and dialectic along with the related concepts like reason, understanding, sense – certainty and dialectic, it will be appropriate to come to Hegel's theory of sign more precisely. Hegel's semiology is situated in the first movement of spirit, i.e. subjective spirit that in general is formulated by Hegel in three phases:

1. *Subjective Spirit*: The spirit's relation to itself, an only ideal totality of the idea. This is being-near-to itself in the form of only internal freedom.
2. *Objective Spirit*: As a world to produce and produced in the forms of reality, not only ideality. Freedom here becomes an existing, present necessity.
3. *Absolute Spirit*: The unity, that is *in itself and for itself,* of the objectivity of the spirit and of its ideality or its concept, the unity producing itself eternally, spirit in its absolute truth–absolute spirit (Hegel 1977: Section 385).

We can say that Hegel's notion of the Absolute is essentially embodied in his doctrine of spirit and the dialectic along with the onto-theological or onto-teleological synthesis. Hegel's *aufhebung* depends on his doctrine of spirit in as much as it rests on dialectical principles and it is within human experience in the world – the phenomenology – that it begins to progress until it reaches the Absolute.

To bring the paper to a close, we can present a brief comparison among Śaṅkara, Kant and Hegel. In the Upaniṣadic philosophic thought, we come across a conflict among the metaphysicians; some regarding the Self as an entity entirely distinct from the Absolute, others regarding it as a part of the Absolute and yet others regarding the Self and the Absolute as entirely identical. These constitute respectively the fundamental positions of the three great metaphysical schools – the dualistic, the quasi-monistic and the monistic. It is the monistic metaphysics, as already explained in Part I, which Śaṅkara has advocated and which has come very close to what Hegel has to say on the Absolute.

The *Chāndogya Upaniṣad* arrives at the conception of self-consciousness as constituting the Ultimate Reality. In the *Taittirīya Upaniṣad* the identification of the Absolute with consciousness has been brought out like this – the Absolute is Existence, Consciousness and Infinity (S. 12.9). In the *Aitareya Upaniṣad*, we find, "of the gods, of the heaven, and the beings of the earth, whether produced from the eggs, or embryo, or sweat, or from the earth, everything that moves, or flies, or is stationary–Self-consciousness is eye of the world; it is self-consciousness which is Absolute". (S. 12b). With an extensive survey of the different approaches to the notion of Absolute and the Ultimate Reality, the Upaniṣadic seers have established Ultimate Reality firmly on self-consciousness. God to them is not God unless he is identical with self-consciousness. Existence is not existence if it does not mean self-consciousness. Reality is not reality if it does not express throughout its structure the marks of pure self-consciousness. On the cognition of the Absolute, the *Taittirīya Upaniṣad* says:

> That, from which our speech turns back along with mind, being unable to comprehend its fullness, is the Ultimate Reality.

The *Kenopaniṣad* says:

> That where the eye is unable to go, where neither speech nor mind is able to reach – what conception can we have of it, except that it is beyond all that is known, and beyond all that is unknown.

Śaṅkara and Hegel would agree with each other that the comprehension of Being as immanent in all other categories is the most fundamental category of all things. Śaṅkara in his commentary on the *Chāndogya Upaniṣad* (vi.2.1) says: "Existence or Being, it is urged, is pure, subtle, indefinable, all-pervading, one, taintless, indivisible, knowledge". On the concept of Pure Being, Hegel has also to say the same thing: Pure Being is complete indeterminacy, absence of all qualities, a vacuity, an empty concept. Being is the most irrepressible category for both Hegel and Śaṅkara. Hegel's Absolute is the unity, which realizes itself in the differences and it is not in which all differences are lost like that of Schelling. As already stated, Hegel too has to say the same thing like this:

> The True is the whole. But the whole is nothing other than the essence consummating itself through its development. Of the absolute it must be said that it is essentially a result, that only in the end is it what it truly is; and that precisely in this consists its nature, viz. to be actual subject, the spontaneous becoming of itself.

Hegel adds:

> Philosophy is itself, in fact, worship (*Die philosophieist der selbstGottesdienst*); it is religion, for in the same way it renounces subjective notions and opinions in order to occupy itself with God. ... The object of religion as well as of philosophy is eternal truth in its objectivity, God and nothing but God and the explication of God. ... In philosophy, religion gets justification from thinking consciousness.

For Hegel, nothing could be external to consciousness; but as consciousness exists through its opposition to the "other" which it at the same time sublates and this process goes on until it reaches to the Absolute Unity.

Immediate experience is the very heart of Śaṅkara's absolutism, whereas Hegel would never accept pure immediacy in the Absolute. In Hegel's dialectic, the thesis is always regarded as "immediate" or as characterized by "immediacy". The second term, the antithesis, is "mediate" or "mediation". The third term, the synthesis, is the merging of "mediation" and emerging as a new "immediacy". And this process goes on. The "Absolute idea" in its final form is the "free-subject", the Notion or *Begriff*. Its otherness or negation is the object. Both the *Begriff* and its otherness are constantly overwhelmed by the ontological conception of Hegel's Absolute idealism. Hegel's *Science of Logic* thus ends where it began with the category of Being and through all its meditations. But for Śaṅkara, Absolute is nothing if it is shorn of immediate experience.

This is the position of Absolute Monism. Whether this state of Absolute Monism is to be intellectually apprehended as Hegel does or expressed in self-realization as Śaṅkara does, both the ways are of the same spiritual pilgrimage.

References

George, Michael, 1984, "Marx's Hegelianism: An Exposition", in *Hegel and Modern Philosophy*, ed. David Lamb, London: Croom Helm.

Hegel, G.W.F., Georg Wilhelm Friedrich, 1977, *The Encyclopaedia of the Philosophical Sciences: An Outline*, tr. M.J. Petry, Dordrecht and Boston: D. Reidel Publishing Company.

——, 1973, *Phenomenology of Spirit*, tr. A.V. Miller, Oxford: Clarendon Press.

——, 1909, *Science of Logic*, tr. A.V. Miller, Book Two, London: George Allen & Unwin.

——, 1895, *Lectures on the Philosophy of Religion*, vol. III, tr. E.B. Speirs and J.B. Sanderson, London: Kegan Paul.

——, 1892, *The Encyclopedia of the Philosophical Sciences*, tr. W. Wallace, 2nd rev. edn, London: Legare Street Press.

Kant, 1973, *Critique of Pure Reason*, Avii, tr. N.K. Smith, London: Macmillan.

Kolb, David, 1986, *Critique of Pure Modernity: Hegel, Heidegger and After*, Chicago: The University Press.

Mukherjee, A.C., 1943, *The Nature of Self*, Allahabad: The Indian Press.

Śaṅkara, 1970, *Pañcīkaraṇam*, Bombay: Gujarati Printing Press.

Shastri, A.K. (ed.), 1933, *Brahmasūtra-Śāṅkarabhāṣya*, Ahmedabad: Metropolitan Printing and Publishing House.

Taylor, Charles, 1979, *Hegel and Modern Society*, London: Cambridge University Press.

5

Consciousness

What It Is and How It Is to Be Realized (A Study in Tripura Rahasya)

Shakuntala

Abstract: Consciousness is the knower and is considered as the only real. It alone is considered as real for in any case of knowing while the known is revealed by knowledge, knowledge depends on the knower.

In any case of knowledge, the object referred to, being precisely an object of knowledge, cannot be but mental. Thus this object is nothing but a notion in the mind. Now, the fact of object of knowledge being a notion brings with it the associated fact of the knower of object as well as knowledge being notions. And the physical is nothing except the materialization of the mental which makes even the physical unreal – be it the thing known or the embodied knower.

Consciousness in its pristine state is that subject where these notions are not present. This is the Self. This Consciousness or Self being pure subject remains unknowable. However, it is realizable by the mind emptied of thought.

This mind emptied of thought is not to be equated with mind of sleep where too there are no objects to be cognized. The

* All quotes are from the *Tripura Rahasya*.

reason for this is not that consciousness is not present in sleep – the presence of consciousness is indicated by awareness of unawareness in sleep. But sleep admits of duality – knower and the known which is a blank.

The mind cleansed of thought is called *samādhi*. *Samādhi* is distinguished from sleep on the ground that while sleep is awareness of the blank containing no objects, *samādhi* is pure awareness. *Samādhi*, however, to be considered as proper has to be continuous. This is known as *nirvikalpa samādhi* where there is no more possibility of rising of any further thought.

Keywords: Consciousness, Self, mind without thought, *samādhi*.

CONSCIOUSNESS is considered as knower which alone is taken as real. Objects and their knowledge are considered to be mere reflections on this consciousness.

> Objects and their knowledge are only reflections in the eternal. Self-luminous, supreme Consciousness which is the same as the knower and which alone is real. – IX.89-91

It is the factor of indubitablity of knower that goes to make for identification of consciousness and knower. This is so because to be real it is required that it is indubitable and knower alone is indubitable. Any talk, any discussion is possible only on the ground of knowledge. It is said:

> He who denies knowledge has no ground to stand on and so no discussion is possible. – Ibid

And knowledge necessarily implies knower. Knowledge, however, not only implies knower, but also brings with it the notion of "known" whose knowledge it is. Of the three factors involved in knowledge, knowledge of object and object of knowledge are said to constitute the world. While knower being subject of knowledge is termed as Self, object of knowledge being object is termed as opposite of subject, the not-Self. Further, amongst the three, the existence of object is proved by knowledge of it and knowledge automatically implies subject whose knowledge it is. In other words, knower cannot be denied. This subject thus remaining indubitable is considered as real. It is said:

> The world consists of knowledge and the objects known, of these the objects are non-self and perceived by senses; knowledge is self-evident; there is no world in the absence of knowledge. Knowledge is the direct proof of the existence of objects which are therefore dependent on knowledge. Knowledge is dependent on knower for its existence. Knower does not require any test for knowing his own existence. Knower therefore is the only reality behind knowledge and objects. That which is self-evident without the necessity to be proved, is alone real; not so other things.
>
> – IX.86-88

That knower is indubitable becomes evident from the fact that its rejection is impossible. Any rejection of knower is self-contradictory. This is so because rejection of knower also involves knowledge. As to reject, one has to perceive the idea of what is being rejected, it is tantamount to admitting knower. Thus, denial also being knowledge, denying existence of knower becomes ridiculous:

> Denial implies the formation of the mental image of the denied thing and it is absurd to deny its existence. – XVIII.22-27

The other reason why consciousness is regarded as real is because it endures. To say anything is, is to admit that it exists and to deny is to say that it does not. But in case of consciousness, while to say it exists is to admit its existence, to deny its existence is also to admit its existence. This is so because to deny it is to admit its conception which is admitting consciousness. Thus, it is said:

> Reality must endure forever and ever. "Consciousness either is or is not." In the former case, it is obvious and in the latter, it is implied, for the conception of its absence implies consciousness. (Therefore consciousness cannot be established to be transitory. It is permanent and therefore real.) – XVIII.145-48

However, the objects of knowledge require that there is knowing of them by the knower. This is the reason why it is said that objects of knowledge exist so long as they are perceived by knower:

> Their existence depends upon perception of them by conscious being. – XI.51

In other words, they do not exist independently. Thus, they are considered as not real; they are mere images, mere reflections:

> Cognition of things implies their images on our intelligence. They are only images. The creation therefore is an image. It is not self-shining; and thus it is not self-aware, but becomes a fact on our perception of it. Therefore, I say that the universe is nothing but an image on our consciousness. – XI.55-63

Object of cognition, even if it is physical, cannot escape from being a mere image. The reason is the same. It is not real being not independently existing. Only that physical is solid image. But image it is not real. An image is drawn and drawn over till the image becomes stronger to attain solidity:

> The repeatedly drawn image becomes clearer until it appears solidly as the object. – IV.68-69

The solidification or physicalization of images, however, require that they are forceful:

> One should forget the old association in order to make one's new conceptions effective, and this endures only so long as it is not obscured by the old one. A conception is forceful unless obscured by an antecedent one, and thus destroyed. It is effective only when forceful; in that way even great things may be achieved.
> – XIV.10-15

Further, objects of knowledge are not permanent – be they objects of dream or objects of waking state. And it is permanence which is test of reality. Illusion is called illusion because it is transitory. Thus object conceived and object perceived, that is, objects of dream state and objects of waking state must be considered as illusory because they do not endure. It is said:

> I ask you what illusion is? It is determined by the transitory nature, which is nothing but appearance to, and disappearance from, our senses. – XIII.71-76

Objects of waking state confirm their unreality by the fact of their undergoing constant change:

> Do you suggest that the hills, the seas and the earth itself are really permanent phenomena, in spite of the fact that their appearance is constantly changing? The ever-changing objects like the body, trees, rivers and islands are easily found to be transitory. Even mountains are not immutable, for their contour changes owing to the erosion of waterfalls and mountain torrents. ... You will see similar change in the seas and on earth.
> – XIII.60-70

Again, if dream objects are considered as unreal or illusory because they are not found in waking state, then the same is true of waking state objects – objects of waking state are not available in dream state. In other words, neither objects of dream state nor objects of waking state are enduring as they are not found in all states of consciousness. The things of both dreams and waking states are false, illusory; their unreality indicated by their not being available in the other state of consciousness:

> Do you mean to say that the dream is rendered false after waking from it? Is not the waking world similarly rendered false in your dream state? – XIII.60-70

Again, in deep sleep, neither things of dream nor things of waking state remain. It is said:

> Is not everything obliterated in deep sleep? – XIII.71-76

Here, it may be mentioned that, sleep, though without object of perception or conception, is not without consciousness and thus does not prove that consciousness is not permanent. That sleep is not without consciousness is revealed in awareness of unawareness.

> Will anything be apparent to you, if there be no consciousness? Even to say that nothing is apparent to you (as in sleep) requires the light of consciousness. Is not your awareness of unawareness (in sleep) due to consciousness? – XV.85

In other words, consciousness endures even in deep sleep.

Nevertheless, as it is because of consciousness that the world appears, it is said that the universe is covered by consciousness:

> Moreover, this consciousness is the only existence, covering the whole universe, and perfect all through. Just as there cannot be breakers apart from the ocean and light without the Sun, so also the universe cannot be conceived without consciousness. – XI.31-32

And because the universe in true sense of the term does not exist, there being only Self, it is said that the universe is Self only – that in reality there is nothing else but the Self:

> Thus, the universe is only the *Self* – the *One* and the only. – XI.85

The question now emerges is how this Self is known? This Self being pure subject cannot be cognized. In fact, it is said that if anything is capable of being cognized, it cannot be considered as Self. In other words, capability of being cognized stays as the standard to discard anything as Self:

> What is not self-luminous can only fall within the orbit of intelligence and cannot be intelligence itself. Intelligence is that by which objects are known; it cannot be what it is if it becomes object of knowledge. What is intelligible must always be different from intelligence itself, or else it could not be made known by it. Intelligence in the abstract cannot admit of parts, which is the characteristic of objects. Therefore, objects take on shapes. Carefully watch absolute intelligence after eliminating all else from it. It cannot be known as such and such, for it is the supporter of one and all. – XVI.15-19

This is the reason why it is said that the Self in the sense of being an object of knowledge, falls within the world. It is said:

> Just as the dream creations are pictures moving on the mind screens, so also this world, including yourself, is the obverse of the picture depicted by pure intelligence and is nothing more than an image in a mirror. – XIII.90

Actually, the objects and *me* being mere illusions, consciousness, the Self is non-dual in its true nature:

> Be also free from the thought "I see"; remain still like a blind man seeing. What transcends sight and no sight, *That* you are. – IX.99

From this fact of consciousness, that in its true pure state it is non-dual, it follows that it cannot be known. That is, in case of the self, there can be no knowing of *it* by *me*.

> As long as you are contaminated with notions of *me* and *mine*, the Self will not be found, for it lies beyond cognition and cannot be realized as "*my* Self". – IX.13

It, i.e. consciousness per se, is the maker without the made. It is subject without objects. It is the Self as pure intelligence. Thus, it is said:

> The Self is Abstract Intelligence free from thought. Knower, knowledge and the known are not real as different entities. When differentiation among them is destroyed, their true nature is evident in the resulting non-dual consciousness. – XX.72-77

Moreover, as the permanent, enduring reality, the Self is also not something to be gained. It is merely to be found:

> Gain is of something which is not already possessed. Is there any moment when the Self is not the Self? – IX.70
>
> Just as things unseen in darkness are found on its removal by means of lamp, and are therefore said to be recovered from oblivion. – IX.72

Now the Self can be found in elimination of perceptions. That is,

Self-realization merely requires that perceptions are eliminated. And that is all. Self-realization does not require concentration as required by other perceptions. It is said:

> The other perceptions require the two conditions, viz. elimination of other objects and concentration on the one. But Self-realization differs from them in that it requires only one condition: elimination of all perceptions. – XVI.33

As there is discarding of everything which can be considered as *mine*, there is the revealing of the Self itself. In other words, whatever is left after discarding is to be understood as the Self:

> Analyse and see what those things are which are cognized as *mine*; discard them all and transcending them, look for the Real Self. – IX.14

> Analyse everything in this way and discard it. What remains over, transcending it all, beyond conception, appropriation – know That to be the Self. – IX.16

Thus, it is said that though pure consciousness remains unknowable as an object, nevertheless, it remains realizable by pure mind:

> Although consciousness is unknowable, it is still realizable by pure mind. – XVI.34

By pure mind is meant the mind that is without thought and desire. It is said that it is a mind that turns inward by which only the Self can be realized. But by "turning inward of mind" is meant the mind without thought, desire. It is said:

> As long as thoughts crop up, so long has the turning inward of the mind not been accomplished. As long as the mind is not inward, so long the Self cannot be realized. Turning inward means absence of desire. – XV.85

This pure mind, however, is not to be mistaken or confounded with sleep. In sleep, mind knows – it knows the blank which contains no things, the void without things. This is called the exterior as the Self considers the void to be exterior to it. It is said:

> Sleep is the first born from Transcendence and also called *unmanifest*, the *exterior*, or the great *void*. – XVI.73

In truth, cognition of exterior is nothing but objectification of consciousness by withdrawing oneself from the non-dual consciousness. Thus, it is said:

> When you say "outside the hill" the hill is withdrawn from the space beyond; it is not included in it. – XIV.34-40

But, Pure Mind is knowledge without objects, pure awareness:

> Pure mind entirely divested of all objective knowledge (or thoughts) is pure intelligence. Awareness is its nature. – XIII.3-5

It is that where no object is found:

> Knowledge devoid of thoughts is like the canvas used in painting; the canvas remains the same whatever picture may be painted on it. Unqualified knowledge is simple light; the objects are manifest by and in it. – XVII.27-29

It is said that the Self can be discerned between the intervals of perceptions. It is said:

> Realize with a still mind the state between sleep and wakefulness, the interval between the recognition of one object after another or the gap between two perceptions. This is the real Self. – IX.94-95

This state without thought is called *samādhi*:

> *Samādhi* is simply absence of thoughts. Such a state prevails in sleep and at odd moments of wakefulness. – XVI.87

It is said that *samādhi*s actually keep happening. Only that one is not aware of it. The states without thought in wakeful states experienced without knowing that they are *samādhi*s are called fleeting *samādhi*. Such *samādhis*, it is said, are experienced by all. But they go undetected as people are not acquainted with it:

> But fleeting *samādhi* goes undetected because people are not so conversant with it. Fleeting *samādhi* is indeed being experienced by all, even in their busy moments; but it passes unnoticed by them, for want of acquaintance with it. Every instant free from thoughts and musing in the wakeful state is the condition of *samādhi*.
> – XVI.85-86

Some examples of fleeting *samādhi* are:

> When a man remains unaware of "in and out" for a short interval and is not overpowered by the ignorance of sleep; the infinitesimal time when one is beside oneself with joy; when embraced by one's beloved in all purity; when a thing is gained which was intensely longed for but given up in despair; when a lonely traveller moving with the utmost confidence is suddenly confronted with the utmost danger; when one hears of the sudden death of one's only son, who was in the best of health, in the prime of life, and at the apex of his glory.
> – XVII.4-11

However, *samādhi* in true sense of the term is supposed to be awareness of the Self unbroken. It is the state in which consciousness continuously shines:

> In *samādhi*, *Brahman*, the Supreme Consciousness, is continuously glowing.
> – XVI.93

Fleeting *samādhi* is not considered as proper *samādhi* because of this reason. Actually, in fleeting *samādhis* thoughts do not end and thus the Self does not reveal Itself all the time.

> Yet it is not called *samādhi* proper, because all the proclivities of the mind are still there latent, ready to manifest the next instant.
> – XVI.88

This desired for knowledge, i.e. continuous Self-knowledge that destroys thought or ignorance, is *nirvikalpa samādhi*. It is said:

> Knowledge born of *nirvikalpa samadhi* generates wisdom by the eradication of ignorance and objective knowledge. – XVII.35-38

Nirvikalpa samādhi is the experience of or practical knowledge of the Self:

> *Nirvikalpa samādhi* is characterized by the experience of the true Self alone, viz. Pure Intelligence. – XVII.110

Nirvikalpa samādhi is the state where there is not only eradication of thoughts but also where there would be no more arising of thoughts:

> When the mind does not create pictures due to thoughts, it is in the unmodified state, which is its primal and pure condition. [T]he mind remains pure when thoughts are eliminated. Therefore, the unqualified state is restored if the present disturbance is ended. – XVII.72, 74

Nirvikalpa samādhi requires that there is theoretical knowledge, attention of the seeker and contemplation. *Nirvikalpa samādhi* is to be necessarily preceded by theoretical knowledge. In fact, absence of theoretical knowledge in casual *samādhi* is a factor that prevents it from providing right kind of knowledge to destroy thought. It is said:

> Just as a man, ignorant of qualities of emerald, cannot recognize it by the mere sight of it in the treasury, nor can another recognize it if he has not seen it before, although he is full of theoretical knowledge on the subject, in the same way, theory must be supplemented with practice in order that a man might become an expert. Ignorance cannot be eradicated by mere theory or by the casual *samādhi* of an ignorant man. – XVII.39-47

Another requirement for *nirvikalpa samādhi* is attention. In absence of attention, even scholarship cannot help one to realize the Self. Once one is taught how *samādhi* is to be discerned, it is left to the seeker to discover these states. And this requires attention and alertness. For the want of it, as it has been pointed out, it may go by without people realizing it:

> Again, want of attention is a serious obstacle; for a man looking up at the sky cannot identify the individual constellation. Even a learned scholar is no better than a fool, if he does not pay attention when a thing is explained to him. On the other hand, a man though not a scholar, but yet attentive having heard all about the planet Venus, goes out in confidence to look for it, and so is able to recognize the same whenever he sees it again. Inattentive people are simply fools, who cannot understand the ever-recurring *samādhis* in their lives. They are like a man, ignorant of the treasure under the floor of his house, who begs for his daily food. – XVII.39-47

However, theoretical knowledge and attention are not sufficient for practical knowledge of the Self. Further, *nirvikalpa samādhi* requires the help of *dhyāna* (contemplation). In other words, *dhyāna* is the practice that leads to it:

> *Dhyāna* has been said to develop into *nirvikalpa samādhi*. – XVII.71

Reference

Saraswathi, Swami Sri Ramananda (tr.), 2021, *Tripura Rahasya or The Mystery Beyond the Trinity*, Tiruvannamalai: Sri Ramanasramam.

6

On Sartre's Theory of Consciousness

A Phenomenological Approach in "The Transcendence of the Ego" and "Being and Nothingness"

Akoijam Thoibisana

Abstract: Sartre, in his early writings, particularly his philosophical essay on "The Transcendence of the Ego" (1936) developed a theory of consciousness that became an important background for his major works like *Being and Nothingness* (1943) and other literary productions. This early writing of Sartre was motivated by the phenomenology of Husserl. Following Husserl's account of consciousness as intentional, Sartre developed a "new" conception of a consciousness that is phenomenological but different from Husserl's transcendental consciousness. Sartre's consciousness is absolute, non-substantial, and exists *for itself*. It is not a mode of Being, and can never be reduced to Being; except in the sense of "the Being of Nothingness". Consciousness for Sartre is also different from ego. The ego appears to consciousness only when it is *reflective*; that is on the level of *the cogito*. Sartre argues that consciousness is just a *pure intentionality*; directed towards the world of Being (which it is not). The paper seeks to bring out Sartre's account of the phenomenology of consciousness. His commitment to phenomenology and application of the phenomenological method in questioning the transcendental ego will be discussed. At the crux of the paper is the phenomenology of Sartre's consciousness that also constitutes his phenomenology of the self.

Keywords: Sartre, phenomenology, consciousness, intentionality, ego, self.

Introduction

SARTRE'S early philosophical work was highly embedded in his intensive reading of Husserl's phenomenology. Sartre's *theory of consciousness* was first developed in his account of questioning and criticizing the *transcendental ego* of Husserl in his philosophical essay "The Transcendence of the Ego" (1936) (hereafter TE). In this essay, Sartre argues that the ego is not transcendental but transcendence. Holding on tight to Husserl's phenomenological account of intentionality, Sartre illustrated how the ego is like any other object, an object of intentionality for consciousness. He developed a phenomenology of consciousness which explains the nature of consciousness in terms of the two levels of consciousness, viz. the reflective consciousness and the unreflective consciousness, in order to set up his position that the ego is transcendence and not transcendental. He elaborated on the constitution of the ego (that is always transcendent) in terms of the phenomenological account of the intended object. In his later work *Being and Nothingness* (1943) (hereafter *BN*) Sartre continues to work on the nature of consciousness in the pursuit of Being. He defines consciousness in terms of the Being-for-itself that carries within itself its own nothingness.

In this background, the paper is set to give a brief exposition of how Sartre developed his essay on the phenomenology of consciousness. It also underlies Sartre's reading of Husserl's phenomenology. At the heart of the paper is Sartre's phenomenological account of consciousness (that is structured intentionally) and also provides a legitimate interpretation even for his fundamental project of *Being and Nothingness*. This paper is divided into four main sections. First is a brief overview of Husserl's phenomenology and Sartre's account of the relation between consciousness and ego. Second is an exposition of Sartre's version of Husserl's phenomenology that (also) explicates Sartre's criticism of the transcendental ego as discussed in "The Transcendence of the Ego". Section III gives an account of Sartre's discussion on the nature of consciousness and the constitution of the ego. Fourth is an exposition of the phenomenological account of consciousness that Sartre developed in his *Being and Nothingness.*

I

Preamble to Phenomenology, Consciousness and the Ego

Phenomenology as a movement founded by Husserl has undergone profound transformation not only in the hand of his fellow-student Heidegger, but also with Sartre and Merleau-Ponty.[1] There are also thinkers like Levinas, Derrida and Ricoeur, among others who have extensively contributed to the tradition of phenomenology. Each of them has made a distinctive reading of Husserl's phenomenology. Sartre's phenomenology is also one such reading.

Husserl's phenomenology is an exhaustive work that has made him one of the most influential philosophers of the twentieth century.[2] Whereas it is not possible to give a detailed account of

---

1 Whereas Heidegger's fundamental ontology in his masterwork *Being and Time* (1927) was a phenomenology analysis of Being that examines "what it means to be" as disclosed through *Dasein*; Sartre's *Being and Nothingness* (1943/2003) adopted phenomenology in his existential philosophy of Being. There is also Merleau-Ponty presentation of a phenomenological version of the philosophy of the body in his *Phenomenology of Perception* (1945/1962).

2 His phenomenology is usually studied in three major periods. The first period of Husserl's phenomenology constitutes his *Logical Investigations* that appeared in two volumes, the *Prolegomena to Pure Logic* (vol. 1) and the Six Phenomenological Investigations (vol. 2). The second period is his transcendental phenomenology →

Husserl's phenomenology, some of its basic characteristics can still be noted. Phenomenology, for Husserl in his *Logical Investigations,* (1900-01) has been a descriptive science of experience and its objects (in a manner in which they are experienced). In his Introduction to the book, Husserl writes:

> Pure phenomenology represents a field of neutral research in which several sciences have their roots. It is, on the one hand, ancillary to *psychology*, conceived as an *empirical science.* Proceeding in a purely intuitive fashion, it analyses and describes in its essential generality – in the specific guise of a phenomenology of thought and knowledge – the experience of presentation, judgement and knowledge, experience, which are treated as classes of real events in the natural context of zoological reality, receive a scientific probing at the hands of empirical psychology. Phenomenology, on the other hand, lays bare the "sources" from which the basic concepts and ideal laws of pure logic "flow", and back to which they must once more be traced, so as to give them all the "clearness and distinctness" needed for an understanding, and for an epistemological critique, of pure logic.
>
> – 1900-01: 166

Following Brentano's account of psychological intentionality, Husserl's phenomenological investigation sets out a theory of intentionality as the essence of consciousness. In *Ideas Pertaining to a Pure Phenomenology and to a Phenomenological Philosophy* (Book I), also popularly known as *Ideas I* (1913), Husserl worked out the concept of *epoche* or bracketing that featured the development of his phenomenology in terms of "transcendental ego". He establishes the faculty necessary for the conditions of experience. His concept of "bracketing" and "transcendental reduction" became a topic that is highly debated. Husserl's notion of the

← most popularly worked out in his *Ideas I* and *Cartesian Meditations.* Third period presents his phenomenology of life-world in his posthumously published work *The Crisis of European Sciences and Transcendental Phenomenology.*

transcendental ego also raises questions on the problem of solipsism, other and intersubjectivity that he tries to address in *Cartesian Meditations* (1931/1960). It opens up his new realm of transcendental subjectivity. Thereafter, his phenomenology is (un)popularly known as "transcendental phenomenology". The last stage of Husserl's work, viz. *The Crisis of European Sciences and Transcendental Philosophy* (1970), addresses the crisis of European culture that was brought about by the alienation of modern science, including philosophy. In this work, Husserl seeks to restore the (lost) life-world within which all human activity arises. This was his phenomenology of the life-world.

Sartre, in his essay "The Transcendence of the Ego", gave a critical account of Husserl's transcendental ego (as it was given in *Ideas I*) as not only false but inconsistent with Husserl's own phenomenology.[3] So, whereas Sartre's early philosophical writings were highly indebted to Husserl's phenomenology, particularly the latter's fifth investigation of *Logical Investigations* (vol. II), Sartre, however, drifted his attention from Husserl in his latter writings. Sartre's major work *Being and Nothingness* has even been given the subtitle "An Essay on Phenomenological Ontology", where he applied phenomenological methods and approaches in his study of the ontology of Being. It was a study on the phenomenological ontology of Being. He applies phenomenological approaches to arrive at the fundamental existential features of the human condition, like freedom and bad faith. However, it was not in *Being and Nothingness*, but in earlier philosophical works, mainly his

---

[3] "The Transcendence of the Ego" was an outcome of Sartre's detailed study of Husserl's phenomenology during a nine-month sabbatical in Berlin, August 1933. The Routledge publication 2004 even has the subtitle of the essay as "A Sketch for a Phenomenological Description". The New York publication in 1957 gave the subtitle "An Existential Theory of Consciousness". This, however, was taken to be misleading since Sartre did not adopt the trade name of existentialism until after the writing of *Being and Nothingness* in 1943 (Robert and Doran 1967: 308).

philosophical essay "The Transcendence of the Ego", that he gave a detailed sketch of his phenomenology.[4] Sartre accepted many of the major ideas and concepts that make up Husserl's phenomenology; he was however equally critical of Husserl's phenomenology, particularly the latter's conception of transcendental ego. What follows first is an account of the relation between consciousness and ego that Sartre has developed in his essay "The Transcendence of the Ego".

Sartre: Between Consciousness and the Ego

Sartre, even before the writing of this essay "The Transcendence of the Ego" found Husserl's concept of intentionality as the key to his philosophical analysis. He followed Husserl's phenomenology in his attempt to come out of the tradition of ancient Western philosophy (going back to Plato and Aristotle, which presents "knowing" on the basis of the metaphor) that was based on an illusion common to both realism and idealism. Sartre's phenomenological account is exhibited in his analysis of Husserl's phenomenology of perception (from Husserl's *Ideas I*). Sartre accepts both Brentano and Husserl's intentionality as the defining features of consciousness and strongly argues that "all consciousness is always consciousness of something". That is, consciousness is consciousness of whatever phenomenon it is directed towards. And, the phenomenon that is intended by consciousness is called an "intentional object" for consciousness. An intentional object is whatever consciousness is *of* or *about*. It is perceived, imagined, believed or felt.[5] Sartre also argues that the paradigm of "perceptual object" that is given to consciousness always transcends "the act of consciousness". That is, the perceptual object that is given to the act of consciousness is always "presented" as having other sides (and having different

[4] Other early philosophical works of Sartre are *The Psychology of the Imagination* (1936) and *Sketch for a Theory of the Emotion* (1939).

[5] Sartre's phenomenological account is adhered to various types of intentional object that is intended by consciousness.

aspects). It is, therefore, not an isolated act of perception. It is always "appresented" to us as any given object of perception at any instance (than is actually and immediately presented from a particular necessary perspective). Hence, for Sartre, any "perceptual objects" is never given at once and we can never fully perceive all (possible) aspects of any object. It is always subject to confirmation of future experience. It, therefore, always transcends the act of consciousness to which it is presented (only partially).

Ego: Between the I and the Me

Hitherto, Sartre also argues that the ego is like any other thing in the world. It is not in consciousness. He writes:

> ... it [Ego] is outside, in the world; it is a Being in the world, like the Ego of another. – *TE*: 1

And, because the Ego is like any object presented to consciousness and is a product of consciousness, it can never be transcendental. It rather is "transcendent". Following Husserl, Sartre noted that the term "transcendent" refers to "an object of consciousness", that is immanent and has an aspect which always "exceeds" or "transcends" a particular experience (TE: ix). For Sartre, the ego, insofar as it is not an "inhabitant" of consciousness, is transcendent. The ego here (that is the transcendent ego) has the double reference of "Self as subject" as well as a "Self as object" of consciousness. Sartre adopts the terminology of the "I" and "Me" to explain these two types of egos. He uses the "I" when the ego is referred to the self as experience in the "stream of consciousness"; and the "Me" to refer to the Self as an object which falls under the scope of phenomenological reduction. The former has the nature of Husserl's transcendental ego, whereas in the latter the ego is transcendent. However, Sartre argues that in both cases, the ego is transcendent and there is no need for a transcendental ego.

Here, it is important to note that Sartre reads Husserl's "transcendental" in terms of the "purely intentional ego" through which we become aware of the transcendent things (in the intentional activity of the Ego). That is, Sartre sees Husserl's transcendental ego as that "experiencing ego" that provides the "unity of consciousness". It exists independently of the "empirical ego" and underlies all our experience. It is this nature of the "transcendental ego" (Husserl *Ideas I*) that Sartre questioned (in his "The Transcendence of the Ego"). Also known as transcendental consciousness in Kant, it is not a real entity that is an inseparable companion of each of our consciousness, but merely the set of conditions necessary for the existence of empirical consciousness. The structure of this transcendental consciousness in principle is not different from Kant's idea of the "Transcendental Unity of Apperception" (*TE*: 2-3). It is not "yours" or "mine"; or "anyone's"; it is an impersonal, necessary, universal, *eidetic* structure. However, Husserl, in around 1931, grasped a distinction between the "empirical ego" (our Being-in-the-world) and the "transcendental ego', also known as "pure ego" in his *Ideas I*. So, for Husserl (at least in *Ideas I*) this transcendental ego is unique "for each separate stream of experiences". It is lived in and through each unique conciseness; in each ego-life.

Sartre argues that Husserl's notion of the transcendental ego is not only false; it also contradicts Husserl's own phenomenology.[6] According to Sartre, there is no need for "I" (or

6 However, in defence of Husserl's transcendental ego, Edie in his paper "The Question of the Transcendental Ego: Sartre's Critique of Husserl" noted that there is no need to make a distinction between two different egos (as Sartre reads it as I and me). It is rather a distinction between two attitudes, the natural attitude and the transcendental attitude. The transcendental ego is not, therefore, some hidden, innermost, ego behind consciousness; it is, rather, an attitude which consciousness can and for the purpose of philosophical reflection must take towards its own empirical experience. The point is that there has to be an aspect, an attitude, of consciousness which escapes the reduction, viz. the ego that performs the reduction. The ego has to be able to transcend its

→

transcendental ego or self as subject) for the unity of consciousness. That is, there is no ego/I inside consciousness to account for the synthesis of all our experiences over time. He also insists that an "I" is also not required to separate it from the consciousness of other people. Both these arguments will render Sartre's consciousness (as) impersonal (*TE*: 3).

In order to discuss the issues of phenomenology and transcendental ego, Sartre in the first part of the essay, section "The I and the Me" formulated two questions. He asks:

> ... is the *I* which we encounter in our consciousness made possible by the synthetic unity of our representations, or is it the *I* that in fact unifies the representations among themselves? – *TE* : 3-4

Sartre turns towards Husserl's phenomenology to address this question of the existence of the *I* in consciousness. Hence, what follows is an exposition of Sartre's account of phenomenology that also lays the ground for the nature of consciousness.

II

Sartre's Revision of Husserl's Phenomenology

Phenomenology, according to Sartre, is a scientific and not a "critical" study of consciousness. It is essentially proceeded via intuition (of the things). He writes:

> Phenomenology is a scientific, and not a "critical", study of consciousness. Its essential way of proceeding is via intuition. Intuition, according to Husserl, puts us in the presence of the thing. We must therefore recognize that phenomenology is a *de facto* science, and that the problems it raises are *de facto* problems – and this is something that can also be seen from the way that Husserl calls it a descriptive science. – *TE*: 4

← momentary experiences of Being a consciousness since it unifies these experiences and enables us to constitute them as acts, states and dispositional of one single, unique, conscious flow, viz. our own, one, ego-life (Edie 1993: 115).

For Sartre, the relation between the I and consciousness is always existential. Consciousness is not a set of logical conditions but an *absolute* fact that is accessible to everyone through the performance of "reduction". Hence, Sartre writes:

> The fact remains that it is indeed this transcendental consciousness that constitutes our empirical consciousness, consciousness "in the world", consciousness with a psychical and psychophysical me.
> – Ibid.

Sartre goes along with Husserl and indeed admires the latter's account of transcendental consciousness that constitutes the world by imprisoning itself in empirical consciousness. Sartre accepted the account of the physical and psychophysical me, that is a kind of "transcendent object" which like any other object comes under the scope of the *epoche*.

The problem arises when Husserl, in his *Ideas I* reverts to what Sartre calls "the classical thesis of a transcendental I", according to which, behind each of these transcendental I, there is a *necessary structure of consciousness that falls onto each phenomenon* that is presented to the field of attention (*TE*: 5). The problem that Sartre has is with the idea of this "necessary structure of consciousness"[7] that is required for the synthesis and unification

7 Here, the notion of the necessary "structure of conscious experience" may be read either as making a claim about the "structure of conscious experience" or as going beyond the structure of experience to analyse the "structure of mind-independent reality". Webber in his paper "Sartre's Critique of Husserl" noted that the latter is about the metaphysical structure that objects of experience have independently of our experience of them; whereas the former can be taken as the phenomenological reduction to restrict the purview of inquiry to the structure of conscious experience itself. It is, he argues, the latter that is preferable for his analysis of Husserl's phenomenology (Webber 2019: 5).

of all consciousness.[8] It is this new transcendental I, or rather this transcendental ego that Sartre says contradicts Husserl's own phenomenology. To put it in other words, we have, in short, the theory of the transcendental ego of Husserl that presupposes that there is a transcendental "I think" that unifies each moment of consciousness, ideas and representation into a single consciousness. It (I think) provides a synthesis of all experience and recognizes all of my experience as mine. In fact, it must be present on all occasions in order for consciousness to be possible. This, however, argues Sartre, contradicts Husserl's own account of phenomenology. Sartre tries to show this from the phenomenological account of the theory of intentionality as well as inner time-consciousness.

So, first, Sartre argues that if intentionality is the theory that asserts that "consciousness is consciousness of ..." and if consciousness is nothing beyond a directness towards the world;[9] if it is nothing but a revealing intuition; then there cannot be an aspect of consciousness that has the form of a transcendental ego (that does not direct towards the world). If so, the next question then is, how does Sartre (then) account for the unity and individuality of consciousness?

Addressing the above question of the unification of conscious experience, Sartre argues that Husserl's notion of intentionality "unifies itself by escaping itself". That is, the unity of consciousness is constituted by the consistency of the objects that are experienced. Sartre gave the example of "counting". In counting, objects appear to consciousness in a series. Counting would not be possible if we

---

[8] He argues that there is no need for any transcendental ego for the unification of consciousness. This is done by the intentional structure of consciousness itself.

[9] According to Sartre, "consciousness as an intentional directedness towards the world" cannot effort to "bracket off" the world. Doing so would render no consciousness at all. It is this understanding of the impossibility to bracket "Being" that Sartre later adopted in his *Being and Nothingness*.

had to start over again at every unit that is counted. That is, for counting to be possible, the immediate past experience needs to be retained in the current experience. This retention of our immediate past experience is part of our inner time-consciousness. This, however, for Sartre, does not mean that inner time-consciousness is akin to some kind of "transcendental I" that actively unifies all our experiences. It, rather, argues Sartre, is the process of "perpetual synthesis of past consciousness with the present consciousness (*TE*: 6). This again does not mean that all past experience (that plays an active role) is retained in constituting the meaning of the things that are given to consciousness. The same goes for anticipating experiences that go in the direction of protention. This process of retention and protention is what Sartre understood by the notion of inner time-consciousness.

Hence, for Sartre, consciousness is perpetually in a process of unification. He argues that it is not the case that things in the world form a series before they are encountered by consciousness. Consciousness also is not that unity that comes before it encounters continuous objects. That is, the immediate past and future are not the object of consciousness; they give meaning to the objects that come before consciousness. Hence, Sartre writes:

> The *object is transcendent* to the consciousness that grasp it and it is within the object that their unity is found. – *TE*: 6

He continues:

> It will be objected that it is necessary for there to be some principle of unity in duration if the continual stream of consciousness is able to posit transcendental objects outside itself. – *TE*: 6

Sartre, however, notes:

> Consciousness must be a perpetual synthesis of past consciousness with the present consciousness. And this is perfectly true. – Ibid.

He refers to Husserl when he further writes:

> But it is typical of Husserl – who studies this subjective unification of consciousness in *On the Phenomenology of the Consciousness of Internal Time* – that he never resorted to any synthetic power of the I.
>
> – Ibid.

Hence, Sartre writes:

> It is *consciousness that unifies itself*, concretely, by an interplay of "*transversal consciousness that are real, concrete retentions of past consciousness*".
>
> – Ibid.: 6-7

Sartre, here, does not claim that the "intentional object" itself unifies the experience. He also does not claim that "consciousness" unifies the intentional object, whose unity in turn explains the unity of consciousness. This would lead to a circular explanation that cannot be accepted just by declaring that consciousness and its object are inseparable (Priest 2000: 41). Sartre's claim is rather that it is part of the sense of each aspect of the presentation of the object that it is related to the other aspects as aspects of the presentation of one object. That is, it is the "unity of presentation, and not of the presented, that unifies a conscious experience". In other words, the various aspects of my experience at a given time are unified into a single experience *by Being aspects of a single presentation of one intentional object*. And, my experience across time is unified into a single stream of consciousness by an interplay of "transversal" consciousness that are real and concrete retention of past consciousness. Hence, what Sartre is claiming is that *the structure of experience* ensures that experience is a single coherence flow. There is therefore no role for a transcendental ego or anything else to play in unifying experience (Webber 2019: 5-6).

Third, Sartre also gave another argument to prove that there is no transcendental ego in conscious experience. He noted that if consciousness is essentially an intentional presentation of its objects and if it were to include a transcendental ego, then this would be either a structure of this presentation or an "inhabitant" of it. The former makes it "a translucent quality of consciousness" that shows up as an experienced feature of the object (which it does not) (*TE*: 8); the latter would be a centre of opacity which would separate consciousness from itself that would divide it and slice it through each consciousness. This itself would be inconsistent with the unity and translucency of experience. Hence, Sartre writes:

> Indeed, this superfluous I is actually a hindrance. If it existed, it would violently separate consciousness from itself, it would divide it, slicing through each consciousness like an opaque blade. The transcendental I is [therefore] the death of consciousness.
>
> – *TE*: 7

This claim of the "no transcendental ego" escapes the objection that such an ego might stand behind experience without featuring in its structure. This is because Sartre's argument is restricted to inquiry concerning analysing the structure of conscious experience. It is not about metaphysical inquiry or about a brain that exists for some kind of visual experience of other objects (Webber 2019: 7).

Sartre, in the second part of the essay "The Constitution of the Ego", resorts to giving a positive account of the transcendental ego as a synthesis of actions, states of mind and qualities (*TE*: 21). He claims that the relation between the ego (the way the *me* appears as the pole of these transcendence) and consciousness can be described only in "magical" terms (*TE*: 26). He argues that the ego produces its qualities, states and action through "poetic production" that mostly takes the form of a "magical procession" which "always retains a ground of unintelligibility" (*TE*: 32-33). This (spontaneity of the ego), argues Sartre, must not be confused with consciousness. The ego, after all, noted Sartre, "Being an object" is passive. It is a pseudo-spontaneity; a mere appearance. It is an object apprehended and also "constituted" by reflective knowledge.[10] It is given only to "reflective consciousness" and never appears except when we are not looking at it.

---

10 The notion of reflective consciousness is discussed in the next section of the paper.

Hence, it may be concluded that, through his critique of Husserl's phenomenology, Sartre laid the foundations for a theory of consciousness. Sartre thereafter developed his new account of "consciousness *of* consciousness" that is pre-reflective, non-positional or non-thetic. And, it is this notion of non-positional consciousness that became a central element of his theory of consciousness that was later propounded in his *Being and Nothingness*. What follows is an account of Sartre's theory of consciousness in terms of the two levels of consciousness as outlined in his "The Transcendence of the Ego".[11]

III

On Sartre's Nature of Consciousness: Reflective and Pre-Reflective

In the above section, it has been shown that phenomenology renders the unifying and individualizing role of the I totally useless. Rather, it is consciousness itself that makes possible the unity and the personality of my I. There is therefore no need for the transcendental I. According to Sartre, the analysis of the structure of consciousness renders the non-existence of transcendental I. This section seeks to bring out the nature of Sartre's consciousness.

The nature of consciousness, according to Sartre, is like Spinoza's substance. It cannot be limited except by itself. Consciousness, for Sartre, is a synthetic, individual totality that is completely isolated from other totalities (of the same kind). It can merely be an expression (and not a condition) of incommunicability and inwardness of consciousness (*TE*: 7). Sartre, therefore, noted that it is this phenomenological conception of consciousness that renders the unity and individualization of my I possibility. The role of the transcendental I is completely useless.

Sartre in his "The Transcendence of the Ego" also argues that the nature of consciousness is *absolute* because "consciousness is

[11] It has also become the cornerstone of his existential phenomenology, that is his existentialism.

conscious of itself". That is, consciousness is not only "conscious of its object" but also "conscious of itself". That is the type of existence consciousness has is that "it is (also) conscious of itself". And it becomes conscious of itself "*insofar as it is consciousness of a transcendent object*" (ibid.). He writes:

> Everything in consciousness is thus clear and lucid: the object lies opposite it, in its characteristic opacity, but consciousness, for its part, is purely and simply the consciousness of Being consciousness of this object: such is the law of its existence.
>
> – Ibid.: 7-8

This notion of "consciousness of consciousness" according to Sartre, is not *positional*. That is, "consciousness" is not its own object. Its object is outside itself by nature. It is for this reason that consciousness in one and the same act can "posit" as well as "grasp" its object. It knows itself only as "absolute inwardness". It is what Sartre calls a "first order" or "unreflective" consciousness. The I (or rather the *cogito*), on the other hand, inhabits the consciousness. Sartre calls it reflective consciousness. The *cogito* as reflective consciousness for Sartre is like the "I" of Husserl's transcendental ego that is "an object *for* consciousness" (ibid.: 9). It occurs when the consciousness reflects upon itself. It is concrete and *psychophysical* in me. Sartre reads the *cogito* as "undeniably personal". He writes:

> In the "I think". There is an I which thinks. – *TE*: 9

The *cogito* or the "I think" therefore bears within itself an "egology" that is (can be) taken as the starting point of our all thoughts and experience by intuition (immediate or memory). It is also this "I" that is Being grasped and gives itself as transcending (this) thought and thoughts. Sartre here gives the example of "remembering a certain landscape that he saw from the train". He argues that it is possible to bring back the memory of that landscape. It is also possible that "I can also remember that I saw that landscape" (*TE*: 9). Husserl calls this "the possibility of reflecting in memory".[12] The

[12] Sartre refers to Husserl's work *On the Phenomenology of the Consciousness of Internal Time* (1929/1990).

"I" immediately occurs whenever there is a personal mode of an "act of remembering". The point of Sartre's argument is that the "I" appears as a "psychic object" in every "act of consciousness". It is not a "psychic subject", but an "intentional object of reflective consciousness". That is, I appear in reflective consciousness to myself as an ego.[13] It is presented in a reflective operation. It is, therefore, called "the second-order" operation. Sartre writes:

> ... all authors who have described the *cogito* have presented it as a reflective operation, i.e. a second-order operation. This *cogito* is performed by a consciousness *directed towards consciousness*, which takes *consciousness as its object.* – Ibid.: 10

So far, Sartre does not have an issue with the notion of the *cogito* as a product of reflective consciousness that gives the illusion of I/ego in me. However, he drew our attention to Husserl's cogito as "an indissoluble unity between the reflecting consciousness and the reflected consciousness" (ibid.). The complication that Sartre sees here is first that "every consciousness is consciousness of existing". Second, is that "the reflecting consciousness cannot exist without reflected consciousness" (*TE*: 10).

Sartre reads Husserl's "reflective consciousness" as an intermittent consciousness of pre-reflective consciousness. He writes:

> The fact remains that we are in the presence of a synthesis of two consciousnesses, one of which is consciousness of the other.
> – Ibid.: 10

This, according to Sartre, also maintained the essential principle of phenomenology, that "all consciousness of consciousness of something". However, the problem is that my "reflecting consciousness" does not take itself for an "object" (when I carry out the *cogito*). That is, what it affirms concerns "the reflected

13 Without reflective consciousness the *I is the me* (that is, I am a psychophysical totality with flesh and blood thinking, feeling, moving human Being) and not an ego.

consciousness". And, insofar as my "reflecting consciousness" is "consciousness *of* itself" (and not consciousness *for* itself), it is a "non-positional" consciousness. As Sartre writes:

> It becomes positional only if directed at the reflected consciousness which, in itself, was not a positional consciousness of itself before it was reflected.
>
> – Ibid.

Sartre, therefore, concludes:

> Thus the consciousness that says "I think" is precisely not the consciousness that thinks.
>
> – Ibid.

In other words, the conscious experience that reflects is not the one it reflects upon (Gusman 2020: 69). Sartre gave the example of Peter saying to Paul, "I love Mary". He argues that when Peter says "I love Mary" to Paul, Peter becomes fully aware of the "conscious act" of loving Mary. Before this, he was just loving Mary. And, now he says "I love Mary" to himself and to Paul. The point of Sartre's argument is that when Peter says "I love Mary", the consciousness which says "I love Mary", is not in the "act of loving Mary". It is not even having Mary as the "object of a particular emotive act". It is rather the *consciousness* of loving Mary. This is what Sartre means by "absolute" consciousness. It does not say "I" until after the fact that takes place in its "pre-reflective acts as objects". And, there is no infinite regress here. That is, at each moment of full reflection the absolute consciousness moves up into the position of Being a fully "reflected" object of the "non-positional, pre-reflective, absolute, non-egological consciousness" which remains a "pure, free, spontaneous intentionality" (Edie 1993: 111).

If this state of "loving Mary" continues as the series of "conscious acts of love directed towards Mary" in Peter's behaviour; this state of consciousness of Being in love, becomes a general mode of having Mary as an "object". It became a fixed disposition of Peter to love Mary, even when he is immersed in other activities and not even thinking of loving Mary. That is, it becomes a part of the way he defines himself in the world, his way of Being-in-the-world. It became a simple, inert quality of his Being an object to himself, insofar as he is a thing among things that is open to the free gaze of intentional consciousness. In other words, it is a Being in the world with the characteristic of dubitability, incompleteness and contingency of any other possible object of consciousness. It is therefore a transcendent, inexhaustible and "infinite" object (ibid: 112). This is what Sartre means by the "transcendence of the ego".

The transcendence of the ego is this ego, even when taken in itself as an "object", finds itself to be an "object in the world" like any other. That is, the experiencing ego, who is the "objectifies of things" is also able to take itself, its own acts, states and "qualities or dispositions as objects". Just as with the experience of external objects, it experiences itself both pre-reflectively and in acts of full reflection, of fully reflective awareness.[14] Hence, in the transcendence of the ego, there is a movement of the I from the pre-reflective state of consciousness to the fully reflective state. So, the I is no longer a pure, disembodied, consciousness-experiencing-the-world. It no longer is the dominant subject, the sole objectifier of the world. The I is also (or rather became) an "object", a "me" who is Being seen by others. Hence, the I is no longer the centre of the universe. The I take myself as an object and is capable of experiencing shame, guilt and otherness. The I is also an "object" to other consciousness who drains the world away from me, and out of me.[15]

It follows that the fundamental law of consciousness that holds that "all consciousness is consciousness of an object" does not exclude "objects" on the pre-reflective level. So, when Peter says to himself that he likes or loves Mary, he is formulating in a fully reflective act of awareness a manner of having Mary as an

14 In *Being and Nothingness*, Sartre gives the famous example of "the look" in which the I as a pure mode Being, eventually modified his structure by means of the reflective *cogito*.

15 The I, therefore, is not transcendental, but transcendence the ego.

object which would have been preceded by any number of pre-reflective acts of the same kind directed towards the same object (Edie 1993: 111).

Hence, it can be concluded that the principal argument of the "The Transcendence of the Ego" is the nature of consciousness that always pertains to the intentional attitude that is always capable of taking ourselves as objects and of going beyond ourselves, and of becoming "unstuck" of ourselves. And my experience of myself is always "what I am not" and not "what I am".[16] This is, for Sartre, also the experience of freedom that he developed in *Being and Nothingness*.

IV

Consciousness in "Being and Nothingness"

The conception of consciousness formulated in "The Transcendence of the Ego" can legitimately be considered as the epistemological starting point of Sartre's philosophy. In his later work *Being and Nothingness*, Sartre diverts his attention from the "descriptive science of consciousness" and turns his attention to the question of the pursuit of Being (or the Being of consciousness). He also grounded the "Being of consciousness" (as different from the phenomenon of Being,[17] that is the Being of appearance) in the pre-reflective *cogito* (or consciousness (of) self).[18]

---

16 The act of consciousness is the "nihilation" of Being.

17 The phenomenon of Being is an appearance of Being (different from the phenomenon of a table) which one can describe. It is disclosed to us by some kind of immediate success like boredom and nausea. Ontology is the description of the "phenomenon of Being" as it manifests itself. But the question that Sartre raises is: is the "phenomenon of Being" thus achieves identical to the "Being of phenomena?" – *BN*: 4

18 Consciousness (of) self or the Being of consciousness that concerns the pre-reflective *cogito* is a form of self-consciousness that examines subjective selfhood.

Consciousness Is Intentionality

Here too, Sartre begins with Husserl's principle of intentionality according to which "all consciousness is consciousness of something". It is always a relation of "aboutness" that never exhausts the experience of a thing. For Sartre, "there is no [act of] consciousness which does not *posit* a transcendent object". Or, as Sartre would say, "if you prefer, that consciousness has no 'content'" (*BN*: 7). Sartre gave the example of a table to illustrate the point. He says that the "table is not *in consciousness* – not even in the capacity of a representation" (ibid.). The existence of the table (i.e. if it exists *in* consciousness) is a "centre of opacity for consciousness" that furthermore makes "consciousness a thing" and "deny the cogito" (ibid.). Hence, for Sartre, the first procedure of a philosophy, in order to know that "consciousness is a positional consciousness of the world", was to "expel" all things from consciousness (and thereafter re-establish its true connection with the world). Hence, Sartre also writes:

> All consciousness is positional in that it transcends itself in order to reach an object, and it exhausts itself in this same positing.
>
> – Ibid.: 7-8

He continues:

> All that there is of intention in my actual consciousness [that is] directed toward the outside, toward the table; all my judgements or practical activities, all my present inclinations transcend themselves; [that is] they aim at the table and are absorbed in it.
>
> – *BN*: 7-8

Following which, Sartre concluded that not all consciousness is knowledge. However, all knowing consciousness can be knowledge only of its object. This is the first sense in which the Husserlian notion that "all consciousness is consciousness of something" is explicated by Sartre in the introduction of his *Being and Nothingness*. Consciousness, therefore, has no "content". It is also not a mode of particular knowledge which may be called an inner meaning or self-knowledge[19] (ibid: 7).

Consciousness, for Sartre, is also not dual in the sense of knower–known series. Sartre rejected the interpretation of "consciousness of consciousness" in terms of "to know is to know that one knows". This, for Sartre, will introduce a kind of subject–object dualism (the knower–known dyad) that will lead to an infinite series of – the known, the knower known, the knower known by the knower and so on. Sartre argues:

> If we wish to avoid an infinite regress, there must be an immediate, non-cognitive relation of the self to itself. – Ibid.: 8-9

That is, the intentionality of consciousness is also "conscious of itself". This self-consciousness, Sartre writes:

> [it is] the *only mode of existence which is possible for a consciousness of something.* Just as an extended object ... so an intention, a pleasure, a grief can exist only as immediate self-consciousness. [that is] If the intention is not a thing [not an external object/thing] in consciousness, then the *Being of the intention* can be only consciousness. – Ibid.: 10

Sartre refers to this as the "transphenomenal Being of consciousness".[20] That is, consciousness implies in its Being, "a non-conscious and transphenomenal Being". In other words, consciousness, therefore, is also conscious of itself. Following Heidegger's line of the question of Being by the Being, Sartre formulates:

---

19 It is as he would later argue the transphenomenal dimension of Being in the subject.

20 Transphenomenal is described by Sartre as the infinite series of aspects or possible appearances of an object that is not presently appearing (to someone) but which by turn could appear. He also noted that the transphenomenal Being of consciousness cannot be the ground for the transphenomenal Being of the phenomenon. – *BN*: 16

> Consciousness is a Being such that in its Being, its Being is in question insofar as this Being implies a Being other than itself.
>
> – *BN*: 18

This also implies that consciousness is a Being whose *existence posits its essence* or its existence implies its essence. That is, the existence of consciousness for Sartre comes from consciousness itself. Sartre writes:

> Consciousness is a plenum of existence, and this determination of itself by itself is an essential characteristic [of consciousness].
>
> – Ibid.: 11

In other words, its "appearance" [that is the existence] lays claim to *Being* (essence). And, consciousness insofar as it is structured intentionally, can, for Sartre, always pass beyond the existence (not towards its Being), but towards the "meaning of this Being". This is what Sartre means by the ontic–ontological, in which the fundamental character of its transcendence is to transcend the ontic towards the ontological (*BN*: 18). Hence, consciousness is the transphenomenal dimension of Being in the subject.

It may, however, be noted that this Being is not a "noumenal Being" which is hidden behind them. This mode of Being is also not the same as encountering any absolute form of Being or the Being of phenomena.[21] In this way, Sartre rules out a

---

21 For example, it is different from the encounter of the "Being of a table" wherein a "synthesis of subjective impressions" still accounts for the fact that it appears as a table. And, also the principle of a "series of manifestations" appears to consciousness as essence, with the fact that the "series need to be accounted for". Here, the series for Sartre cannot be reduced to consciousness. This is because the "mode of the *percipi*" here is passive. In other words, things which are perceived are encountered but do not act upon consciousness. For Sartre, when things go modification (of which it is not the origin), it is passive. And, in consciousness, this is the way things appear; relative to consciousness. Hence, when I walk around a table, the other side gets manifested. Here, the relation →

realistic conception of the relations of the phenomenon with consciousness (*BN*: 19).

Sartre also refers to the example of writing a book to illustrate this point (that is the relation between the transphenomenal Being of consciousness and the phenomenon of transphenomenal Being). Once the book is written, it exists independently. It has its own Being once it has been created. He argues that the same is true for consciousness. And because everything is active and entirely spontaneous, nothing can bite into it. Hitherto, consciousness also cannot act on anything. Consciousness rather is pure activity. It is not a thing which acts. It itself is an act. It does not, however, act on the thing it is conscious of. That is, for example, a table is not altered in any way by the act of consciousness (that is by the way it is perceived about existing things and not about non-existent objects). Taken this way, consciousness is also passive in its relation to the perceived thing. Hence, for Sartre, the transphenomenal Being of consciousness cannot provide the foundation for the phenomenon's transphenomenal Being. It also implies that the self-consistency of Being is beyond the active as well as it is beyond the passive (ibid.: 20).

So, when Sartre notes that "consciousness is consciousness of something", he also means that "transcendence" is a constitutive structure of consciousness. That is, consciousness is born *bearing on* a Being that it is not. So, when consciousness implies the Being of this table, of this package of tobacco, or of the lamp and, more generally, the Being of the world, the Being of that which appears (to consciousness) does not exist only in its appearance. It rather transcends beyond what is given to what is also not given. Now, it is also important to note that this mode of apprehension is not phenomenal but the structure

---

← of passivity is always relative to the Being that acts upon it. That is, consciousness can only act on something of this Being that supports action and exists on its own.

of conscious experience. The *esse* of the phenomenon therefore cannot be its *percipi* too[22] (*BN*: 15).

Hence, the Being of phenomenon lies beyond consciousness. And it is when we encounter the "phenomenon of Being" rather than the "Being of phenomenon" that meaning arises. Hence, without consciousness, there would be *no thing*. In other words, it is consciousness that causes there to be things. That is, it is only through consciousness that there is differentiation, there is meaning, and there is also plurality for Being. All this is because consciousness has nothing substantial. It is what Sartre would say, "a non-substantial absolute" (ibid.: 12). It is an appearance, a merely "pure appearance" in the sense that it "exists only to the degree to which it appears" (ibid.: 12). And, consciousness is precisely pure appearance because it is "total emptiness" (since the entire world is outside it).[23]

The intentionality account of consciousness that "all consciousness is consciousness of something", according to Sartre, does not account for "consciousness as constitutive of the Being of its object". This is because consciousness in terms of "consciousness of something" or "to be conscious of something" is to be at the same time "confronted with a concrete and full presence [of that] which is [also not] consciousness" (*BN*: 16). In other words, one can be conscious of "an absence" that necessarily implies a precondition of presence. Hence, the nature of consciousness (in terms of its intentional structure) is rational of a "transcendent Being", that transcends any definition of Being to include even its absence or the non-being. Sartre writes:

---

22 Sartre rather argues that it is not the reflective *cogito* but the pre-reflective Being of the *percipients* that would provide the ontological proof of the Being of phenomena (*BN*: 16).

23 This identity of "appearance" and "existence" within it, also constitutes consciousness (ibid.: 12).

> ... the Being of the phenomenon [to be] depend [end] on consciousness, the object must be distinguished from consciousness not by its presence but by its absence, not by its plenitude, but by its nothingness. – Ibid.: 16

He continues:

> If Being belongs to consciousness, the object is not consciousness, not to the extent that it is another Being, but that it is non-Being. – Ibid.: 16

This also explains the notion of "consciousness is consciousness of something" in terms of the "transcendence" that "constitutes the structure of consciousness". It is the nature of consciousness that orients towards a Being "which is not itself".[24] It also means that there is no Being outside the revealing intuition of a transcendent Being (ibid.: 17). Consciousness even as "pure subjectivity" also fails to transcend itself to posit the objective. Because subjectivity in terms of "consciousness (of) consciousness" qualifies "consciousness (of Being) consciousness" in what Sartre calls the "revealing intuition" that implies (within itself) something (that is) revealed. And, since the intentional structure of consciousness (already) implies in its Being "a non-conscious and transcendental Being", it must produce itself as a "revealed-revelation of Being", "which is not it" but which also gives itself as "already existing" when consciousness reveals it (*BN*: 18). That is, consciousness implies in its Being, "a non-conscious and transphenomenal Being". In other words, consciousness, therefore, is also conscious of itself. Following Heidegger's line of the question of Being by the Being, Sartre formulates:

> Consciousness is a Being such that in its Being, its Being is in question insofar as this Being implies a Being other than itself – Ibid.: 18

[24] This is also what Sartre means by ontological proof (*BN*: 17).

Consciousness Is Nothingness

Another main assertion of Sartre in his *Being and Nothingness* is the discussion of consciousness as nothing. The phenomenological precepts set up in the introduction of the book provide particular insight into his conception of the Being for-itself, consciousness as a nothingness.[25] That is, Sartre's phenomenological principles that have the role of which "things present themselves" reveal that consciousness is nothingness. The first way in which consciousness is nothing lies in the claims that for every positional consciousness of an object, there is a "non-positional consciousness of itself". That is, consciousness (that is always pre-reflective) recognized its object as "not itself". It is taken to mean that its self-consciousness is derivative from its recognition of an object as transcendent (what it is not). Again, consciousness insofar as it is the "sum of its appearance or effect" is nothing that adds to the "appearance of the existing human Being". It adds no new substance to the world, no mental substance, because it is non-substantial, unlike the Cartesian consciousness that is a substance. Hence, consciousness if at all it adds anything is "nothing". The conception of consciousness as a "transcendence of facticity" is a "nothingness" in the sense that it is not an existent thing but an occurrence or a movement. As an action, consciousness is always a projection towards the future; it is always moving beyond the finite series towards the further constitution of the infinite essence. Hence, consciousness as the pre-reflective consciousness of self participates in the level of transcendence; it is, in other words, a transcendence in the sense that it is not the appearance, but the appearance's consciousness of itself. And, consciousness insofar as it is not an appearance (effect) that makes up the human Being as a thing, is rather the self-consciousness of these appearances. Hence, it is no-thing. And, the Being of consciousness insofar as it exists – always at a distance from itself, bears within its Being the nothingness. As Sartre would

25 The phenomenon is revealed to consciousness, which Sartre refers to as Being-for-itself or simple for-itself.

later in the section, "The Problem of Nothingness" asserts that "nothingness haunts Being" (*BN*: 35). It is neither before nor after Being. It is also not outside of Being. Nothingness rather lies coiled in the heart of Being – like a worm[26] (*BN*: 45).

It can be concluded that consciousness exists in such a way that it carries within itself its own nothingness. It is the for-itself that must be its own nothingness. Because while the in-itself simple "is", consciousness on the other hand is "what it is not" and "is not what it is" (ibid.: 21). That is, consciousness does not coincide with itself.[27] And, it does not coincide with itself because it carries nothingness within itself. Consciousness, therefore, is also nothingness; it does not have any definitive set of characteristics. It can change its relationship with the things around it. It also is not fully determined by those things. Consciousness, therefore, is free.[28]

The theme of freedom is Sartre's fundamental project in his *Being and Nothingness*. Freedom, as the condition required for the

---

26 Hence, the Being by which nothingness comes to the world must be its own nothingness. It is, for Sartre, not a nihilating act. It is not a foundation in Being. It is rather an ontological characteristic of the Being required (*BN*: 47).

27 Sartre gave the example of "believing". He noted that to have an experience of believing something, and to be conscious of this belief at the moment I am having the experience are one and the same thing (ibid.: 125). However, it is not one and the same thing in the sense that it coincides with itself. That is, my belief is a conscious (of) belief. It is not something that I can confine myself to say that "it is a belief", in other words, my belief is a conscious (of) belief (ibid.: 123). The conscious experience of my belief is both a belief as well as a presence of this Being. Sartre calls this the "mirror-mirroring" structure of consciousness (ibid.: 125).

28 Here, free is not some mental faculty that human Beings have. It rather means that our conscious experience itself is freedom. It has the freedom to escape the rigidity and self-coincidence of the in-itself (Gusman 2020: 120).

nihilation of nothingness, is not a property which belongs to the essence of a human Being. It precedes man's essence. It rather makes it possible. That is, the essence of a human Being is suspended in his freedom. It is therefore impossible to distinguish freedom from the *Being* of human reality (*BN*: 49). Hence, the famous quotes of Sartre:

> Man does not exist *first* in order to be free subsequently; there is no difference between the Being of man and his Being-free.
>
> – Ibid.

The question of freedom also entails the question of "what it is to act?" And, since an action, for Sartre, is by definition "intentional" (ibid.: 455), it is [also not different from] consciousness. Action, for Sartre, is a projection of the for-itself towards "what is not".[29] And, nothing "that is" can ever determine by itself "what is not" (ibid.: 458). In other words, anything "this is" cannot determine (that) "which is not". And insofar as action involves a "negative Being" (i.e. an end which implies a state of the world which is not), all actions are by definition free. That is, once nihilation becomes an integral part of the positing of an end, Sartre acknowledges that an indispensable fundamental condition of any action is the "freedom of the Being who acts" (ibid.: 459). He argues that reason, motive and end are the three indissoluble terms of a "free consciousness" projects itself towards its possibilities. And, since consciousness is intentionality, there is no pure desire, emotions and passion. They are all directed towards an object or towards a more fundamental project. Freedom does not entail the ability to choose literally anything.

Sartre refers to the example of hiking when one man chooses to end the hike because he was plagued with fatigue. He writes:

> I start out on a hike with friends, at the end of several hours of walking my fatigue increases and finally becomes very painful.

---

[29] It is not a type of behaviour in which a person tries to achieve a certain goal.

> At first, I resist and then suddenly I let myself go, I give up, I throw my knapsack down on the side of the road and let myself fall down beside it. Someone will reproach me for my act and will mean thereby that I was free – that is, not only was my act not determined by anything or person, but I also could have succeeded in resisting my fatigue longer, I could have done as my companions did and reached the resting place before relaxing. I shall defend myself by saying that I was too tired.
>
> – *BN*: 475-76

Here, Sartre argues that it is not "freedom" of my action (not to continue to hike) that alone can explain the case. It is something else, what Sartre calls the "larger project"; the fundamental projects that determine the case. Hence, whereas all our actions have their own projected ends, they form the totality of the "fundamental project". This fundamental choice is not a deliberate choice. It exists against the background of consciousness. That is, for Sartre, the fundamental choice is one and the same as the consciousness we have of ourselves (ibid.: 483). Hence, for Sartre, my choice of not to continue the hike, in this case, cannot be reduced to any external motives, nor can it be viewed as unpredictable. And, since our choice can only be explained by a fundamental choice, Sartre concludes that "choice and consciousness" are also one and the same thing (ibid.: 484).

Hence, we are free because our consciousness is self-presence and entails its own nothingness (which allows it to break away from the in-itself). This also allows us to posit ends and act in light of these ends. The choices we subsequently make can be related to each other in the form of a fundamental choice. This works both ways. However, we act in light of our fundamental choice and since every conscious experience contains nothingness within it, it is also a choice. Thus, he concluded that every conscious act gives the world (its) meaning in light of (its) posited ends (Gusman 2020: 125). Hence, the world necessarily appears to us as we are and indeed it is by surpassing it towards ourselves that we make the world appear the way it is. In other words, we choose the world not in its in-itself consciousness, but in its meaning, by choosing ourselves (*BN*: 485-86). This consciousness for Sartre is expressed by the twofold feeling of anguish and of responsibility. They also constitute the *quality* of our consciousness insofar as it is pure and simple freedom (*BN*: 486).

References

Deutscher, M. 2001, "Sartre's Story of Consciousness", in *A Hundred Years of Phenomenology*, ed. R. Small, Ashgate: Routledge.

Edie, M. James, 1993, "The Question of the Transcendental Ego: Sartre Critique of Husserl", *Journal of the British Society for Phenomenology*, 24(2): 104-20.

Gusman, S., 2020, *Sartre on Subjectivity and Selfhood: The Self as a Thing Among Things*, New York: Palgrave Macmillan.

Heidegger, Martin, 1927, *Being and Time* (*Sein und Zeit*), Tübingen: Max Niemeyer Verlag.

Husserl, Edmund, 1970, *The Crises of European Sciences and Transcendental Philosophy*, Evanston, IL: Northwestern University Press.

——, 1900-1901, *Logical Investigations,* 2 vols, Halle: M. Niemeyer.

Levy, L., 2016, "Intentionality, Consciousness, and the Ego: The Influence of Husserl's Logical Investigations on Sartre's Early Work," in *The European Legacy*, Taylor and Francisa Online, 21, (5-6): 511-24. (Can be excessed through https://www.tandfonline.com/doi/full/10.1080/10848770.2016.1169606)

Merleau-Ponty, M., 1945 (1962), *Phenomenology of Perception*, London: Routledge and Kegan Paul.

Morris, P.S., 1985, "Sartre on the Transcendence of the Ego", *Philosophy and Phenomenological Research*, XLVI(2): 179-98.

Priest, S., 2000, *The Subject in Question: Sartre's Critique of Husserl in the Transcendence of the Ego*, in Routledge Studies in Twentieth Century Philosophy, London: Routledge.

Robert, M. and M. Doran, 1967, "Sartre's Critique of the Husserlian Ego", *The Modern Schoolman*, XLIV: 307-17.

Sartre, J.-P., 2004, *The Transcendence of the Ego*, London: Routledge.

——, 2003, *Being and Nothingness*, Routledge Classic.

——, 2001, *Basic Writings*, ed. S. Priest, London and New York: Routledge.

Webber, J., 2019, "Sartre's Critique of Husserl", *British Journal for the History of Philosophy*, Routledge.

7

The Problem of Alienation and Its Overcoming in Hegel

Arup Jyoti Sarma

Abstract: In his paper, I shall discuss the problem of alienation and its overcoming considering the development of consciousness in Hegel's *Phenomenology of Spirit*. The phenomenological growth of consciousness undertakes the journey that consciousness must take to overcome its self-alienation. While alienation is an undesirable aspect of consciousness's existence, the experience of alienation is an essential one if consciousness is to fully understand itself. In this paper, I shall attempt to highlight that (1) alienation is an important aspect of every shape of consciousness before Absolute Knowing; and (2) it is the experience of alienation that prompts consciousness to change its understanding of itself and its object until it overcomes its alienation in Absolute Knowing. While discussing the problem of alienation, I shall also refer to two German terms *entfremdung* and *entaüsserung*. *Entfremdung* will be translated as "estrangement" and *entaüsserung* will be translated as "externalization". The distinction between these two terms takes us to understand the multi-faceted role that alienation plays in the phenomenological progress of consciousness.

Keywords: Consciousness, alienation, unhappy consciousness, work, recognition.

Introduction

ALIENATION is an unpleasant aspect of consciousness's existence, but the experience of alienation is an essential one if consciousness is to fully understand itself. Alienation is vital to this process because, for Hegel, consciousness does not simply know itself with certainty; consciousness must develop its self-understanding to fully understand itself. As such, consciousness starts from a position where it does not fully understand itself; consciousness is, initially, alienated from itself. The phenomenological growth of consciousness undertakes the journey that consciousness must take to overcome its self-alienation. Gavin Rae (2012: 1, 24) argues:

> Alienation is a key to Hegel's phenomenological development of consciousness because: (1) alienation is a fundamental aspect of every shape of consciousness prior to Absolute Knowing; and (2) it is the experience of alienation that drives consciousness to alter its understanding of itself and its object until it overcomes its alienation in Absolute Knowing.

Alienation necessitates the mind's incapability to recognize itself in an externalization that it nevertheless knows to be its own (Dupré 1972). It enters into the life of consciousness from a variety of different angles, outlooks and events. Significantly, however, the experience of alienation constitutive of each shape of consciousness before Absolute Knowing contributes to the process whereby consciousness overcomes its alienation. This is necessarily so because, as Hegel explains, "it is the nature of spirit, of the Idea, to alienate itself in order to find itself again" (Hegel 2003: 80).

Consciousness initially does not understand that it is constituted by a subjective and an objective aspect with the relationship between its two aspects mediated and unified by spirit. Since consciousness only fully realizes its ontological nexus in Absolute Knowing, consciousness is alienated from itself in each shape it adopts before Absolute Knowing. Needless to point out that in each shape of consciousness before Absolute Knowing alienation does not stem in the same relation or is revealed in the same manner. The various ways that consciousness understands itself, as described in the various shapes of consciousness constitutive of its development process, shows that consciousness comprehends itself and its object differently in each shape it adopts. While each shape of consciousness understands its object differently, each shape of consciousness before Absolute Knowing fails, in some way, to properly understand that its object is an aspect of its ontological structure and that spirit grounds and intermediates its subjective and objective aspects. Consciousness is alienated in each of the shapes it adopts before Absolute Knowing because of this lack.

While in the shape of itself before Absolute Knowing consciousness fails, in some way, to fully understand its ontological structure, its constant lack leads consciousness to a better understanding of its ontological structure. Because consciousness's failings teach it something about what it is *not* and because consciousness learns from its failures, consciousness gradually learns what it *is*. As Hegel remarks, consciousness

> wins its truth only when, in utter dismemberment, it finds itself. It is this power, not as something positive, which closes its eyes to the negative, as when we say of something that it is nothing or is false, and then, having done with it, turn away and pass on to something else; on the contrary, Spirit is this power only by looking the negative in the face, and tarrying with it. – 1977: 19

It is the experience of being alienated from itself, by failing to understand that it is an organic spiritual unity of subjectivity and objectivity that pushes consciousness to adopt a new shape of itself to fully understand itself. Consciousness's experience continues to lead it to adopt new shapes of itself until it reaches Absolute Knowing where its experience reveals that it does fully understand its ontological structure. It is only from the position of Absolute Knowing we can understand the *ontological* nexus between subjectivity and objectivity. We can also say that this nexus is also a spiritual synthesis between the two.

The intentionality of Consciousness in the Phenomenology of Spirit

The *Phenomenology of Spirit* calls for the logical movement of consciousness to fully understand itself. To justify the necessity of philosophical consciousness, Hegel starts with the most abstract and minor shape of consciousness and traces the movement that will bring consciousness from the path of abstract truth of sense-certainty to the certainty of Absolute Knowing. However, Hegel wants to point out that while consciousness's journey to full self-understanding is a struggle, it is a struggle that also describes consciousness.

Consciousness consists of two aspects:

> Consciousness is, on the one hand, consciousness of the object and on the other, consciousness of itself; consciousness of what for it is the True and consciousness of its knowledge of the truth.
>
> – Hegel 1977: 54

Thus, consciousness is intentional; it always relates to an independent object. But significantly, Hegel holds that, because consciousness's existence depends on its intentional relation to an independent object, its independent, intentional object is an aspect of its *ontological* structure. This, however, does not mean that Hegel collapses the object into the subject. Rather, because consciousness's ontological structure always includes a relation to an independent object, consciousness is dependent on this relation (Rae 2012: 25). Because of its dependency on its intentional relation to an independent object, Hegel holds that consciousness's independent object is an aspect of its ontological structure. But ironically, consciousness does not initially realize that its independent, intentional object is an aspect of its ontological structure, consciousness understands itself to be in some way distinct from its intentional object and so is, initially, alienated from what *it truly is*.

Consciousness's preliminary failure to understand that its intentional object is an aspect of its ontological structure leads Hegel to claim that there is, initially, a distinction between the object as it appears *for consciousness* and the object as it is *in-itself* (Hegel 1977: 52-53). While this distinction results from consciousness's failure to understand itself, it also comprises the means that will allow consciousness to judge for itself when it has fully understood both itself and its object. Because the object as it appears *for consciousness* and the object as it is *in itself* belong to the same consciousness, consciousness itself can determine "whether its knowledge of the object corresponds to the object or not" (ibid.: 54). It does this by comparing whether the way the object appears *for consciousness* corresponds to the way the object is *in itself.*

Hegel, however, points out that while the movement between different shapes of itself is a necessary one if consciousness is to fully understand its ontological structure, the movement itself is not an easy one. Each new shape it adopts requires that consciousness renounces the certainty of itself that its previous shape gives it. If it is to fully understand itself consciousness must not adhere to the understanding that a particular shape of itself gives it or to the ease it has attained in a particular shape of itself. While consciousness can exist in a state of estrangement and indeed can find a degree of satisfaction in its estrangement, to fully understand its ontological structure, consciousness must be willing to alter its self-understanding. This takes courage, Hegel argues (Rae 2012: 29). It is not easy for consciousness to let go of what it considers to be the truth. However, consciousness will only learn what it truly is if it is willing to alter its self-understanding to accord with its experience.

It should be noted that what constitutes a moment of alienation in one shape of consciousness takes on a different meaning in another shape. Several commentators comment on the intricacy and multi-dimensionality of Hegel's analysis of alienation. Stanley

Rosen (1974: 172) maintains that "alienation" means "becoming another". Rosen argues that

> man undergoes alienation when he is separated from the products of his own labour, not by a voluntary contract but by a failure to grasp (...) the significance or essence of his life as a worker. ... Nature is the "otherness" or externalization of the Idea in which Spirit is merely implicit. – Ibid.: 173

Philip J. Kain aptly remarks that an aspect of alienation occurs when consciousness experiences reified sociocultural structures but fails to understand that not only does alienation not need to be experienced by consciousness, but that there are other sources of alienation besides reified social structures (2005: 156-69) Louis Dupré maintains that alienation consists in the mind's inability to recognize itself in an externalization which it nevertheless knows to be its own and so fails to understand that alienation does not need to be explicitly experienced by consciousness, nor does it solely arise when consciousness externalizes itself in objective form. Eric von der Luft (1989) states a tripartite division of alienation into "cultural", "spiritual" and "perceived" forms of alienation and so recognizes that different forms of alienation occur in different shapes of consciousness.

Two Forms of Alienation: Estrangement and Externalization

To understand appropriately the role that alienation plays in the *Phenomenology of Spirit* necessitates that we must know two German words: *entfremdung* and *entaüsserung*. There is a significant distinction between the two to know the fully multi-faceted role that alienation plays in the phenomenological growth of consciousness. *Entfremdung* defines a process or state where consciousness is separated from, at least, one of the aspects that are required for consciousness to fully understand itself. *Entfremdung* will be translated as "estrangement". In contrast, *entaüserung* designates the process whereby consciousness externalizes itself in object form and, through this objectification, develops a better form of itself. *Entaüserung* will be translated as "externalization".

Estrangement (*entfremdung*) is essentially known as alienation. Rae (2012: 31) says:

> Consciousness is alienated whenever it does not openly recognize that it is constituted by an objective and a subjective aspect and that, because spirit grounds and unites both aspects without negating their independence, it is fundamentally spirit.

In its immediate form, the estrangement of consciousness is negative. The negativity of estrangement originates from consciousness's failure to appropriately understand its ontological structure. However, while estrangement is negative, this is not to say that consciousness always *experiences* it negatively. Nor is it to say that it is always experienced at all by consciousness.

Since consciousness undergoes different understandings of its ontological structure, can we contend that whether Hegel's phenomenological expansion of consciousness talks of degrees of estrangement? Yes, it does. The various shapes of its journey to full self-understanding are constituted by different degrees of estrangement. Different degrees of estrangement originate from how the shapes of consciousness form a hierarchy of development. An earlier shape of consciousness is more alienated than a later shape of consciousness because, in the earlier shape of consciousness, consciousness is more abstract and further away from fully understanding its ontological structure. The process of determinate negation allows consciousness to gradually understand its ontological structure. The closer consciousness gets to Absolute Knowing, the less its existence is constituted by alienation. In a sense, "sense-certainty" is a more estranged form of consciousness than revealed religion, according to Hegel. "Sense-certainty" has a less developed understanding of itself than other shapes of consciousness and it is the most estranged form of consciousness.

This is not to say, however, that consciousness willingly experiences a lower level of intensity in its estrangement as it progresses through the shapes of consciousness. Consciousness does not need to explicitly experience its estrangement for it to be estranged. Whether experienced or not, the phenomenological development of consciousness establishes that consciousness is constituted by the greatest degree of estrangement when it adopts a shape of itself that is at the lowest levels of self-understanding.

Hegel recognizes that consciousness's estrangement from itself is undesirable. He upholds that the experience of estrangement plays an essentially positive and constitutive role in the developmental process that allows consciousness to overcome its self-alienation. If consciousness is estranged from what it truly is then it will be motivated to change its self-understanding to discover what it truly *is*. Murray Greene points out that Hegel recognizes that consciousness's journey to full self-understanding is not an easy or happy one. The experience of

> pain, [...] self-estrangement, homelessness in the world [...] is necessary moments to be lived through by the individual consciousness [so] that it may ascend to higher levels of self-consciousness and freedom. – Greene 1966: 367-68

The shape of consciousness, called the "unhappy consciousness", exhibits that consciousness can explicitly experience estrangement as negative. The unhappy consciousness develops from the consciousness's previous experiences. The unhappy consciousness is "the consciousness of self as a dual-natured [...] contradictory being" (Hegel 1977: 126). This duality takes the form of an essential objective aspect called the "fixed" and a contingent subjective aspect called the "changeable". But the duality of the unhappy consciousness is not a static binary opposition; it is a division constituted by motion. Consciousness takes the objective fixed aspect to be an essential moment, while it takes the subjective changeable aspect to be unessential. Despite both aspects belonging to the same consciousness, consciousness does not explicitly recognize this. For consciousness, each aspect is completely alien to the other. Because it is aware of the essential fixed aspect, consciousness takes itself to be the unessential subjective changeable aspect. Because it privileges the objective fixed aspect of itself, this shape of consciousness seeks to set aside the subjective changeable aspect.

This privileging, however, does not overcome its fundamental difference. Because this shape of consciousness is constituted by a duality, to negate one aspect of itself is to immediately reaffirm its opposite aspect. The unessential changeable moment is always present; consciousness cannot escape it. Whenever it seeks to negate the subjective changeable aspect and affirm the objective fixed aspect, because this act is an act of consciousness of which the subjective changeable aspect is a part, consciousness's negation of its subjective changeable aspect is also an affirmation of its subjective changeable aspect. This reaffirmation sets the whole process off again. The unhappy consciousness is this continuous movement; it is constantly thrown back and forth between its two contradictory aspects. It is because this shape of consciousness cannot reconcile the two aspects of itself in a peaceful and harmonious relationship that is "unhappy".

While the unhappy consciousness experiences its estrangement and while each shape of itself before Absolute Knowing fails to *initially* recognize that its understanding of itself is alienating, the discussion of the "heart of the matter in the shape of consciousness called "The Spiritual Animal Kingdom and deceit" or the "matter in hand" itself demonstrates that consciousness does not necessarily need to explicitly experience its estrangement (Hegel 1977: 237-52).

The "heart of the matter" springs from a discussion of the role and constitution of work. Consciousness's past experiences have taught it that "an individual cannot know what he [really] is until he has made himself a reality through action" (ibid.: 240). In other words, coming to fully understand itself requires that consciousness work on and shape its objective reality following under its ends. By coming to see that it has created its objective reality, consciousness will recognize itself in its objective world and so will no longer see its objective world as something simply alien to itself. The importance of work and recognition will be further explicated in connection with the "lord and bondsman or popularly known as the "master–slave" dialectic of Hegel.

The process of overcoming alienation is the process of externalization. Let me explain alienation as externalization. Externalization (*entaüsserung*) defines the process whereby consciousness externalizes itself in objective form and through this self-objectification develops a better understanding of itself. While the experience of estrangement, constitutive of each shape of consciousness before Absolute Knowing, leads consciousness to alter its self-understanding, externalization is the means through which consciousness objectifies itself and learns that it is not simply a pure subject, but that its ontological structure always incorporates a relation to objectivity. As Hegel explains, consciousness must

> externalize itself, have itself as an object, so that it knows what it is, in this way [it] exhausts all its potentialities, becomes entirely its object, wholly discloses itself and plumbs and reveals its whole depth. – 2003: 80-81

By externalizing itself in the world and seeing itself manifested through its object, consciousness understands that it is not simply opposed to itself; rather its ontological structure is always dependent on and incorporates a relation to objectivity. This allows consciousness to overcome the strict ontological binary between itself and its object that it originally holds to be constitutive of its relation to its object.

Consciousness can come to meaningfully externalize itself in an objective form because its previous experiences have taught it that externalization can augment its self-understanding. This can be realized in the shape of consciousness entitled "Individuality which takes itself to be Real In and For Itself" (Hegel 1977: 236-52). The famous section that underscores the lord and bondsman relation emanates from consciousness's experience of previous shapes of itself.

Work and Mutual Recognition: Lord and Bondsman Dialectic

Hegel explains the dialectic of self-consciousness with the famous dialectic of the lord and the bondsman. It is also sometimes referred to as the dialectic of the master and the slave relationship. Hegel says that the lord or the master on the one hand is "... the independent consciousness whose essential nature is to be for itself" (ibid.: 115). And the bondsman or the slave, on the other hand, "... is the dependent consciousness whose essential nature is simply to live or to be for another" (ibid.).

The lord is self-consciousness or simply the being for self. It is an immediate consciousness that excludes itself from everything else. Hegel says that

> ... its essence and absolute object is "I"; and in this immediacy or in this [mere] being, of its being-for-self, it is an *individual*.
>
> – Ibid.: 113

The bondsman is the consciousness that exists for another. The lord and bondsman exist as two opposite forms of consciousness.

The relationship between the lord and the bondsman has to be understood with the help of a third term, thinghood. The lord is the consciousness that exists for itself and is mediated through the aid of another consciousness, the bondsman. The bondsman is by nature bound up with an existence, which is independent, or thinghood. Hegel says that the lord is related to both of these moments, the thinghood and to the bondsman, whose essential nature is in this thinghood. In his words:

> The lord relates himself mediately to the bondman through a being [a thing] that is independent, for it is just this which holds the bondsman in bondage; it is his chain from which he could not break free in the struggle, thus proving himself to be dependent, to possess his independence in thinghood. – Ibid.: 115

The lord is related to the material reality through the bondsman. The relation of the lord to what surrounds him is that of a pure consumer. The task of the bondsman is to transform things and prepare them for the consumption of his lord. The bondsman is the one who experiences the independence and resistance of his master. The bondsman works for his master. The master enjoys the work of the bondsman. Hegel states this point in the following words:

> But the lord is the power over this thing, for he proved in the struggle that it is something merely negative; since he is the power over this thing and this again is the power over the other [the bondsman], it follows that he holds the other in subjection. Equally, the lord related himself mediately to the thing through the bondman; the bondman, *qua* self-consciousness in general, also relates himself negatively to the thing, and takes away its independence; but at the same time the thing is independent vis-à-vis the bondman, whose negating of it, therefore, cannot go the length of being altogether done with it to the point of annihilation; in other words, he only *works* on it. For the lord, on the other hand, the *immediate* relation becomes through this mediation the sheer negation of the thing, or the enjoyment of it. What desire failed to achieve, he succeeds in doing, viz. to have done with the thing altogether, and to achieve satisfaction in the enjoyment of it. Desire failed to do this because of the thing's independence; but the lord, who has interposed the bondsman between it and himself, takes to himself only the dependent aspect of the thing and has the pure enjoyment of it. The aspect of its independence he leaves to the bondsman, who works on it. – Hegel 1977: 115-16

The lord achieves his recognition from the activity of another consciousness, the bondsman. The bondsman, Hegel argues, sets aside his being-for-self and recognizes the works of the lord. The bondsman is doing the activity for the lord (Hegel 1977: 116).

But the relationship between the lord and the bondsman is one-sided. The bondsman works for the lord. The lord is simply the enjoyer of the works of the bondsman. The lord receives his due recognition from the works of the bondsman. But the lord does not recognize the activities of the bondsman and out of this subjugation, the bondsman is alienated from the objective reality that surrounds him. Hegel realizes this and explains, "The outcome is a recognition that is one-sided and unequal" (Hegel 1977: 116). Charles Taylor thinks (1975: 154) that the bondsman or slave is forced to recognize his master, but not vice versa. But for this very reason, the outcome is of no value to the master. His vis-à-vis is not seen to be a real other self but has been reduced to subordination to things. Recognition by him is therefore worthless; the master cannot see himself in the other. Rather, he is reduced to the parlous condition of being surrounded by beings that to him cannot be self-conscious; so that the surrounding world on which he continues to depend cannot reflect him as a human visage. His integrity is thus radically undermined just when it seemed assured.

We know that the lord has advantages over things. He is simply the enjoyer of the things that surround him. The bondsman experiences their independence and resistance. Hegel however argues that in course of time, the situation reverses. The lord cannot see himself in other things. The lord is in face of a world, which offers him no effective resistance. He is simply the being-for-self or self-consciousness (I = I). He is the consumer. Taylor explains this in the following words:

> The master we saw above has the advantage that his relation to things is that of simple enjoyment (...). It is the slave who experiences their resistance and independence. But with time,

> the advantages reverse. The master being in face of a world which offers him no effective resistance tends to sink back into a stupor of self-coincidence. He approaches the stagnant pole where I = I. He is simply the consumer. – Taylor 1975: 156

At the same time, the bondsman always wants to transform himself to rise to the level of universal. According to Hegel, one of the fundamental factors for transforming bondsman to the level of universal is the fear of death. The possibility of death always quakes him. Hegel says that the bondman

> ... has been fearful, not of this or that particular thing or just at odd moments, but its whole being has been seized with dread; for it has experienced the fear of death, the absolute Lord. In that experience it has been quite unmanned, has trembled in every fibre of its being, and everything solid and stable has been shaken to its foundations. – 1977: 117

Hegel states that the bondsman passes through the fear of death because he is at the mercy of his lord. But the fear of death is not alone enough to transform the bondsman to the highest stages of self-consciousness. He must do the work for the service of his lord. Work also plays an important role in transforming the lower levels of existence into the self-conscious embodiment of the universal. Therefore, it is the service and the fear of the lord that lead to transforming the bondsman to attain the universal spirit. The fear of the lord always reminds the bondsman of his existence and his services to the lord make him conscious of his existence. The slave by transforming himself through his work becomes a free thinker. He sees in the world of objects made by him the reflection of himself as universal, as a thinking being. Hegel, therefore, argues that

> ... the fear of the lord is indeed the beginning of wisdom, consciousness is not therein aware that it is a being-for-self. Through work, however, the bondsman becomes conscious of what he truly is. – Ibid.: 117-18

Through this discovery of himself by himself, the bondsman realizes that it is precisely in his work wherein he seemed to have only an alienated existence that he acquires a mind of his own (Hegel 1977: 118-19). For this reflection, the two moments of fear and service as such are necessary. Without the discipline of service and obedience, fear remains at the formal stage and does not extend to the known real world of existence. The bondsman works with the hope to get due recognition from his master.

Concluding Remarks

The problem of alienation is central to Hegel's account of the development of the spirit (*Geist*) and consequently of the process of human development. Hegel rejects the atomistic individuality of the enlightenment period, which opines that the self has a nature that is before society and which flourishes best when unrestricted by it. Hegel's view is that the self is a historical and social being. It develops through a process of self-alienation and its overcoming; self-estrangement and self-externalization through recognition. Subjectivity, individuality and freedom grow through a process in which the self is alienated from itself and then comes to identify itself in its alienation so that in the end, the self feels at home with itself.

References

Dupré, Louis, 1972, "Hegel's Concept of Alienation and Marx's Reinterpretation of It", *Hegel-Studien,* 7: 217-36.

Greene, Murray, 1966, "Alienation within a Problematic of Substance and Subject", *Social Research,* 33: 355-74.

Hegel, G.W.F., 2003, *Introduction to the Lectures on the History of Philosophy*, tr. T.M. Knox and A.V. Miller, Oxford: Oxford University Press.

——, 2003, *Introduction to the Lectures on the History of Philosophy*, tr. T.M. Knox and A.V. Miller, Oxford: Clarendon Press.

——, 1977, *Phenomenology of Spirit*, tr. A.V. Miller, Oxford: Oxford University Press.

Kain, Philip J., 2005, *Hegel and the Other: A Study of the Phenomenology of Spirit*, New York: State University of New York.

Rae, Gavin, 2012, "Hegel, Alienation, and the Phenomenological Development of Consciousness", *International Journal of Philosophical Studies*, 20(1): 23-42.

Rosen, Stanley, 1974, *G.W.F. Hegel: An Introduction to the Science of Wisdom*, New Haven and London: Yale University Press.

Taylor, Charles, 1975, *Hegel*, London: Cambridge University Press.

von der Luft, Eric, 1989, "An Early Interpretation of Hegel's Phenomenology of Spirit", *Hegel-Studien*, 24: 183-94.

8

Transcendence of Subjectivity

A Contemporary Exploration of Epistemological Social Self in Neohumanism of P.R. Sarkar

Sindhu Poudyal

Abstract: The question of being and becoming/one and many are thc approach to the impression of that aspect of reality that underlies one's being in the world and also sets apart this being beyond the world of phenomena. Hence, it has been revived because of the finitude of perception of the infinitude of reality in scientific explanations. Indian philosophy (of classical antiquity) has seen it as an all-inclusive consciousness *aham brahmāsmi* which "is" in the world yet beyond the given finitude of existence and associated the transcendence[1] of it linguistically as a state

---

1 The term transcendence though appears frequently in Western philosophical tradition; more so, in pure and hermeneutical phenomenological philosophies. The usage of the term however is borrowed from the phenomenological tradition of Husserl, Levinas, Marion, Buber and even Derrida. For phenomenologists, the concept of transcendence could be the very ground of phenomenological subject which transcends its own consciousness: the nature of which seems objective at least within the domain of understanding. It is a fascinating idea that similar is to the approach of knowledge of *Brahman*. *Ātman* is brahman that transcends itself at the transcendental experience. It transcends the finitude of the →

of knowledge, being and bliss, i.e. *Saccidānanda.* This paper aims at exploring the development of Advaitic consciousness (both classical and contemporary) in several dimensions in the name of "transformed subjectivity" bearing a profoundly meaningful approach and rigour. However, I shall confine these meanings and dimensions to the epistemological and social paradigm in classical and contemporary Indian tradition on consciousness vis-à-vis P.R. Sarkar's neohumanism.[2] In doing so, there are frequent terms I shall be revisiting like consciousness, *ātman, Brahman, brahmānubhūti, mokṣa,* subjectivity, phenomena, microvita, authenticity, transcendence, transcendental PROUT. This paper aims to analyse these dimensions (at least two dimensions) and

← objective validation and tries to get into its authentic meaning. It is very close to the spiritual/divine experience which has been the foundation of neohumanism of P.R. Sarkar. His humanism promotes spiritual cult as one of the pillars of neohumanist society. He believed until and unless a being is elevated spiritually, his/her subjectivity cannot be transcended to see oneness in the multiplicity. And if that does not happen, there cannot be social progress.

2 Neohumanism (sounds as a Western theory) is a universal philosophical approach has been theorized by P.R. Sarkar in the twentieth century. He defines its meaning as the "liberation of the intellect". Which is somewhat similar to the absolutism of Advaitic philosophy – reaching beyond the logic and reason in a way transcending the limitation of the intelligence. Neohumanism tries to extend the spirit of humanism, i.e. the subjective experience of humans to a universal philosophy. He holds, it is the therapeutic approach of love towards all beings (both animate and inanimate). The intellect of humanism when transcends (in phenomenological terms), it is extended to everything and he calls it a neohumanist moment. All sociality and holism are possible within this transcendence of the subjective experience. This paper intends to analyse how this transcendence of subjective experience evolves in a profoundly meaningful way in the social self and in return creates a new dimension of the epistemically social self, the whole movement P.R. Sarkar calls as neohumanism.

find the underlying conjectures to answer – why there are different approaches to the same reality – if all we intend is to culminate within the metaphysical realm – which cannot be spoken in terms of discourse yet available in subjective consciousness and, second, to search for an alternative theory that is essential for twenty-first century understanding of the transcendence of the self as socially available/accepted self. Hence, this paper puts forth the transcended self as an epistemologically ethical self. Along these lines, it explores the epistemologically ethical self (a social self) which is a neohumanist theory and an offset of a post-humanist theory of P.R. Sarkar. Hence, the methodology of the paper is critically analytical and hermeneutical.

Keywords: *Brahmānubhūti, mokṣa*, post-humanism, PROUT, microvita.

Consciousness, Subjectivity and Its Transcendence

CLASSICAL Indian philosophy profoundly expresses the fundamental aspect of reality being non-dual (Advaita/*bhedābheda rahita*), non-physical (*cit/cetanā*), beyond the spatio-temporal and linguistic domain (*anirvacanīya*) – yet there is an emphasis on an urgent need to "know" about this reality "as it is". But the real paradox begins once it is known, nothing is remaining to know yet there is "silence" (*mauna*); after knowing it.[3] The real quest starts from here

---

[3] That *ātman* (self, soul) is indeed *Brahman*. It is identified with the intellect, mind and even the breath, with the eyes and ears, with earth, water, air and *ākāśa* (sky), with fire and with what is other than fire, with desire and the absence of desire, with anger and the absence of anger, with righteousness and unrighteousness, with everything – it is identified, as is well known, with this (what is perceived) and with that (what is inferred). This *ātman* does and acts, so it becomes: by doing good it becomes good and by doing evil it becomes evil. It becomes virtuous through good acts and vicious through evil acts. Others, however, say, "The self is identified with desire alone. What it desires, so it resolves; what it resolves, so is its deed; and what deed it does, so it reaps". – *Bṛhadāraṇyaka* →

as a knower tries to know the given/that which is hidden how to go about it? Original/manifestation, etc. how it comes into "being". Classical scriptures prescribed – *śravaṇa, manana* and *nididhyāsana* as the modes of knowing/realization of that reality. The second quest which is equally important yet not answered satisfactorily is what is next for the knower who becomes one with the knowledge itself? There the *Gītā* prescribes – reap your *prārabdha* and settle the score with *karma* and be liberated from the cycle of birth and death which has been considered as *mokṣa.* Like classical Indian philosophical exploration of reality as *Brahman* or pure consciousness, P.R. Sarkar too believes:

> Reality is *Brahman* that exists – It is *Paramātman, Bhūmācaitanya,* Universal Consciousness or Consciousness in its totality.[4]

However, his notion of reality is not merely transcendental. What appears to me in P.R. Sarkar's notion of reality is – immanent rather than only transcendental and does not remain an enigma for intellect and expression which is otherwise believed to be so. P.R. Sarkar in contemporary times attempts to provide a more approachable explanation of reality and this immanent approach could be seen in his foundational text – *Ānanda Sūtram* (1962). In the opening verse of the *Ānanda Sūtram*, Sarkar holds:

śivaśaktyātmakaṁ brahma ।

Brahman is the composite of Śiva and Śakti. *Brahman*, i.e. the cosmic entity, is the composite of Śiva which is consciousness and Śakti that which is an operative principle. Now the question is: if Śiva is a conscious element, then what is the status of phenomenal human existence in the world? The universe has been created out of *Puruṣa.*

← *Upaniṣad* 4.4.5, extracted from *The Bṛhadāraṇyaka Upaniṣad*, third edn, Madhavananda (tr.) Almora: Advaita Ashrama, 4.4.5, p. 712, 1950.

4 P.R. Sarkar, 1988, "What Is the Cosmic Entity?", in *Ananda Marga Elementary Philosophy*, 5th edn, pp. 14-25, Kolkata: Ananda Marga Publication.

In other words, *Puruṣa*, when qualified by the *guṇa* of *prakṛti*, has created the universe out of His self. *Puruṣa*, we know, is a subtle entity that can be appreciated only as an idea. Yet the moon, the sun, the stars and the planets, the atmosphere and the earth, made of subtle *Puruṣa*, are all found in this creation. We have to admit that this creation has been formed by a subtle entity gradually becoming crude. We have already established by logical reasoning that *Puruṣa* is subtle. So if the crude universe has been created out of this subtle entity, its seed must have existed in this subtle entity, and, on being qualified by *prakṛti*, germinated into this expansive universe. In the same way, we get butter from milk only because it existed in milk in another form. If the seed of the crude universe existed in Him, *Puruṣa* could not be called subtle or understandable only as an idea. Subtle is something that can be understood or appreciated as an idea only and contains no crudeness. The ethereal factor in which no perceivable crude substance can be found is called crude because sound can travel through it. The ethereal factor has no dimensions and no perceptible existence, yet merely because of the presence of the quality permitting sound waves to travel through it, it is called crude. The presence of something makes it identifiable; it cannot be said to be subtle or understandable only as an idea. *Puruṣa* cannot be said to be subtle if the seed of the universe exists in Him. He has to be crude, but it has already been established that *Puruṣa* is subtle, and so the seed of the crude universe cannot exist in Him (Sarkar 1962).

Unlike the classical philosophies, P.R. Sarkar tries to explore the more convincing relationship of *Brahman* with the world and holds:

brahma satyaṁ jagadapi satyamāpekṣikam ।

Brahman is the Absolute Truth; the universe is also truth, but relative.[5]

---

[5] The purport of the *sūtra* is – *Brahman* is *satya* (truth), i.e. unchangeable. But we cannot say that the changes that are perceived apparently on the body of *Brahman* under the influence of *prakṛti* and the three fundamental relative factors of time, space →

This relative nature of the world seems extremely complex and because of the complexity, the comprehension of the subtlest essence becomes a misnomer – a common expression we have been hearing from classical times.

The contradictory situation in knowledge and realization arises because of the pre-established understanding that being knowledgeable means having some extraordinary perception. However, the experience is so private (subjective) that, its comprehension of language and objectivity is incomplete. But the novelty of this expression has been propagated by P.R. Sarkar in his neohumanism where he defines neohumanism as the liberation of the intellect. It is the humanism of the past, the humanism of the present and humanism – newly explained of the future – the philosophy which will make people understand that they are not merely ordinary creatures and that the meaning of human existence is not merely physical, psychic or spiritual; it comprises all three (Sarkar 1982: 94-99). If the universe has been created out of *Puruṣa*, but if the seed did not exist in *Puruṣa*, how could the universe have been created? This sounds illogical and unreasonable, and the only logical thing to say is that the universe was never created as *Puruṣa* is subtle by nature and the crude universe could not have been created out of Him. It was however said earlier that the universe was created out of Him and as it has been logically proven to be true, the only other rational statement would be to say that the crude universe was never a created reality. Yet, the existence of

---

← and person are false, nor can we say that they are eternal truths. All that we can say is that they are relative truths, for the apparent changes are dependent on the relativity of these three factors, i.e. time, space and person. The unit-entity or the unit mind, also, in its progressive bearing, is involved with these three factors, hence its existence also is a relative factor. One relative entity appears to be a spiritual truth to another relative entity and so the changeable world appears to be a truth to the changeable living unit.

– Sarkar 1962: 22

this visible universe cannot be ignored. This crude universe is created only as a thought projection of *Puruṣa*. When influenced by *Prakṛti*, a wave arises in the mind of *Puruṣa* and, as a result, the entire creation becomes an imaginary entity filled with different forms. The universe comes into being only as an imaginary entity in the mind of *Puruṣa* and no crude stuff is required for its creation. Imaginary objects are not crude realities, for the creation of which crude stuff may be necessary. Hence, *Puruṣa*, who is subtle, can easily create the universe out of His self. Accepting the creation to be only a thoughtwave gives rise to the following doubts:

1. How do we experience this world as real if it is not a crude reality and exists only as a thoughtprojection of *Puruṣa*?
2. The creation should come to an end the moment the thoughtwave of *Puruṣa* ceases to exist. Thoughtwaves or imaginary entities are only momentary, and their cessation should bring about complete annihilation.[6]

To this, he further states that among the species:

> Human beings are the highest-evolved beings. They possess clearly-reflected consciousness and this makes them superior to animals. No other being has such a clear reflection of consciousness. Human beings can distinguish between good and bad with the help of their consciousness and when in trouble they can find a way out, with its help. Everyone is in quest of happiness; in fact, it is people's nature to seek happiness. The acquisition of something limited only creates the want for more, and the quest for happiness finds no end. The hunger for possessing is unending. It is limitless and infinite. He further holds that however dignified or lofty the achievement, it fails to set at rest people's unlimited quest for happiness. The world itself is finite and cannot provide infinite objects. Naturally,

---

6 Originally published in "What Is This World?", *Ananda Marga Philosophy in a Nutshell*, Part 1 and Supreme Expression, vol. 1, Extracted from the electronic edition version 9.0.15.

> therefore, the greatest worldly acquisition, even if it be the entire globe, would not secure anything of an infinite and permanent character. What then is that infinite, eternal thing which will provide everlasting happiness?[7]

The Cosmic Entity alone is infinite and eternal. It alone is limitless. And the eternal longing of human beings for happiness can only be satiated by the realization of the Infinite. The Infinite can be only one and that is the Cosmic Entity.[8] Hence it is only the Cosmic Entity that can provide everlasting happiness – the quest for which is the characteristic of every human being. In reality, behind this human urge is hidden the desire, the longing, for the attainment of the Cosmic Entity. It is the very nature of every living being. This alone is the *dharma* of every person. The word *dharma* signifies "property". The English word for it is "nature", "characteristic" or "property". The nature of fire is to burn or produce heat. It is the characteristic or property of fire and is also termed the nature of fire. Similarly, the *dharma* or nature of a human being is to seek the Cosmic Entity.

Transcendence of the Subjectivity: Neohumanism and PROUT

P.R. Sarkar's social self can be seen as the transcendence of the subject to "being human" – it can be seen as a return of the spiritual subject to the world for the constitution of a neohumanist world order. As Sarkar asserts – the degree of divinity in human beings is indicated by their clearly-reflected consciousness. Every human being, having evolved from animals, has, therefore, two aspects – the animal aspect and the conscious aspect – which distinguish a person from animals. The difference between the two is due to the

---

7 P.R. Sarkar, "What Is Dharma?", in *Ananda Marga: Elementary Philosophy, Universal Humanism and Ananda Marga Philosophy in a Nutshell Part 1* [a compilation]. Electronic edition version 9.0.15.

8 P.R. Sarkar, "The Dharma of Human Beings", in *Prout in a Nutshell, Volume 1, Part 1* [a compilation]. Electronic edition version 9.0.15.

possession by the human being of a clearly reflected consciousness, something which animals lack. The infinite nature of the human urge for absolute happiness is due to their consciousness alone. It is this consciousness alone that is not satisfied with the physical pleasure of possession, power and position – things which despite their huge proportions, are only transitory.[9] It is their consciousness that creates in human beings the longing for the Cosmic Entity.

As Sarkar affirms though the world is full of complexities, the individual embodied self constantly wishes to break the confinement of the compartment in which it is. The essential propensity in a human being is to set itself free from its finitude and merge into the infinite. Hence, the essential nature of the objects of the world – physical enjoyment – does not quench the thirst of the human heart for happiness. Yet, we find that people are attracted by them. The animality in people draws them towards gratification of animal desires, but the rationality of their consciousness remains ungratified since all these are transitory and short-lived. They are not enough to set at rest the unending and unlimited hunger of the human consciousness. There is, thus, a constant duel in humans between their animality and rationality. The animal aspect pulls them towards instant earthly joys, while their consciousness, not being satisfied with these, draws them towards the Cosmic Entity – the Infinite. This results in the struggle between the animal aspect and consciousness. Had the carnal pleasures derived from power and position been infinite and endless, they would have set at rest the eternal quest of consciousness for happiness. But they do not, and that is why the fleeting glory of temporal joys can never secure a lasting peace in the human mind and lead people to ecstasy.[10]

It is only the well-reflected consciousness that differentiates human beings from animals. Is it then not imperative for human

---

9 P.R. Sarkar, "The Dharma of Human Beings", in *Prout in a Nutshell, Volume 1, Part 1* [a compilation]. Electronic edition version 9.0.15.

10 Ibid.

beings to make use of their consciousness? If their consciousness lies dormant behind their animality, people are bound to behave like animals. They become worse than animals as, even though endowed with well-reflected consciousness, they do not make use of it. Such people do not deserve the status of human beings. They are animals in human form.

The nature of consciousness is to seek the Infinite or realize the Cosmic Entity. Only those who make use of their consciousness and follow its dictates deserve to be called human beings. Therefore, every person, by making full use of his or her reflected consciousness, earns the right to be called a human being and finds his or her *dharma* (nature) to be only the search for the Infinite or Cosmic Entity.[11] And so people derive real happiness only when they can attain the Cosmic Entity or get into the process of attaining it. Consciousness does not want earthly joys because being finite none of them satisfies it. The conclusion we arrive at is that the *dharma* of humanity is to realize the Infinite or the Cosmic Entity. It is only by using this *dharma* that people can enjoy eternal happiness and bliss.[12]

Human beings form the last stage in the evolutionary ladder of creation. In human beings consciousness is fully reflected in a physical body made of the five rudimental factors derived from the Cosmic body of the Qualified Supreme Entity (*Saguṇa-Brahman*). This clear reflection of consciousness is unit consciousness (*ātman*) and the physical body of the five factors which receive this reflection is called the human body. Thus, a human being has unit consciousness (*ātman*) and body. Being the possessor of these two shows that a human being is neither of these. If human beings were *ātman* (unit consciousness) they could not claim it as their *ātman* and alternatively where the body only, they could not say, "This is

---

11 P.R. Sarkar, "The Dharma of Human Beings", in *Prout in a Nutshell, Volume 1, Part 1* [a compilation]. Electronic edition version 9.0.15.

12 Ibid.

my body". They are different from these two. There is some other entity in human beings which claims the possession of *ātman* and body. That other entity appears to be the owner of *ātman* and the body. What then is that other entity? Foundational philosophy and the development in P.R. Sarkar can be traced in four central domains – ontological, metaphysical, epistemological and ethical (specifically socio-economic) which are the constituents of the concept called human life in general. The entire metaphysical orientation of P.R. Sarkar's philosophy can be seen from four central elements comprising phenomenal and transcendental aspects of an integrated system of creation[13] which have been highlighted by Sarkar himself – The universe, the mind, the spirit, the society in which we live alongside our social life – integral to each other, bearing both phenomenal and transcendental essence and how Sarkar aims at offering a cosmic connection amongst all animate and inanimate things and beings in the world. Sarkar extended his practical philosophy in the form of a new cult/tradition, without any intention to destroy the traditional/existing practices of ancient India. His favourite subject "humanism" runs through his discourse in society with the introduction of his new theory of neohumanism. He holds that, if humanism as a theory tries to emancipate humans in an anthropocentric view, this neohumanism aims to elevate the existing philosophies of humanism to universalism. Sarkar (2012) says:

> When the underlying spirit of humanism is extended to everything, animate and inanimate, in this universe – I have designated this as "neohumanism".

This neohumanism, according to Sarkar, will elevate humanism to universalism – the cult of love for all created beings of this universe.

Neohumanism is said to prefer existential value over

---

[13] Comprehensive of individual and collective life of the creation; more specifically it is for human as it is only for the human being his existence and meaning to the existence are an issue.

utility value for all living beings. Sarkar's neohumanism places great emphasis on rationality and encourages what he calls a "protospiritual mentality", a process of continually recognizing each object with which we come in contact, externally or internally, as a manifestation of the Supreme Consciousness (*Brahman*) (Sarkar 2012). According to Sarkar, rationality helps to give rise to devotion, which he considers to be the "highest and most valuable treasure of humanity". In Sarkar's view, neohumanism leads to the liberation of human intellect from the constraints of imposed dogma and the principle of selfish pleasure and psychic complexes helping to bridge the gap between the inner and outer worlds.

According to Sarkar, the pure feeling of "I" is only an abstract idea – a little introspection would show that this feeling of "I exist" is an idea. It comes about as a result of thinking. This feeling of "I" can come only when there is consciousness, and it is with consciousness or *jñāna* that one can take an idea and think or perform some action. The feeling of "I" is, therefore, a mental projection of consciousness; or, to be explicit, it can be said that without consciousness, or *jñāna*, the knowledge of the existence and thereby the idea of the feeling of "I" cannot be formed. *Ātman* is unit consciousness or unit *Puruṣa* and as it is within the scope of *Saguṇa-Brahman*, it will be qualified by the principles of *prakr̥ti* in the same way as has occurred in the case of *Puruṣa* in *Saguṇa-Brahman*. It is due to the qualifying influence of the sentient principle of *prakr̥ti* that *ātman* acquires the knowledge of the existence or that the pure feeling of "I" comes into being. It is by this idea of existence that the feeling of "I" is formed and, hence, the individual identity as "I" is this idea only. This is thus only a projection formed due to the qualifying influence of sentient *prakr̥ti* on unit consciousness. This feeling of "I" is, therefore, not *ātman* or unit consciousness.[14]

---

14 P.R. Sarkar, "What Is My Relation with the Universe and the Cosmic Entity?", in *Ananda Marga: Elementary Philosophy and Ananda Marga Philosophy in a Nutshell, Part 1* [a compilation]. Electronic edition version 9.0.15.

The human beings' individuality or their feeling of "I" is not unit consciousness. It is only an objective idea of unit consciousness, the knowledge of which comes about by the qualifying influence of *prakṛti*. A human being's feeling of "I" is thus entirely dependent on unit consciousness, just as the existence of a plank of wood is dependent on a tree. The plank cannot be called a tree, similarly, this entity of "I" cannot be unit consciousness. It is only an idea dependent on unit consciousness, formed as a result of the qualifying influence of sentient *prakṛti* on it.

Bodhisattva comes into being due to the qualifying influence of the sentient principle of *prakṛti* on the unit consciousness. This also brings about the feeling of "I" and creates the knowledge of the existence of unity consciousness. The individual entity of "I", therefore, is not unit consciousness; it is *bodhisattva*, which is only a part of his or her mind. For this, the "I" entity of human beings is *bodhisattva*, which is subtler than *ahaṁ-tattva* and *citta*. What then are *ahaṁ-tattva* and *citta*? It has been explained by Sarkar that *ahaṁ-tattva* (ego) comes into being as a result of the qualifying influence of the mutative principle of *prakṛti* on *bodhisattva*, whereupon the latter manifests itself as *ahaṁ-tattva*. The *ahaṁ-tattva*, on being further qualified by the static principle of *prakṛti*, is manifested as *citta*.[15] It is, in fact, *bodhisattva*, or the pure feeling of "I", which is manifested as *ahaṁ-tattva* and *citta* due to the qualifying influence of the mutative and static principles of *prakṛti*. *Ahaṁ-tattva* and *citta* are only cruder functional forms of the human being's "I" entity. The human being's mind is, therefore, a further projection of his feeling of "I" (*bodhisattva*) and is made of that entity only. Unit consciousness or *ātman* is reflected only when there is a physical body made of the five rudimental factors of the macrocosm.[16]

---

15 P.R. Sarkar, "What Is My Relation with the Universe and the Cosmic Entity?", in *Ananda Marga: Elementary Philosophy and Ananda Marga Philosophy in a Nutshell, Part 1* [a compilation]. Electronic edition version 9.0.15.

16 Ibid.

Sarkar further holds that *buddhi-tattva* comes into being as a result of the influence of sentient *prakṛti* on unit consciousness and so *bodhisattva*, or the feeling of "I", is also dependent on the physical body. Since *buddhi-tattva* pervades every bit of the body, one feels the presence of "I" in every part of the body and is prone to identify this "I" with the body.[17] It has, however, been explained earlier that this feeling of "I" and the body is not the same entity. They are different – the feeling of "I" is *bodhisattva* and the physical body merely forms a shelter (*ādhāra*) for it.[18] A human being's feeling of "I" is thus neither his nor her unit consciousness nor his or her body; it is only the mental creation of unit consciousness, termed as a *bodhisattva* and this "I" is further manifested as the other two functional forms of mind – *ahaṁ-tattva* (ego) and *citta*.[19]

Prout can be understood as the path of socio-economic emancipation for humanity. PROUT should go side by side with the psychic approach of neohumanism. Neohumanistic ideas give human beings the impetus to move. They create a longing for subtler pabula, and that pabula are supplied by PROUT. The spirit is to maintain a balance between the physical and psychic worlds and take human beings to the threshold of spirituality.[20] For, Sarkar holds, there must be balance, equipoise and equilibrium between the physical, psychic and spiritual realms. There must be a balance between PROUT, neohumanism and spiritual practices. He suggests, one must maintain a balance among these three. PROUT is the socio-economic approach; neohumanism is the psycho-intellectual approach and spiritual practice is the spiritual-intuitional approach. This threefold approach will take human

17 P.R. Sarkar, "What Is My Relation with the Universe and the Cosmic Entity?"

18 Ibid.

19 *Ananda Marga Philosophy in a Nutshell, Part 1* [a compilation]. Electronic edition version 9.0.15.

20 P.R. Sarkar, "Prout and Neohumanism", in *Prout in a Nutshell, Volume 4, Part* 17 [a compilation]. Electronic edition version 9.0.15.

beings along the path of salvation. The goal of humanity is the supreme stance in *Parama Puruṣa* (the Supreme Entity).[21] Our goal is a state of complete composure and complete spiritual unification. On the one side is the socio-economic approach of PROUT and on the other is the psychic approach of neohumanism. The mid-point is the path of spirituality. In both the socio-economic and psychic realms there are imperfections. Prout and neohumanism cannot surmount the threshold of spirituality.[22] The path of spiritual practice enables one to surmount the threshold and enter the realm of spirituality. This proto-spiritual philosophy can be interpreted as a transcendence of subjectivity of the postmodernist approach to the self. If transcendence of the self culminates in the realization of consciousness, then this unit consciousness (embodied self) transcends itself into a transformed subject which culminates in a social self in P.R. Sarkar which is eventually actualized in Prout. Hence, in nutshell, Prout can be seen as an extension of subjectivity.

The Novelty of P.R. Sarkar: The Microvitum

"Microvitum, the Mysterious Emanation of the Cosmic Factor" (Sarkar 1987: 1). It is one of the human wants that whatever we do not know, to conceal our limitations or hide our imperfections, we either say that it is non-existent or in a more intelligent style, we will say it is abstract. In this universe of ours, whatever comes within the scope of our senses or within the periphery of our perception, we say, "it is" and whatever is beyond the arena of the senses or the jurisdiction of perception, we cannot say anything. Hence, our world functions within the limitations of our senses and perceptions. We know in the realm of cosmic introvert or extrovert that in the first phase – in the phase of an extrovert – "subtle" is transmuted into "crude" and in the returning phase of an introvert, "crude" is metamorphozed into "subtle". In this progress, rather

21 P.R. Sarkar, "Prout and Neohumanism", in *Prout in a Nutshell, Volume 4, Part* 17.

22 Ibid.

in this semicircular approach, there may be subtler objects in the scope of matter – many objects subtler than electrons or protons, [neutrons] or positrons – but we find no alternative but to say that they are either electrons or protons or positrons or neutrons. And, similarly, in the psychic sphere, there may be entities subtler than ectoplasm or its extra-psychic coverage, endoplasm.

These entities that come within the realm of both physicality and psychic expressions are smaller or subtler than atoms, electrons or protons, and in the psychic realm they may be subtler than ectoplasm. For such objects or for such entities I use the term "microvitum". This microvitum, or in plural microvita, is not of protoplasmic order and, as such, they have got little to do with carbon molecules or carbon atoms, which are treated as the initial point or initial stage of life in this universe. So far as physicality is concerned, the position of the microvita is just between ectoplasm and electron, but they are neither ectoplasm nor electron.

It is a human want that whatever we know regarding any subject or any object when we know that it exists but its characteristics or other particulars are not known to us, we say it is "mysterious". So regarding these microvita, we may say it is mysterious. That is why I used the term "microvitum, the mysterious emanation of the Cosmic Factor". They are not of protoplasmic order and hence the question of their protozoic structure or metazoic structure does not arise.[23] They are something mysterious. Now the question is can we say

---

[23] These explorations were scientific terms to signify the first emanation of life in this planet around 2,500 to 570 million years ago. For millions of years, only bacteria and single-celled organisms existed and the early invertebrates that followed were soft-bodied and rarely left any trace in the form of fossils. This may sound speculation to many as we have no ways to refer to those structures but scientific evidences certify the factual reference of it. However, these references in this paper were taken specifically from P.R. Sarkar's text *Microvitum in a Nutshell* and he himself used these terms from the scientific usage.

that these microvita have the element/trace of consciousness that we have been continually searching for? If it is, then the riddle of the mind and matter/consciousness and the matter can be reduced to a great length so also the missing dots in the understanding of the cosmos in scientific temper. Well, P.R. Sarkar himself quotes this concept of microvita remains a concept of philosophical and mythical speculation if it is limited to discourse. Hence, he proposed a method for understanding the integrated system of the cosmos in a theory that he named mictovitum. However, it is important to note that microvitum constitutes one of the major and mature theories contributed by P.R. Sarkar to make it a common platform for scientists, social science researchers, theologians, as well as spiritualists to work together for a better understanding of the post-humanist and trans-humanist world. This theory of microvita can be seen as a holistic approach to theorizing the contemporary and future of Indian philosophy and science.

References

Sarkar, P.R., 1962, *Ānanda Sūtram*, Kolkata: Ananda Marga Pracharaka Samgha (Central).

——, 1982, *The Liberation of the Intellect: Neo Humanism*, 4th edn, Kolkata: Ananda Marga Pracharaka Samgha (Central).

——, 1987, *Microvitum in a Nutshell*, Kolkata: Ananda Marga Pracharaka Samgha.

——, 2012, *Neohumanism: Principles and Cardinal Values, Sentimentality to Spirituality, Human Society*, Kolkata: Ananda Marga Publications.

9

The Idea of Self and Mahāyāna Buddhism

A Special Reference to Nāgārjuna's Mādhyamaka

Saumya Kanti Biswas

Abstract: S. Radhakrishnan mentions very significantly in his *Indian Philosophy*, vol. 1: "the ethics of Buddhism is based on its *psychology*. All sound philosophy and true ethics requires correct psychological analysis" (p. 418). A critical psychological analysis is the meta-ethics in Buddhism. It had been claimed by studies made earlier that critique of reason and the analysis of the self in the Mahāyāna Buddhism and especially by Nāgārjuna not only have a practical presupposition but also refer to a soteriological implication.[1] Hence, the proposed paper is a re-reading of the Mahāyāna school in the context of Nāgārjuna's intension in his methodological criticism against the categorical foundations of self-hood and the ethical implications that thus follow.

Keywords: *Skandhas*, critique, self-awareness, meta-ethics, psychology, dependent co-arising.

---

1 "For Nāgārjuna ... as for Buddhist thinkers in general, the emptiness of the self constitutes a central philosophical position with major practical and soteriological implications. Its realization, that is not just the intellectual understanding of the absence of *svabhāva* in the self but the cognitive shift accompanying the ability to stop concerning of oneself as a substantial self, is taken to be an essential step on the road to liberation." – Westerhoff 2009: 157

ātmā skandhā yadiyadi bhaved udaya-vyaya-bhāg bhavet ।
skandhebhyo 'nyo yadibhaved bhaved askandha-lakṣaṇaḥ ।।
– *Mūlamādhyamakakārikā* 18.1

If the self were to be identical with the aggregates, it will partake of uprising and ceasing. If it were to be different from the aggregates, it would have the characteristics of the non-aggregates.

Again,

memetyaham iti kṣīṇe bahirdhādhyātmameva ca ।
nirudhyata upādānaṁ tat kṣayāj janmanaḥ kṣayaḥ ।।
– Ibid. 18.4

When views pertaining to "mine" and "I", whether they are associated with the internal and the external, have waned, then grasping comes to cease. With the waning of that [grasping], there is waning of birth.

Introduction

It seems, from a good amount of conversations among scholars, that a critical psychological analysis is the foundation of the Buddhist ethical enquiry. Radhakrishnan thus says in his discourse on the conditions of the time of the flourishing of Buddhism:

> The salvation of the soul does not depend on minute distinctions of metaphysical conceits, or the habit of restless questioning, or the refinement of reason by the subtle disputes of sects. The indecision of thought, though it may not be taxing to the intellect of man, was injurious to his ethical interests. Anarchy in thought was leading to the anarchy of morals.... Buddhism is essentially psychology, logic and ethics. – 1985: 353

D.T. Suzuki (1908: 52) says, "... psychologically, Nirvana is enlightenment, the actualization of the Bodhicitta (Heart of Intelligence)". While T.R.V. Murti says:

> The essential prerequisite of spiritual awakening is the awareness of the intensity and universality of suffering. ...

> There is suffering; but it can be helped, because it is conditioned (*pratītyasamutpanna*). If it were a brute fact of nature and not the result of *avidyā* and *karma*, our efforts would be unavailing, and there could be no spiritual life. – 1955: 260-61

The psychological enquiry basically echoes the meta-ethics in Buddhism[2] – Buddhism finds its ethical foundation in the critique of reason. When reason gives up, understanding must be left to the hands of moral cognitivism.[3] This statement can be reckoned

---

[2] "Mahayana condemns the vulgar view that denies the consubstantiality and reciprocal transformation of all beings, not only because it is scientifically untenable, but mainly because, ethically and religiously considered, it is fraught with extremely dangerous ideas. ... Because this view, born of egoism, would dry up the well of human love and sympathy, and transform us into creatures of bestial selfishness; because this view is not capable of inspiring us with the sense of mutuality and commiseration and of making us disinterestedly feel for our fellow beings. Then, all fine religious and humane sentiments would depart from our hearts, and we should be nothing less than rigid, lifeless corpses, no pulse beating, no blood running. And how many victims are offered everyday on this alter of egoism! They are not necessarily immoral by nature, but blindly led by the false conception of life and the world, they have been rendered incapable of seeing their own spiritual doubles in their neighbors. Being ever controlled by their sensual impulses, they sin against humanity, against nature, and against themselves." – Suzuki 1908: 44

[3] "For the human heart, being a reflection of the Dharmakāya which is love and intelligence, recovers its intrinsic power and goodness, only when the veil of ignorance and egoism is cast aside. The animation, energy, strenuousness, which were shown by the self-centered will, and which therefore were utterly desplicable, will not surely die out with the removal of their odious atmosphere in which egoism had enveloped them. But they will gain an ever nobler interpretation, ever more elevating and satisfying significance; for they have gone through a baptism of fire, by which the last trace of egoism has been thoroughly consumed. The old evil master is eternally buried, but the willing servants are still here and ever →

as the foundation of compassion in the epistemological analysis of the Mādhyamaka. Compassion is thus a rational category of understanding in its transcendental form.[4] Rationalism is understood in this context as the intellectual (dialectical) apprehension of the unity of contradictions. As Suzuki says: "... when the cursed barrier of egoism is broken down, there remains nothing that can prevent us from loving others as ourselves" (1908: 54). The Mahāyāna psychology has the peculiarity of aiming to general salvation by transcending the modification of substance selfhood in both sentient and non-sentient objects. When the intellect is freed of the veils of ego-consciousness it results in the unconditional apprehension of the *dharmakāya*, the source of all pervasive, unselfish, pure compassion. *Nirvāṇa* is thus defined as the unconditional realization of *dharmakāya*; it is neither bondage nor release; bondage and release are but the modifications of the unreal. All types of discursive modifications are negated to be left with the transcendental compassion or universal fellow-feeling. Thus, a compassionate understanding of the cosmic order is the only cognitive category of reason that synthesizes the intellect in understanding the Real. Knowledge has been claimed as contrary to the understanding as compassion by Buddhist scholars and mystics.

Radhakrishnan quotes from the Larger *Prajñāpāramitāhr̥daya-sūtra*:

> The *skandhas* are empty, all things have the character of emptiness, they have no beginning, no end, they are faultless and

---

← ready to do their service, now more efficiently, for their new legitimate and more authoritative lord." – Suzuki 1908: 55

[4] "Nirvana, according to Buddhists, does not signify an annihilation of consciousness nor a temporal or permanent suppression of mentation, as imagines by some; but it is the annihilation of the notion of the ego-substance and of all the desires that arise from this enormous conception. But this represents the negative side of the doctrine, and its positive side consists in universal love or sympathy (*karuna*) for all beings." – Ibid.: 50-51

> not faultless, they are not imperfect and not perfect, therefore, Oh Sāriputta, here in this emptiness there is no form, no perception, no name, no concept, no knowledge. – 1985: 657

The Real can only be apprehended by the intellect not through the arbitrary categories of reason, but by the understanding enhanced in reason by the dialectic and thus compassion.[5] The Buddhist examination of the self is critical to an intellectual understanding of the self as a separate autonomous entity. Mahāyāna Buddhism challenges the notion of intellectuality in terms of having a rational understanding of the world of phenomena in terms of self-existent entity, because it thinks that the primordial ignorance in terms of *bhāva* is inherent in reasoning with postulation of the arbitrary conditions of understanding. This is a problem when reasoning is confined to the conditions of *bhāva* (inherent existence) in terms of understanding. This, according to the Mahāyāna thinkers, is a reductionist concept of understanding.[6]

The subjective aspect of action is the ground of the development of the theory of all the five *skandhas*.[7] The five *skandha*s are the constituent factors of individuality:

> To postulate an independent atman outside a combination of five Skandhas, of which an individual being is supposed by Buddhists to consist, is to unreservedly welcome egoism with all its pernicious corollaries. – Suzuki 1908: 32

5 "The whole show of Nagarjuna's logic is a screen of his heart which believed in an absolute reality. The outer scepticism is in the interest of the inner truth. Nature is an appearance, yet there is the eternal foundation, the infinite, from which everything springs and into which everything retires. Only when talking about it we must drop all categories relative to our empirical life."
– Radhakrishnan 1985: 656

6 The term concept is a repository of an infinite dimension of the thing it denotes.

7 The five *skandhas* are: 1. form or materiality (*rūpa*), 2. sensation (*vedanā*), 3. perception (*saṁjñā*), 4. mental activity or formation (*saṁskāra*), 5. consciousness (*vijñāna*).

The *pudgala* or the entity that reincarnates on its kārmic forces is considered to be the subjective principle of action and the compound of several interdependent causes and conditions coming together in the form of a phenomenal experience of the world. Action is considered to be the formative principle of the universe. Action is considered to be the root cause of the formation of the chain of interdependent laws of causal factors leading to bondage.[8] Action is neutralized in the exhaustion of its both subjective and objective phenomenal aspirations – in a productive concept. *Karma* becomes *karma* in the mundane sense of the term when it is executed in *ignorance*;[9] and kārmic forces are bound to wield their possessions binding the individual consciousness into a deeper realm of the web of *saṁskāra*. *Karma* thus formed would also side-effect a subjective aspect in the form of the agent or the *kartā*. The ethical significance of the concept of agent in Buddhism is in basic, the individual who is not the so-called subjective aspect of the *karma*; the one who is not empowered by *karma* or its forces.

The unity of consciousness is an amalgamation of different interconnected and interdependent causal factors that come

---

8 "The conception of Karma plays the most important role in Buddhist ethics. *Karma* is the formative principle of the universe. It determines the course of events and the destiny of our existence."

Again,

"The doctrine of Karma may be regarded as an application in our ethical realm of the theory of the conservation of energy. Everything done is done once for all; its footprints on the sand of our moral and social evolution are forever left; nay, more than left, they are generative, good or evil, and waiting for further development under favorable conditions." – Suzuki 1908: 33-34

9 Our earthly existence is the true meaning of ignorance. Suzuki says, "Ignorant are they who do not recognize the evanescence of worldly things and who tenaciously cleave to them as final realities ..." (ibid.: 36).

together because of the kārmic forces on objective adherences.[10] *Vijñāna skandha*, as a systematic coordination of different mental apparatus/interdependent causal factors, appears to take the connotation of consciousness while outdating the concept of *ātman* as only the ego conceived as an eternal entity. Buddhism does not deny the existence of a combination of different causes and conditions in order to have an explanation about the different forms of experiences and their recognitions. The disintegration of the ego-categories would be possible with the cessation (exhaustion) of the kārmic forces that keeps them associated in the *saṁskāra.*

The practicality that would be discussed in this sequence does transcend the theoretic forms of intellectual rigidity; the practicality attempted to be theorized here is a dialectical interpretation of it. It is not something that enhances any exhaustive or exclusive categorical apprehensiveness, but reveals itself in the understanding as criticism of its highest form.

The chief purpose of the present paper is to analytically represent the psychological aspects of the problem of emancipation according to Mādhyamaka. And, therefore, it is assumed under sufficient evidence that "practical" or emancipatory necessity of accepting the Mādhyamaka argument is to consider the notion of the negation of the self-substance from a cognitive shift. All the other kinds of discussions regarding the arguments concerning the absence of *svabhāva* presuppose a cognitive dimension static on the notion of the reality of the substance. But, on the other hand, a sufficient amount of discussion has been conducted by the

---

10 "It (Buddhism) does not deny that there is a unity of consciousness, for to deny this is to doubt our everyday experience, but it refuses to assert that this unity is absolute, unconditioned and independent. Everything, in this phenomenal phase of existence, is a combination of certain causes (*hetu*) and conditions (*pratyaya*) brought together according to the principle of karma; and everything that is compound is finite and subject to dissolution, and, therefore, always limited by something else." – Suzuki 1908: 41

advocates of Mādhyamaka about the notion of self-substance to be a purely psychological contingency. Thus, it is quite evident that only a cognitive shift can be an antitode to that problem of soul substance and the grasping it enhances.

A Brief Outline of Mahāyāna Psychology[11]

The *pudgala* and *dharma* do not have any substantial basis – this statement itself in turn does not claim any substantial basis. The Mahāyāna rational psychology is consistent on freedom from speculations of cosmic ontology. "Buddhism is essentially psychology, logic and ethics, and not metaphysics" (Radhakrishnan 1985: 353). The psychological framework of Mahāyāna makes way for the theoretical foundation of dependent origination and thus makes important footings on the concepts of *nirvāṇa* (both *jīvanmukta* and *videha-mukti*) as primary to moral aspirations than other theories of moral importance. *Mukti* or *nirvāṇa* as freedom from the cycle of birth and death, whether for oneself or for others is something that makes philosophies practical in their approaches. The practical concern of the Mādhyamaka belongs to the critique of the dogmatic consciousness which is subject to and conditioned by illegitimate grasping resulting to craving and the effects of bondage. The Mahāyāna psychological foundation emphasizes upon the decategorization of the intellect in order to escape the course of *vikalpa* or grasping those results in obsessional grounds of *saṁsāra*. Decategorization of the intellect is the critique of the ordinary functionality of the intellect under analytical–rational categories. It is pure criticism in itself. The critique of the self is a consistent effort of such a radical criticism of the very concept of existence as conceptualized by the cognitive consciousness. It is not refutation of the concept of the self, rather disowning the contradictions of the reason. "The Mādhyamaka dialectic is not refutation; it is pre-

---

[11] "Mahayanism, against this egoistic conception of the world, extends its theory of non-atman to the realm lying outside us." – Suzuki 1908: 42

eminently a critique of reason."[12] The psychology of the critique of reason is, as Murti describes, as the critique of dogmatic reasoning by the critical reasoning which is self-consciousness of the highest order (Murti 1955: 145, fn 4).

The categorical format of logic that is in use for the *pramāṇa* theorists gives way to Nāgārjuna's refutation of the concept of an uncaused cause. The non-caused is a contradiction in Nāgārjuna, which has been successfully demonstrated and well-defended by him. If nothing is uncaused, then the general definition of an (uncaused) substantial self stands absurd. *Substance view* is therefore a transcendental illusion. Substance view, thus claimed, is the root cause of all attachments. Liberty in Buddhism is primarily a psychological phenomenon. It insists in freedom from the undue attachment of the soul substance and its contingent ego. Consciousness is thus nothing apart from the five *skandhas* which are themselves transcendental and not immanent conditions of the consciousness. The self and the other assertion of the consciousness are devoid of the absoluteness, the strict categorical foundation of analytical logic and participates in the logic of the transcendent. The moral characteristic of individuality suggests that an individual is an array of all the changing states which makes him up and there is no central entity underlying the organism.[13] The experiences, the reflections, the impressions (*saṁskāra*) and the volitional motives formed out of the impression of previous set of actions and reflections construct the individuality of that person. The individuality is thus a successive aggregate of these phenomena which has no permanent and transcendental existence.

> A critique is a disinterested analysis of reason by itself. Reason occupies at once the position of the judge and the accused

[12] A critique of reason is the criticism of reason undertaken by reason itself.

[13] "It is only the close interdependence of aggregates of moment-events which makes for their relationship." – Vasubandhu 2013: 57

> brought before the tribunal. All sound criticism is self-criticism. Only then can it serve the spiritual purpose of self-culture.
>
> – Murti 1955: 146

Therefore, Mādhyamaka's criticism is not a refutation of the self, but the critique of the idea, the speculative conceptual concept of the self. Radhakrishnan says on the practicality of the refutation of metaphysics:

> The indecision of thought, though it may not be taxing to the intellect of man, was injurious to its ethical interests. Anarchy in thought was leading to anarchy in morals. Therefore, the Buddha wishes to steer clear of profitless metaphysical discussions.

A metaphysical study of "knowledge" by the *pramāṇa* theorists concerns the substance or substratum in which the properties of an object as qualities inhere. The substance and the qualities are separate realities having independent and individual qualities of their own. But the substantialist theory of knowledge presupposes an essential regressive condition as per the logical categories accepted by the *pramāṇa* theorists themselves.[14] The logical consistency that the reason presupposes, immediately conceives the inconsistency that the analytical reason is subjected to. A critical psychological analysis of the Mādhyamaka philosophy is immediately aware of and theoretically reacts against the substance view both as *pudgala* and *dharma* as *svabhāva* as a result of the pathologies of grasping modified under the transcendental illusion. The Mādhyamaka, therefore, identifies the crisis of modification and aspires to lead reason to a theoretic demodification of the transcendental consciousness.

---

14 "Unlike other forms of infinite regress that Nagarjuna accepts (such as the infinitely extended chain of causes and conditions), this regress is vicious, since the burden of proof is transferred in its entirety to the preceding stage, since preceding means of knowledge would have to establish all the succeeding ones."

– Westerhoff 2009: 167

Aśvaghoṣa's Report

To take recourse to the history of Buddhism, Aśvaghoṣa stands a prominent figure in the exposition and development of the Mahāyāna tradition. It is on this basis of the historical importance of the psychological trend in the development of arguments instrumental to the foundation of the Mahāyāna school of thought that the theory of non-*ātman* takes a significant meta-ethical[15] turn in this. For, it seems to be contrary to a sound logic that while an ego-self is negated, a category of phenomenal things in the sensual world is given an exclusive noumenal status (Suzuki 1908: 41-42). In order to be convincible, the ethical boundaries of theoretic claims of non-*ātman* must also be logically consistent.

The Absolute is a mind form.[16] The mind is all-pervasive and consists in itself the *dharmadhātus* or the Absolute or Real aspect of the universe in its totality. Without a mind, the Absolute does not have any real existential entity. If there is no Absolute, then even the conventional discussion on bondage and liberation is meaningless. It is the mind only that manifests itself in phenomenal consciousness by the virtue of transcendental illusion. The mind as phenomenal consciousness is only the paradigm of bondage

---

[15] To maintain the existence of a soul-substance, which is supposed to lie hidden behind the phenomena of consciousness, is not only misleading, but harmful and productive of some morally dangerous conclusions. The supposition that there is something where there is really nothing, makes us cling to this chimerical form, with no other result than subjecting ourselves to an eternal series of sufferings. – Suzuki 1908: 41

[16] This Mind includes in itself all states of being of the phenomenal world and the transcendental world. On the basis of this Mind, the meanings of Mahayana may be unfolded. ... Because the absolute aspect of this Mind represents the essence (*svabhava*) of Mahayana, and the phenomenal aspect of the mind indicates the essence, attributes (*laksana*), and influences (*kriya*) of Mahayana itself.
– Aśvaghoṣa 1967: 4

and enlightenment, Absolute and relative. It is only because of the transcendental modification of ignorance and the world of appearance as the agora of suffering individuals that the discussion on bondage and liberation is here inevitable and justified. Aśvaghoṣa classifies mind into Absolute and phenomenal mind. The mind in Absolute is the foundation of all existence and non-existence, it is the suchness that is not spoken of; whatever is spoken of is only provisional. The modification of the mind again into forms of objective consciousness is empty in itself in terms of ontological category.[17] The cause and condition of man's being in *saṁsāra* is the storehouse consciousness on which the mind (*manas*) and *vijñāna* (consciousness) develop. Because of the non-enlightenment of the storehouse consciousness man continues to live in ignorance. With enlightenment everything becomes unrelated and rolls back to the deconstructed aspects of *dharmadhātus* or the non-dual Absolute. The non-dual Absolute cannot even be assigned to that ascription because any ascription implies manifestation in the mind itself. Unlike the Vedāntin, the non-attachment to any real concept of the Absolute compels the author of the *Shastra* to categorize the Absolute in a mental form, though in its transcendental/trans-conditional trajectory. The radical critique of Nāgārjuna advances far beyond such categorical attributions by its argumentative demonstration of the untenability of the categories themselves.

The "problem" is denoted in philosophy as an interrelated probable judgements of the intellect.

> All explanations by words are provisional and without validity for they are merely used in accordance with illusions and are incapable of denoting Suchness. – Aśvaghoṣa 1967: 6

There is nothing to be affirmed, and hence there is nothing to be

---

[17] Suchness is empty because from the beginning it has never been related to any defiled state of existence, it is free from all marks of individual distinction of things, and it has nothing to do with thoughts conceived by a deluded mind. – Aśvaghoṣa 1967: 6

negated. Consciousness is an error. The Anirvacanīyakhyātivāda[18] says that error is due to the primordial conflict in mind caused by the beginningless illusion.

> Contradiction is the essence of all appearances, for non-contradiction belongs only to reality which is of the nature of pure knowledge. – Sharma 1987: 232

Knowledge, therefore, is only the removal of the contradiction.

> Error is true as long as it lasts and becomes unreal only when it is contradicted by a higher knowledge. – Ibid.

Nāgārjuna's Refutation of a Rationalistic Concept of Self

Radhakrishnan (1985: 645) observes:

> The Yogācāra accounted for the empirical world by positing a continuous subject. The argument is pushed a step beyond this (in Mādhyamaka) and the very shadow of the soul is given up. If the Yogācāra are right, then there are no objects to be known. No object means no subject. Thus the Mādhyamaka abolishes the constant *ālaya* and sets the stream of ideas adrift.

The effort of Nāgārjuna in his entire philosophical enterprise is dependent on and has a purpose behind it; the moment that purpose is realized by the student of Nāgārjuna the entire structure of the intellectual effort is negated by its root. The purpose itself is a negative process of clearing the mental modifications of consciousness.[19]

---

18 "When the shell is mistaken for silver, the shell-delimited consciousness is the ground on which silver and its cognition are illusorily imposed by beginningless ignorance. This "silver" is not real, because it is contradicted afterwards when the shall is known; and it cannot be unreal, because it appears as silver as long as illusion lasts. It is therefore called *anirvachanīya* or indescribable either as real or as unreal." – Sharma 1987: 232

19 "In the true philosophic spirit Nāgārjuna reveals the paradoxes which our everyday consciousness veils by means of a more or →

Nāgarjuna insisted that the self cannot be an exclusively distinct entity from the aggregates. A radically exclusive entity as self is redundant of any of the qualities of the self as appears to the experience.[20] Once we have abstracted from all the constituents of the person, there seems to be nothing left that could qualify as a self.

Nāgārjuna seems to contradict every aspect of reason that appears a stand in with a categorical framework of understanding – whether it is the concept of dependent arising or the aggregation of the self. Both the argumentative claims of negation and affirmation of the soul-substance are contradictory of the true nature of the Real. A negation of the self would rule out the epistemological foundation of Nāgārjuna himself. Nāgārjuna thus abstains from both affirming and negating the concept of self from that technical point of view. The only idea that the paper assumes to have presupposed the endeavour is the pure ethical access of reason to social integrity in the form of the self-and-the-other where the *self* is not an egoistic/absolutistic self-centre. The *self* is to be realized as transcendental to the substantial conceptual accreditations and appraised inclusively and dependently of the others' existential aggregations. Nāgārjuna, thus, does not negate the self, rather he negates the selfhood as an extension of the speculative reason on

---

← less thoughtless phraseology and indifference to reflection."
– Radhakrishnan 1985: 644

20 "... Nāgārjuna has not given any indication that he recognizes a special intuitive faculty through which one can see beyond the world of change and impermanence. Indeed, all that he has admitted points to his recognition of sense experience as the foundation of human knowledge. The impermanent aggregates constitute not only the human personality, but also its experiences. If the self is considered to be different from the aggregates, Nāgārjuna is here implying that it is unknowable, not merely inconceivable, for it will not have any of the characteristics of the aggregates that are all that we know through sense experience."
– Nāgārjuna 1986: 263

self-consciousness.[21] it is not the self but the attachment towards the self that is the root cause of all sufferings.

Candrakīrti and the Problem of Self

"You need to know that the root of *saṁsāra* is not the self, but attachment to the self" (Candrakīrti 2012: 246). Again, "Candrakīrti is saying that the self is just an idea, without any solid basis, but this idea becomes the base to which our clinging to the self arises" (ibid.: 251). Refutation of the existence of the self by means of reasoning and logic, and the uprooting of the clinging to the self are two different things. The logical reasoning is a means to purify the mind for the uprooting of the idea of the selfness although a purely conditioned self is considered.

According to Candrakīrti, the idea of the self is only because of the wrong notion of the self. The idea is completely without any base; it is because of the idea itself that the notion of the self arise in the mind. For thc *prāsaṅgika*, the root cause of the *saṁsāra* is the ignorance and not the five aggregates that should form the base of the ignorance. It is because of the ignorance that the five aggregates appear to be the base of the idea of the self. It is the attachment to the self and not the self that is the root cause of the *saṁsāra*. The attachment to the self, however, for Candrakīrti is not something without a cause, the cause being the transcendental ignorance (Candrakīrti 2003: 250). The cause of the grasping is the presupposition of the *cogito*. Candrakīrti tries to establish that the cause of the self is thus not the five aggregates but the transcendentally wrong notion about the self on the wrongly assumed basis of the five aggregates. For, there is nothing that could be found as essential quality among the five aggregates and their relations that form the basis (foundation) for the notion of the self. The aggregates are empty of the quality of forming any such notion of the self.

---

21 "The denial of a permanent entity does not mean that Nagarjuna is committed to a rejection of self-awareness or self-consciousness".
– Nāgārjuna 1986: 246

Candrakīrti makes a distinction between the notion of the self and the clinging to the self. According to him and many of his analysers, the root cause of suffering is not the notion of the self or the knowledge of the five aggregates, but the clinging to the self (Candrakīrti 2012: 246-48). The self is merely a dependent imputation. Self is the name of the consciousness' false dependence on the five aggregates. This dependence of the pure consciousness and the five aggregates is the I-ness. "Self-consciousness" as according to Candrakīrti is the imputed self which ultimately becomes the base for all attachments. Like a chariot which has no existence in itself though but depends on the imputation as a chariot, in a similar way, the self is neither independent nor dependent on the aggregates for its existence as a permanent self. Consideration of a self-entity encounters certain logical, empirical as well as psychological problems. The psychological problems are concerned with moral problems which it presupposes. What is important from a philosophical perspective is the fact that human personality for the sake of its practical concerns is considered to be the composite of what makes him up. Logic is the tool by virtue of which Nāgārjuna tries to serve the practical moral purpose that would lead the consciousness to the path of liberation. To show the inner inconsistency of the arguments and concepts of the opponents of the Mādhyamaka is not a positive use of the logical reasoning. *Rūpa*, *vedanā*, *citta*, *saṁjñā* and *saṁskāra* are shown by Nāgārjuna as neither different, nor identical to their causes, neither both identical and different nor the negation of both identity and difference. Therefore, any theoretical concept of the five aggregates is an impossibility. Therefore, cognition and conception are interdependent on each other and ontologically (concerning Absolute) transcend all the qualities of apprehension that claim to assume the form of boundaries in each context.

The critical studies made earlier on the epistemological boundaries of realism claim that the conditions of robust realism dictate that the substance or the substratum must be distinguished from the features, properties or qualities it holds. This also consequently decrees a mental substratum for the so-called psychic episodes of dispositions, awareness, desires, preferences, etc.; and the body, because of its continuously changing nature, cannot be regarded as adequate for such a substratumhood. The two considerations of an independent, uncreated, eternal substance and the distinction of it from the transient, fleeting qualities like attributes and modes is a necessity for the epistemological purposes of human mind and thus these two are categorical (from a psychological point of view of the philosophy of understanding) or natural presuppositions of cognition.[22] The substance concept serves only a conventional epistemological purpose with transitory categories of understanding. The *understanding* ontologically presupposes the critical capacity of transcendental passage of reason to the transcendental realms of the Absolute. The logical tool of *śūnyatā* as used by Nāgārjuna to show the inconsistency of logico–analytical categories of understanding is thus contingent to the critical endeavour of reason itself. The problem that concerns the Mahāyāna thinkers is the unwarranted ontological ascriptions of the epistemological tool to an ontological status. According to Candrakīrti, ontological categories in the sense of an independent self that follows, is a mere category of the mind in convention that results in the cognition of a self without any metaphysical basis. The cause of the origin of consciousness in that ontological fold has been clearly categorized by Aśvaghoṣa. The category of *svabhāva* as a substance is a purely psychological category denoting the "form" of understanding in epistemology. This category consequently needs other categories as substantial as it is to prove its existential qualities such as the principles of causes and conditions. But Nāgārjuna proves that categories as they are considered to be are logically untenable thus negating the logical and ontological

---

22 "It (the substance) provides a procedure for drwing a line between a variety of objects with shared qualities and thereby allows us to tell them apart." – Westerhoff 2009: 23

possibility of the existence of the substance. Thus, the philosophy of Nāgārjuna estimates the entire interdependent framework of psychological, logical, ontological and teleological intensions of the entire Mahāyāna school, consequently representing the theoretic opposition and criticism of the dogmatic foundations of knowledge system. All the streams of philosophical problems concerning the soul-substance as the locus of self-awareness find justice in the *śūnyatā* as a moral presupposition of a civil and self-conscious sets of social networking of egoless individual selves.

References

Aśvaghoṣa, 1967, *The Awakening of Faith in Mahayana: Mahayana-Shraddhotpada Shastra*, tr. Yoshito S. Hakedas, New York: Colombia University Press.

Candrakīrti, 2003, *Introduction to the Middle Way: Chandrakirti's Madhyamikavatara with Commentary by Dzongsar Jamyang K. Rinpoche*, Dordogne, France.

——, 2012, *Introduction to the Middle Way: Chandrakirti's Madhyamikavatara with Commentary by Jamgön Mipham*, tr. Padmakara Translation Group, Boston and London: Shambhala.

Murti, T.R.V., 1955, *The Central Philosophy of Buddhism: A Study of Madhyamika System*, New Delhi: Munshiram Manoharlal.

Nāgārjuna, 1986, *Mūlamādhyamakakārikā: The Philosophy of the Middle Way*, tr. David J. Kalupahana, Delhi: Motilal Banarsidass.

Radhakrishnan, S., 1985, *Indian Philosophy*, vol. 1, London: George Allen & Unwin, reprinted in India by Blackie & Son Publishers.

Sharma, Chandradhar, 1987, *A Critical Survey of Indian Philosophy*, Delhi: Motilal Banarsidass.

Suzuki, D.T., 1908, *Outlines of Mahayana Buddhism*, Chicago: The Open Court Publishing Company.

Vasubandhu, 2013, *Pancaskandha Prakarana, Seven Works of Vasubandhu: The Buddhist Psychological Doctor*, ed. Stefan Anacker, Delhi: Motilal Banarsidass.

Westerhoff, Jan, 2009, *Nagarjuna's Madhyamaka: A Philosophical Investigation*, Oxford: Oxford University Press.

10

The Problematic Mind, Meditation and the Deep Structure of Consciousness

A Buddhist Perspective

Hari Shankar Prasad

Abstract: The title of this essay contains three interrelated foundational terms and concepts, viz. (1) mind (*mano*), which creates the diversified phenomena (*dhammā*); (2) meditation (*jhāna*: absorption) through which the achievements of elimination of mental perversion (*citta-vipallāsa*), mental purity (*citta-visuddhi*), mental development (*bhāvanā*) and the higher mentality (*adhicitta*) are made possible on the path of spiritual powers (*abhiññā*); and (3) the dynamic ontological consciousness (*citta*) and its own created phenomenal concomitants (*cetasika*) rooted in the *citta* itself, both of which together structure and regulate the two worlds of outer and inner hemispheres. Further, there is another similar set of three terms and concepts in the Buddhist literature, interesting but also confusing, as *mano*, *citta* and *viññāṇa* – which are considered synonymous and generally translated as consciousness or mind, but they are also used in different contexts and with different meanings, such as cognitive awareness, cognitive or mental acts, consciousness-moment (*cittakkhaṇa*), independently functional states of consciousnesses (*kiriyā-citta*) considered to be the Noble Roots found in the *arhat* whose deep structure of consciousness is pure (= *a-rāga*, *a-dosa*, *a-moha*), advertence (*āvajjana*), subconsciousness (*bhavaṅga*) as a part of the deep structure of consciousness, mental awareness by the inner faculty (*mano-viññāṇa*) and so on. In such a complex situation, it is not possible to be precise while discussing the fixed meanings and interpretations of the pure and mystical consciousness, which is the necessary condition of *nibbāna*, i.e. freedom from all kinds of impurity of the mind or consciousness and the cycle of suffering across the rebirths.

Every Buddhist scholar knows that the three words-cum-concepts mentioned in the title are not only highly complex but also puzzling, mysterious and unfathomable for the sensory and intellectual faculties alone, but for the internal faculty as well to grasp their natures and functions, because they belong to the deeper inner world, utterly contrary to the external physical world. Among these, the mind is problematic because of its imperfect psychophysical–cognitive constitution within its mind–body integrated system. Its problematic nature may be dull, ignorant and erroneous in cognition, emotion and conation, which range from minor state to extreme state in their manifestations, but conversely, it can also be sensitive and compassionate in the same range and different degrees. (1) Mind is actually problematic for multiple reasons. In the Buddhist process philosophy, it is fluxional, self-unifying, self-manifesting; creates the phenomena out of itself and also reifies them; conceives ideas and objectifies them in the external world; imbued with intentionality; forgetful of its own original status under ignorance; possesses capacity to create ideal and imaginary world in both waking and dream states; deposits within itself dispositions (*saṁskāra*) arising from different forms of its own experiences and so on, on the one hand, and (2) on the other, it is self-aware, self-reflexive, self-reflective, self-knowing, self-correcting, self-planning, spiritually self-developing, self-purifying and so on. It plans meditational techniques for cleansing its own defilements (*kilesa*, *anusaya*, *rāga-dosa-moha*, *akusala-citta*) and developing positive qualities by means of various practices – *pañcasīla*, *sīla-samādhi-paññā*, *brahma-vihāra*, *aṭṭhaṅgika-magga*, *pāramitā*, single-mindedness (*ekaggatā*), mindfulness (*satipaṭṭhāna*), tranquillity (*samatha*), intuitive insight into the nature of reality (*vipassanā*) and nine progressive stages of absorption (four *rūpa-jhāna*, four *arūpa-jhāna* and one *jhāna*-absorption), which together fulfil the preconditions for the spiritual development of its nature, which in turn cultivate and promote the states of being in the modes of the *bodhisattva*, *tathāgata*, the Perfect Buddha and the Supreme Peace (*nibbāna*) of the mind. Finally, against the backdrop of the preceding passages, I have tried to explain and interpret the theme of the present essay, which has three mutually related components – the problematic mind, meditation and the deep structure of consciousness – in the process of the mental development in its culmination.

Keywords: *Paṭisotagāmī, dhamma, mano* (creative mind), *dhammā* (plural, mind-created phenomena), *avijjā, tilakkhaṇa, pañca-khandha, dvādasa-nidāna, citta, viññāṇa, citta-suddhi, bodhi, jhāna, Agaññasutta, bhavaṅga-citta, paṭisandhi.*

Preamble

In the abstract, I have sufficiently discussed the relevant issues related to the present theme. However, in a medium-size article like this, obviously it is not possible to elaborate these crucial issues and answer the related questions in detail even in a particular religious and philosophical system like early Buddhism. Nevertheless, in the backdrop of these issues and questions, I take for granted that the interested readers have some basic understanding of the Buddha's spiritual journey and the basics of early Buddhism. With this hope I venture into the discussion of certain crucial aspects of the Buddhist dynamic world view as I find in the early Buddhist literature (Sutta, Theravāda and Abhidhamma), which is grounded in the Buddha's discourses (*desanā*), keeping the focus on the present theme. Note that the Buddhist concept of mind is radically different from other concepts of mind in various systems of Indian philosophy.

Let us come to the main theme of the essay. In my opinion, metaphorically, mind can be compared with a live kitchen wherein there are different items like grocery ingredients, spices, vegetables, oil, utensils, gas, water, light, exhaust fan and the cook for preparing various kinds of food, which may be hygienic or unhygienic, all within the kitchen. But in the case of a creative mind, it is everything, not in physical but mental forms. Thus, it is itself a kitchen within which it creates ideas as mental food-ingredients and utensils, and other factors, and itself works as a skilled cook who designs conceptual framework, theories, own rationality, perspective, methods and itself enjoys or denies the taste of its own menu, which is within itself, out of itself, by itself and for itself. Alternatively, in this case, everything is the product of mentation and content-wise mental as opposed to the physical. Since Buddhism denies the permanently static soul as an agent of all kinds of empirical formations like mind, the soul is itself replaced by the fluxional series of the mind which gives rise to a false sense of ego (sense of "I") and a minimal or conventional sense of "self". Consequently, all the three concepts – mind, meditation and consciousness – are integrally functional and in the state of ultimate silence and peace (*nibbāna*), which is a state of liberation from all kinds of defilements by means of meditative process; the spiritually transformed mind is then designated as the purified fluxional consciousness (*citta-suddhi*) in this world itself as it is found in the attitudes of the *bodhisattva* or the Buddha.

Needless to say, man has a privileged status in the nature's multiple formulations, which are broadly classified into two groups – physical and mental. In man or any other sentient being, both aspects are mutually interactive as well as integrated. In the Buddhist system process philosophy, everything is constantly changing (*aniccā, anitya*) and also it is a cluster of eventual happenings but in a non-static manner, which (events, happenings) under the natural law of dependent arising (*paṭicca-samuppāda*) are converted into a functional unity and continuity just like a continuously flowing river. For these reasons, every spatio-temporal-dimensional and static empirical thing is considered non-substantial (*anattā, anātmatā*) and non-eternal (*aniccā, anitya*), which marks the characteristics of non-self, non-ego and impersonal status of man. All these characteristics apply to mind and consciousness also, which are not strictly two separate things, because consciousness in its originality is the foundational source of the mind (*mano*) and its concomitants (*dhammās* in plural, *cetasika*). According to the *Dhammapada* (Yamaka-vagga, v. 1), mind is a creative principle, which creates the multiple phenomena (*dhammās*), but it is ignorant of its own creativity out of itself and that is why it becomes the most problematic for itself and for the world. But the mind is self-aware, self-reflexive, self-correcting and self-developing also, all these through the rigorous practice of progressive meditational method. Thus, mind, meditation and deep structure of consciousness are internally interactive and corrective. For convenience to understand the fundamental ideas of the Buddha and the early Buddhist world view, I have listed below some of the most significant doctrines:

1. Understanding of the existence, nature, constitution and the predicament of the person within the most basic framework of the three characteristics of things or existence (*tilakkhaṇa*).
2. The empirical constitution of the human person comprising of the integrated five aggregates (*pañca-khandha*, i.e. psycho-corporeality of the person) in the present life, which defines his status and identity in this world (*saṁsāra*) of suffering.
3. His way of continued temporal existence in the twelve-link formula (*dvādasa-nidāna*) across the three segments of time (past, present and future), which displays each link's "conditioned and conditioning" characteristics on the pattern of the dependently arising schema (*paṭicca-samuppāda*).
4. The extremely complex and mysterious nature, function and various modes of manifestation of mind (*citta, mano, viññāṇa*) throughout the present as well as the continued future life against the background of its past functions evoked by good/ wholesome (*kusala*) and bad/unwholesome (*akusala*) *kammas*

erupted from the factors of defilement and undefilement respectively.

5. Interactive relationship of mind and body in terms of *nāma-rūpa* formula, unlike the Western mind–body theories as found in Descartes.
6. Integral relationship between psychological cosmology and various progressively transformed stages of meditation.
7. Man's intention-(*cetanā*)-based skilful or unskilful kammic activities and their consequences.
8. Kammic determination of his station in the three cosmic realms (*kāma-dhātu*, *rūpa-dhātu* and *arūpa-dhātu*) in the birth–life–death–rebirth process.
9. His birth in one of the five destinies (*gati*) meant for sentient beings, viz. denizens of hell (*niraya*), hungry ghost (*pettivisaya*), animal (*tiracchānayoni*), human being (*manussa*) and demon (*asura*) or God/god (*deva*), through which he moves from one birth to another as per the quality of his *kamma*s performed as a person.
10. However, there is a way of overcoming his predicament by means of moral transformation, reflective thinking, right knowledge, purification of mind from defilements (*citta-suddhi*), etc. and also by practising the meditative techniques in progressive order – all these within the Buddhist way.
11. A Buddhist who is adept in meditation gradually passes through different hierarchical levels: (1) stream-entrant (*sotāpatti*), (2) once-returner (*sakadāgāmī*), (3) non-returner (*anāgāmī*), and (4) *arhat*. The latter attainment is the ultimate journey of the cessation of the cycle of sāṁsāric life.
12. In the very beginning, it would be very important to know that the entire Buddhist schema or the world view or the doctrines are consciousness-centric in a general sense, which is diversified in multiple modes. In Buddhism, the physical picturization of the cosmology or description of the

myths and the narratives are interiorized and psychologized within a human person as his own creations by his own kammic formations, which can be undone only by his own effort (*attakāra*). Moreover, it is the generic consciousness (the base of *citta*, *mano*, *viññāṇa* and so on) which functions in every theory – metaphysical, epistemological, logical, moral, soteriological, etc. In every theory, the influence of the *tilakkhaṇa* formula is the guiding principle. There are some more basic ideas, which must be kept in mind while discussing the theme of this article or any other Buddhist doctrine. I am not going to elaborate all of them in this brief note.

The Basics of the Buddha's Life and Teaching

It is advisable that if one wants to thoroughly understand an aspect of Buddhism, it would be helpful if he understands the Buddha's journey of life, for which we have to *begin at the beginning* in sequence, such as:

1. Siddhārtha's early striking experiences of human existence and life at different stages and in different modes, such as a sick person, an old person, a dead person and the life of an ascetic, which made him deeply reflective as his life was also destined to pass through such existential conditions.
2. His emphatic problematization of human suffering, first time in the history of man.
3. As a prince, the abandoning of his palace to adopt an ascetic life to search for the truth of the human existential predicament and its causes and solution.
4. His way of adopting the rigorous meditational techniques under his two teachers – Ālāra Kālāma and Uddaka Rāmaputta – but with serious differences.
5. His *paradigmatic shift* from rigorous self-mortifying, i.e. body torturing, meditational means to mutually interactive, although integrated system of mind–body duality, which

is actually psycho–corporeal dichotomy, but unlike their separable duality as found in many Indian and Western philosophies like Sāṁkhya–Yoga, Nyāya–Vaiśeṣika and thinkers such as Descartes.

6. The contents of his attainment of awakening (*bodhi*) are the most fundamental ground of his elaborated *Weltanschauung* and the entire development of Buddhism. These are: the realization of the non-substantial universal law of dependent arising (*paṭicca-samuppāda*) and the doctrinal and ethical path of living (*majjhima-paṭipadā*), which later proved to be the radical "Turning of the Wheel of the World View", which he himself called *sailing against the current* (*paṭisotagāmī*).

7. *Paṭicca-samuppāda* is the most complex fundamental metaphysical principle functioning at the deepest level of the dynamically fluxional mind or consciousness, which generates uninterrupted experience, which in turn mirrors the phenomenal world (*dhammas*) and the way of the things as a whole, internal or external. Being an inherent active causal principle, it constitutes, synthesizes and regulates the very process of the things or the so-called unified existence. It is this principle which gives rise to a basic conceptual framework of the trinity (*tilakkhaṇa*) – impermanence (*aniccā*), non-substantiality/soullessness (*anattā*) and subsequent existential dissatisfactoriness (*dukkhatā*).

8. The universal *paṭicca-samuppāda* principle is a natural ubiquitous empirical causal schema, which was apprehended in the Buddha's transcendental *bodhi.*

9. As an awakened liberated person, designated as the Buddha in a cognitive sense, he devoted the next forty-five years of his life to awaken others through his preaching. Thus, he began with a conventional life of experience, passed through different varieties of the stages of life and experiences including physical, psychological, cognitive, emotive,

reflective, hermeneutic, ethical and finally the meditational transformative experience until his demise at the age of 80 when he ended his preaching to his favourite disciple Ānanda in the enlightening *Mahāparinibbāna Sutta* at Kushinagar.

What we learn from this brief narration of the Buddha's life and act is that the uninterrupted experience in the course of one's life is the bedrock, source and foundation of all other forms of expression. Buddhism is the product of that. But it is noteworthy that the transformative meditational experience is the game-changer of the adept's mind, morality and destiny.

In the process, every mental event evokes a bit of experience and thus the perpetual mental events give rise to the continuity of the experience of different varieties. It is a first-person-singular-experience-centric programme to radically reshape an individual's self-view within the framework of no-self-view. Moreover, Buddhism is dominantly more empirical, epistemological, ethical and logical than a variety of absolute metaphysics of transcendent nature like the Upaniṣadic Absolutism. The entire Buddhism, by means of different strategies, aims at disproving the substantial nature of the reality of the immaterial soul or the material entity like a table, and proving the no-soul-theory (*anātmatā*). The Buddhist kinds of meditation are particularly preoccupied with the insightful experience of selflessness (*anātmatā*).

Moreover, Buddhism has a grand teleological cosmic design when it talks of an inseparable relationship between cosmology and meditation, and the kammic destiny of each sentient being who falls within this cosmological network. For the present human being, meditation is a technique to improve the past *kamma*s in the present life. Likewise, the present life gives an opportunity to avail a better life either in the form of rebirth or Ultimate Freedom from suffering (*nibbāna*) by means of meditative techniques. This shows that *life is both beginningless and endless* as per the self-effort in this programme.

Key Pāli Terms

The semantic clarification of the following key Pāli terms and notions are imperative before we go further to present their analysis: *bodhi*, *dhamma* (singular), *dhammas* (plural), *Ariyapariyesana Sutta*, *Dhammacakkapavattana Sutta*, *paṭicca-samuppāda*, *majjhima-paṭipadā*, *hetu-paccaya*, *citta*, *cetasika*, *viññāṇa*, *sota-viññāṇa*, *manas*, *citta-bhūmi*, *āramaṇa*, *bhavaṅga-citta*, *paṭisandhi-citta*, *vīthī-citta* (or *citta-vīthī*), *vīthī-mutta*, *citta-visuddhi*, *pañcakkhandha* (1 *rūpa*; 4 *nāma*: *vedanā*, *saṁjñā*, *saṁkhāra* and *viññāṇa*), 12 *āyatanas*, 18 *dhātus*, *abhisaṁkhāra*, *kamma*, *cetanā*, *dvādasa-nidāna*, *bhāvanā*, *kiriyā-citta*, *akiriyā-citta*, *kusala*, *akusala*, *kilesa*, *anusaya*, *nivaraṇa*, *māra*, *jhāna*, *samādhi*, *samatha*, *vipassanā*, *nirodha-samāpatti*, *tridhātu* (*kāma-dhātu*, *rūpa-dhātu*, *arūpa-dhātu*), *gati*, *loka-dhātu* and so on.

The present article aims at creating an awareness in the mind of a meditation practitioner the necessity of a critical understanding of the complex issues of meditation, which is grounded in the domain of consciousness and its various techniques, temporal causal process, management and first-person temporal experience with desirable results such as awakening, peace, happiness, moral development and soteriological end. Meditation is not only a mental medication, but also a physiological and physical medication through practices. Its real target is purification and development (both behavioural and spiritual) of practitioner's own mind and entire life within the psycho-corporeal system in this world and the sphere of mind alone.

In theory, meditation as a technique is a programme of consciousness – within itself, of itself, by itself and for itself. It has various philosophical aspects, viz. psychological, phenomenological, metaphysical, epistemological, ethical, axiological, culturally contextual and soteriological (*nibbāna*). It has different modes of manifestation like silence, recitation of *mantras*, the devotion of deities and so on. In the Indian context, generally the practitioners' meditations have seated postures with closed eyes so that they can direct their attention inward. This is actually an internal understanding of oneself, a management of the mental process and inner-transformation by means of various progressive stages of *jhāna* (*dhyāna*) involving suppression of various kinds of defilements and obstacles and volatile discursive thought, technically called calmness (*samatha*) and penetrative insight into the non-substantial transient nature of consciousness, which is a mode of intellectual and discursive thinking (*vipassanā*).

The Buddhist Conceptual Framework

In a conventional sense, the given nature of human existence and life is unsatisfactory and full of predicaments because of its transient character and lack of certainty in life whether in the present life or after its death, although life seems to be continuous, yet on reflection it proves to be eventual and so fluxional. But the changing world – material or immaterial sentient or insentient, human or non-human – has a fixed pattern in its multiple manifestations, underlying which there is a continuous, inbuilt, non-divinely natural, inseparable, universal and the dynamic principle of causality, which constitutes and regulates them. More appropriately, we can say that a thing or a human being carries its own destiny by means of its essential dynamism. But the question is: How to explain it? As we know, as a result of his reflection on the human predicament of life and deep concern for its eradication, "Siddhārtha-turned Buddha" went on the quest for knowing the causes of this predicament and its remedy. Subsequently, as said above, his Awakening disclosed the very basic causal principle of the Dependent Arising and the Middle-Path in respect of avoiding the extremely metaphysical doctrines as well as the perverted ethical conduct. His ingenious discovery of the root cause of the human predicament was traced by him in the deep structure of his mind, which in a generic way constitutes every human person and his cosmic set-up. This is an attempt to interiorize within the mind the entire vast physical cosmos. In other words, it is an exceptionally brilliant plan to convert the physical cosmic structure into each human mind's psychological world, which marks the changing position of the destiny, good or bad, across the temporally continuing series of life from past to future via present corresponding to the quality of his mental, vocal and physical behaviour.

Buddhist Cosmology

In his study of the *Agaññasutta*, Gethin (1997) identifies three basic principles regarding the early Buddhist literature (Nikāyas, Āgamas and the *Abhidhamma*) on the Buddhist view of cosmology vis-à-vis meditation attainments in the following passage:

> First, there are a number of different realms of existence that constitute a hierarchy; there are lower realms – the realms of animals (*tiracchānayoni*) and of hungry ghosts (*pettivisaya*) and various hells (*niraya*); there is the realm of men (*manussa*) and above, the various heaven realms of the *devas* and *brahmās*. Second, beings are continually reborn in these various realms in accordance with their actions – the ten unskilful (*akusala*) courses of action (*kammapatha*) lead to rebirth in one of the lower realms, and the ten skilful (*kusala*) courses of action lead to rebirth as a human being or in the lower heavens, while meditation attainments (*jhāna*) lead to rebirth in the higher heavens as a *brahmā*. The third principle is that which is inherent in the formula from the *Agaññasutta*. ... The various levels of existence arrange themselves in "world-system" (*loka-dhātu*); there are innumerable world-systems which all expand and contract across vast expanses of time.
>
> – pp. 186-87

The architectural design of the Buddhist psychological cosmology is entirely teleological pertaining to the different kinds of sentient beings born and living in the cycle of birth–living–death–rebirth in different realms. This schema is particularly meant for human beings according to their *kammas*, which can be qualitatively managed by them by their own self-effort in the scale of descending or ascending order, in the manner of bottom-up or top-down, by transforming their minds by means of their meditational techniques. Here, mind is neither substantial nor static, but a temporally and causally continuing series of the interconnected mental acts (*citta-santati*) which always carries its associates or concomitant factors (*cetasika*). In its originary state, it is single and pure or undefiled, but in its flow, it is joined by numerous defiled factors, which go on *endlessly*. But in the state of awakening, this factual truth is realized and a mechanism is devised by the practitioner to eliminate them, followed by the *recovery of the pure consciousness,* which is the state *of nibbāna.*

We can understand this process on the water simile applied to the origin, journey and the end of the River Gaṅgā. In this case, at its source in Himalayas, its water is pure, but in its passage of flow on the plane when it passes through different areas like muddy field, residential and industrial areas, it gets mixed with lots of dirt and wastes like garbage, sewer water and industrial waste and chemical. These elements make it dangerously polluted and subsequently its water becomes poisonous and unusable for drinking, cooking, bathing and also for agricultural purposes and damages ecological balance. To make it usable, its impurity requires to be removed. Only this way, the river's health and utility can be restored.

Likewise, in its flow in the sāṁsāric life conditioned by ignorance (*avijjā*), mind becomes polluted by numerous defilements (*kilesa, anusaya*), which are the responsible factors for creating suffering. To restore its purity for the sake of happier life and *nibbāna*, a three-pronged strategy is to be devised: first, knowledge of the hazardous character of the defilements, following the Buddha's path with faith in his teachings and their practices; second, development of wisdom, and third, fourfold/fivefold meditations (*jhāna*) in progressive stages. The latter is equated with various schema of human psychology, which will be discussed later, but at this moment it is necessary that we know some more details about the nature and role of defilement (*kilesa*, Skt. *kleśa*).

Defilement has the nature of afflicting both mind and body, which always go together in Buddhism and, in the process, it keeps creating all sorts of suffering. There are different larger lists of defilements mentioned in the Sutta and Abhidhamma literature. But the most fundamental of them are: craving/greed (*lobha*), hatred (*dosa*) and delusion (*moha*). These are the root-motivating moral evils, which afflict the mind and cause overall suffering, both mental and physical body. Needless to say, their consequences are detrimental to peace of mind, moral and spiritual development, social emotions and soteriological goal. It is imperative that their dangerous consequences can be reversed and eliminated by deep transcendental knowledge, moral virtues and meditational techniques. These defilements (*kilesa*) may be latent or active. When these are latent, inactive or sleeping, they are called *anusaya*, but when they are active, they are called *kilesa*. In this respect, it is worth noticing that only their negative restraint (*a-lobha, a-dosa, a-moha*) is not enough, it also requires positive actions like other-regarding charity, friendliness/love and intellectual clarity/ wisdom respectively, which are antidotes to defilements. I present here some other kinds of defilements, which are mentioned in different combinations in the early Buddhist literature: Pride/ conceit (*māna*), wrong views (*diṭṭhi*), torpor (*middha*), sloth (*thīna*), greed (*lobha*), hatred (*dosa*), delusion (*moha*), envy (*issā*), avarice (*macchariya*), moral shamelessness (*ahirika*), moral fearlessness (*anottapa*), restlessness (*uddhacca*), worry (*kukkucca*), doubt (*vicikicchā*) and so on.

To repeat, all such defilements, which are mental phenomenal qualities, are subject to elimination by means of skilful moral conduct, knowledge and meditative techniques.

Moreover, these defilements belong to the desire realm (*kāma-dhātu*), which is dominated by craving for "sensual pleasure" (*kāma-taṇhā*) arising from the material or non-material objects. But craving becomes extremely perverted when one desires for "eternal existence" (*bhāva-taṇhā*) in the higher realms. This kind of craving comes under subtle form-realm (*rūpa-dhātu*) or formless-realm (*arūpa-dhātu*). The three broadly hierarchical realms are the locations wherein human beings, according to their moral qualities (*kamma*), are reborn in the form of different sentient beings, which mark their destinies (*gati*), such as denizens of hell (*naraka, niraya*), hungry ghost (*preta*), animal (*tirayañc*), human being (*manusya*), demons (*asura*) and god (*deva*). All these have complex categories and classifications. In the case of a human being, he/she can acquire a better destiny by means of his/her progressive mental development meditational (*jhāna*) schema. Note that Buddhism develops its philosophical, psychological and religious theories within the cosmological framework, brilliantly converted into psychological cosmology in case of every human being.

Psycho-Corporeal Interactive Relationship

As we know, everything is temporally dynamic in nature and there is nothing which is temporally abiding and static. In the Buddhist natural schema, there is neither any independent reality, nor is there any monistic creator like God. Such is the nature of a human person, who is basically constituted of five aggregates, each of which is a series of causally interactive multiple conditioned (*khandha*) factors. These five aggregates are classified under two groups: (i) name (*nāma, arūpa-khandha*), i.e. immaterial or more appropriately four psychological factors – feeling (*vedanā*), apperception (*saṁjñā*), volition (*saṁkhāra*) and consciousness (*viññāṇa*), and (ii) physical/corporeal body, generally called "form" (*rūpa, rūpa-khandha*): physical or corporeal factor, which is actually not a spatio-temporal material form, rather it designates the combination of separate four basic subtle natural elements, viz. earth/solid element (*paṭhavī-dhātu*), water/liquid element (*apo-dhātu*), fire/heat element (*tejo-dhātu*) and wind/motion element (*vāyo-dhātu*), apart from their twenty-four secondary phenomena. The fundamental difference between *nāma* and *rūpa* is that while *nāma* stands for those factors, which are intentional and formless in character, i.e. it refers to an object and in the range of sensory perception, whereas *rūpa* lacks these characteristics. Thus, the person is an organic synthesis of psychophysical factors. In common parlance, the two are separately called immaterial mind and material body, which is not correct. In reality, for the wise, both are constantly interdependent and interactive. In Buddhism, physical factors (*rūpa*) are the basis of consciousness (*viññāṇa*), which in turn is the basis of the remaining three psychological factors – *vedanā*, *saṁjñā* and *saṁkhāra*. But the phenomenon of *rūpa*, which literally means colour or visual object, is actually derived (*upādā*) from the four constitutive physical elements (*mahābhūta*) and it stands for the corporeal body, which is subject to continuous change, growth, degeneration, disintegration and ultimately death.

It is important to note that in their mutual interactive activity, *rūpa* and *nāma* influence each other both for good and bad, which depends on man's skilful management. It is imperative for the present life that man maintains the sound health of both and keeps his mind alert. Meditation is the most powerful technique in this respect, which also leads to the attainment of the soteriological goal after death when the physical body is disintegrated, but the mind is the principle of life, which continues over to the next life in the state of rebirth within time framework.

According to the *Paṭṭhāna* (vol. I, pp. 5, 8-9), *nāma* and *rūpa* are mutually dependent and interactive, which give rise to consciousness in the sense of *viññāṇa*. *Viññāṇa* is permeated in the entire body, but finding its particular location, such as heart, is debated in the Abhidhamma literature and rejected by the majority of the Buddhist commentators. The production of *viññāṇa* can be understood on the analogy of fire. If we take two dry pieces of wooden sticks and forcefully rub them against each other, sparking of fire will be produced, which can be developed into a blazing fire. Consciousness (*viññāṇa)* is just like that. In our cognitive system, when our attentive sensory organ, say, an eye comes in contact with a material object, an awareness or consciousness of that object arises, which is called (a) visual-consciousness (*cakkhu-viññāṇa*). The same happens with the four other external senses, viz. ear, nose, tongue and skin, with their respective sensible objects – sound, smell, taste and tactile feeling. Thus, there arise four different sensations/consciousnesses respectively like (b) auditory-consciousness (*sota-viññāṇa*), (c) olfactory-consciousness (*ghāṇa-viññāṇa*), (d) gustatory-consciousness (*jīhvā-viññāṇa*), and (e) tactile-consciousness (*kāya-viññāṇa*). Thus, in total, the five consciousnesses (including visual-consciousness) are passively grasped by the internal sensory organ called *manas* (mind), which is also an active organizing principle. The latter characteristic-wise organizes, structures and identifies these five separate consciousnesses, which are five different gates or channels (*dvāra*) through which the sensory awarenesses pass. But this principle derives its power from a further consciousness-principle called *citta*, which although remains in latent mode, yet it is active but in low profile.

Another characteristic of *manas*, unlike the above five consciousnesses, is that it is a mental cognitive faculty (*mano-dvāra*), which grasps the internal objects like emotions and ideas. These two characteristics of mind are more appropriately called *mano-viññāṇa*. The most robust defiled mental principle (later elaborated while discussing *kliṣṭamanas* in Yogācāra), which is manifested in the form of "I" or "ego" or "mine", etc. is also the product of this mind, that is deeply engrossed in the *saṁkhāra*-loaded *citta* subconsciousness. However, the four psychological factors are more complex to analyse and understand. In the present context, Gethin's observations are noteworthy:

> One of the general concerns of the Abhidharma is to provide a detailed and complex hierarchy of consciousness. The classic Theravāda scheme of eighty-nine or 121 "consciousnesses" (*citta*) begins with unskilful consciousnesses at the bottom, followed by consciousnesses that concern the mechanics of bare awareness of the objects of the five senses, and then by skilful sense-

> sphere consciousnesses; next come the various form-sphere and formless-sphere consciousnesses that constitute the *jhānas*, or meditation attainments; finally we have the world-transcending (*lokuttara*) consciousnesses that constitute the mind at the moment of awakening itself. The basic structure of this hierarchy of consciousness parallels quite explicitly the basic structure of the cosmos: consciousness belongs to the sense sphere (*kāmāvacāra*), the form sphere (*rūpāvacāra*), or the formless sphere (*arūpāvacāra*); beings exist in the sense world (*kāma-dhātu, kāma-loka*), the form world (*rūpa-dhātu, rūpa-loka*), or the formless world (*arūpa-dhātu, arūpa-loka*). As well as laying down a more precise hierarchy of consciousness, the Abhidhamma also finalized the structure of the cosmos: both Theravādin and northern sources detail thirty-one basic realms. – 1997: 192-93

Citta, Mano and Viññāṇa

The English translations of these three technical terms are very often highly misleading and incorrect. I, therefore, compound them with the English generic word "consciousness" – *citta*-consciousness, *mano*-consciousness and *viññāṇa*-consciousness, which have their own numerous varieties with different contexts. That is to say, all these technical terms show different modes of consciousness, which is the basic life-principle of all varieties of sentient beings, who keep swinging from one birth to another, i.e. from one destiny to another by means of kammic forces in the cycle of *saṁsāra*. The dynamic nature of consciousness permanently comes to an end when a sentient being is born as a human being and transforms his defiled consciousness through knowledge, moral conduct and meditative technique leading to the blissful state of *nibbāna* following the Buddhist liberating schema. Generally, the entire Buddhism aims at liberating the human beings from their existential predicament, because of their special status and capacity in the hierarchy of sentient beings in the cosmos. A sentient being's rebirth in human being's category clearly shows that he carries his defiled consciousness from his previous life. Now it depends on the quality of his present modes of the *kamma*s (mental–vocal–physical acts) – wholesome or unwholesome in respect of his effort to further enhance the defiling factors already deposited in his consciousness or eliminating them – which will degrade or upgrade his destiny with increasing sorrow or happiness with it respectively.

In Buddhism, mind refers to a synthetic combination of *citta*, *mano* and *viññāṇa*, which function in different modes but interdependently within the domain of consciousness, the generic life-principle. In one sense, the three are considered synonyms, but in other different senses and contexts, they prove to be highly complex and vague. However, for the purpose of meditation and its impact, both mind and body are inseparably mixed up and interactive, which means mind influences body and vice versa. Taken separately in the empirical world, *nāma* and *rūpa* not only lack any purpose but also efficacy. That is why, the maintenance of sound health of both is necessary as we can see in the interactive relationship and mutual dependence in five aggregates (*pañca-khandha*) formula – four immaterial names (*nāma*) and one material form (*rūpa*) – all of which are dependently arising conditioned aggregates, while explaining the impermanence (*aniccā*) and non-substantiality (*anattā*) of the human person. Their inseparable coexistence, efficacy and continuous interaction are seen and felt in day-to-day life in every experiential cognitive process and are self-evident when we have the experience of the interactions with external sensory organs, arising of their respective awareness, attentive focus, mental images, concepts, thoughts, languages, emotive responses and so on. On analysis, we can find that at every moment, multiple supporting conditions are involved.

It is noteworthy that *citta*, *mano* and *viññāṇa* are not static entities, rather they are fluxional and dependently arising conscious series and also cognitive processes of differently related modes of consciousnesses within the psycho-corporeal framework. In order to avoid any ontological commitment, they can be designated as mere series of mental acts, activity, or dynamic process, from which our experience arises, gets conceptually structured, expresses in conventional language, reification takes place, world views are formed, intention and motivation (*cetanā*) are aroused and, subsequently, moral acts (*kamma*) are performed – leading to rebirth in various corresponding hierarchical realms and conditions. The Buddha's awakening is focused more on epistemological experience than metaphysical. In other words, the very beginning of the human existence and life is rooted in experience and its various constructions, which are further rooted in the deeply underlying active constituting and regulating factors.

Nāma and Its Four Constituents

We have seen that *rūpa* is a derived conceptual category (*upādā*) from the four physical bases, and so it is a conceptual and non-ontological generic term. That is, it is a mental construction. On the other hand, *nāma* is also a generic term for the combination of four conditioned consciousness factors (*vedanā*-consciousness, *saññā*-consciousness, *saṁkhāra*-consciousness and *viññāṇa*-consciousness), which are interdependently interlocked in a very complex manner without any clash among themselves. Note that such dynamic schemas are not chaotic or arbitrary. They, meaning a thing or a phenomenon, are governed and regulated in a certain natural way (*dhammaṭṭhitatā*) and as per rule without exception (*dhammaniyāmatā*). In both cases, or in such other cases, causal principle is necessarily inbuilt. However, the four *nāma*-constituents are conditioned factors, but they are also conditioning factors. This mechanism requires explanation so that we can understand their interdependent nature, deontological status and non-substantial continuity of a human person through rigorous mereological analysis and then also by way of synthesis. Being a derived conditioned thing, the person is liable for perpetual change, degeneration and disintegration leading to death. Remember that both *rūpa* and *nāma* undergo perpetual change, but it is the *citta*-consciousness only which goes for rebirth-linking (*paṭisandhi*) with the *kamma*-formations (*saṁkhāra*) enriched by the skilful or unskilful defilements (*kilesa*). *Saṁkhāra* is created by the mental faculty, which after receiving external and/or internal information prepares judgemental statement, wilful intention (*cetanā*) and psychological and physical responses toward their respective objects, as a consequence of which it generates various kinds of root-motivating defilements (e.g. *lobha*, *dosa* and *moha*).

Twelve-link Formula of Man's Consciousness Journey

In the preceding passages, I have discussed five-aggregates (*pañca-khandha*) formula, which explains the very human constitution in terms of impersonal non-substantial characteristics of the person. Now in this section, I am going to discuss the twelve-link formula (*dvādasa-nidāna*), which shows the two-pronged condition-conditioning causal principle (*paṭicca-samuppāda* formula) in the twelve-link sequential order. In other words, we can see that each link is a series of fluxional factors, thus its character is conditioned. But this series, in turn, is the condition of the next series and so it is called conditioning series. Remember that each link or series is a mode of the generic consciousness. As a whole, the whole formula covers the three temporal epochs – i.e. past existence, present existence and life, and future existence – which marks the temporal continuity of the sāṁsāric cycle of birth–life–death–rebirth of a person's *kamma-phala* generated journey.

The twelve-link system, which describes the cycle of one's life continuum across the temporal modes of life, explains a man's journey in accordance with the dependently arising formula. Like the five-aggregates formula, it also shows the existence and life as fluxional, non-substantial and kammic continuum. But unlike the five-aggregate formula, it works out step by step the twelve-links schema in the cyclical sāṁsāric order, which shows the link of the preceding past with two links (*avijjā* and *saṁkhāra*) by entering into the immediately present existence spanning over the ten links (*viññāṇa* to *bhāva*) and finally the two links (*jāti* and *jarāmaraṇa*) into future existence or the next life in the continuing flow of *bhavaṅga*.

Each of these three temporal components shows a normal course of life until the cycle of suffering ends in the state of *nibbāna*. In other words, the structure of *avijjā*-consciousness along with the *saṁkhāra*-consciousness enters into the present, which together with the subsequent ten links provides an opportunity to make the present life kammically better or worse on which the quality of future life depends in terms of moving to lower or higher or the highest destiny. This twelve-link formula has the scope for reversal of the order, which according to the Buddha's teaching is desirable for the deliverance from the suffering. In this process, the whole programme is executed within the domain of fluxional consciousness and by the consciousness itself. In this context, Jeffrey D. Watts makes a genuine critical remark, which is worth noticing:

> This schema has a number of important functions in the context of the teachings. On the one hand, it provides a causal explanation of the genesis of a relatively "new" psychophysical individual, conceived not as an autonomous entity but as a congeries of various causally arisen and interrelated phenomena. On the other, it often stands as a point of focus for an illustration of the causal status of the elements or *nidānas* with which it deals, in terms of their relation(s) – individually and collectively – to the human experience of suffering (*dukkha*). The schema has still other functions in the teachings .... – 1982: 407

Bhavaṅga-citta: Deep Structure of Consciousness

Bhavaaṅga-citta is that specific mode of consciousness, which is the latently flowing bedrock of the conditioned continuity of the existence (*bhāva*) of a sentient being across the three segmented temporality. It is thus called *bhavaṅga-sota*: as it is like a stream of a river which carries all sorts of elements; in this sense, it is the underlying current powered by the kammic forces (*vipāka*), which condition (*kāraṇa*) the structuring process of the appropriate nature of the existence of a new sentient being, i.e. it is a *sine qua non* of a particular continuing life. For this reason, it is a dynamic process, without beginning and end as long as the sāṁsāric life continues because of the consciousness factors like ignorance (*avijjā*) and *kamma-vipāka* (*saṁkhāra*). The *bhavaṅga-citta* is the possessor and carrier of all past impressions of experiences and wilful *kammas*, which have the potentiality to shape the future life, good or bad. It is also the root-cause of the arising of the faculty of memory. It is also the factor to create a bridge between death (*cuti*) and rebirth (*paṭisandhi*). Thus, it is a specific mode of consciousness, which latently sustains the regular flow of a stream of consciousness from past to present to future existence and life. Gethin succinctly explains the characteristics of *bhavaṅga-citta*:

> Consciousness is said to be in its *bhavaṅga* mode whenever no active consciousness process is occurring; in other words, *bhavaṅga* is passive, inactive state of the mind – the mind when resting in itself. Ordinary waking consciousness is to be understood as the mind continually and very rapidly emerging from the lapsing back into *bhavaṅga* in response to various sense stimuli coming through the five sense-doors and giving rise to sense-door consciousness process; these will be interspersed with mind-door processes of various sorts. In contrast, the dream state is understood as essentially confined to mind-door processes occurring in what the texts, following the *Milindapañha*, call "monkey sleep" (*kapi-niddā, kapi-middhā, makkata-niddā*). In deep sleep, the mind rests in inactivity and does not emerge *bhavaṅga*.
>
> – 2005: 162

In the same article, Gethin makes another brilliant observation on the notion of *bhavaṅga-citta*:

> The fact that the Abhidhamma uses the notion of *bhavaṅga* to define both the nature of a given being and also what constitutes a lifetime as that being suggests that *bhavaṅga* is being used to explain not merely the logic of continuity but also why a particular being continues to be that particular being throughout his or her life, rather than becoming some other being – to become another being is to change one's *bhavaṅga*. Thus, why I

> do not suddenly start behaving like an animal is because I have what is essentially a human *bhavaṅga*. In other words, the notion of *bhavaṅga* is, in part at least, intended to provide some account of why I am me and why I continue to behave like me; it is surely intended to give some theoretical basis for observed consistency in behaviour pattern, character traits and the habitual mental states of a given individual. – Gethin 2005: 171

Meditation: The Dynamics of Liberation

On some occasion, the Buddha was asked to summarize his teachings in two words. His remarkable answer, which is worth noticing: "*avijjā* and *ācaraṇa*" (ignorance and moral conduct) and "*dukkha* and *dukkha-nirodha*" (existential predicament and its cessation), which are pregnant with profound meanings and message. The meditation technique and the *jhāna*'s progressive stages keep these two as the core focus of their analysis and practice. The Buddha's three fundamental doctrines, which arise from his Awakening are: *paṭicca-samuppāda* (universal natural law of dependent arising), *cattāri ariyasaccāni* (four noble truths) and *majjhima-paṭipadā* (middle-path), which he designated as *dhammacakkapavattana* (turning of the wheel of the *dhamma*), and *paṭisotagāmī* (sailing his *dhamma* against the current). Note that the Buddha's this approach in Indian belief system proved to be a revolutionary paradigm shift. These points of focus necessarily require "directing the outward attention and movement toward external world" into the inward mental world, which contains the dynamic function of the human suffering or predicament. The Buddha located the roots of their causes and solutions within the domain of mind (*citta*), which is the host of all sorts of its defilements, which are responsible for concealing the purity of the mind and polluting it with the root-motivating factors like greed (*lobha*), hatred (*dvesa*) and intellectual dullness or confusion (*moha*).

Obviously, if these root factors and their associates are the causes of suffering, then cessation of suffering is possible only by means of devising and applying an effective method to eliminate them forever in order to achieve the permanent original purity, which turns out to be the "attainment of cessation" (*nirodha-samāpatti*), i.e. a soteriological attainment. Meditation method is the only method for this purpose. Meditation, a mode of concentration, is a generic term used across the various religious traditions, such as Vedic–Upaniṣadic, Buddhist, Jaina, Sāṁkhya–Yoga, Judaism, Christian, Islamic and Sikhism. All these methods have the same goal of suppressing and purifying the defilements in the creative mind and its concomitants, which are just like a kitchen wherein the cook prepares all sorts of foods according to the taste, choices, situation and culture. These varieties contain both hygienic and unhygienic elements, which are supposed to be cleansed in the right way. In a literal sense, meditation is a method of deep thinking with silence and beyond focused on gaining an uncommon mysterious goal, which may be worldly or other-worldly. It is a combined method of psycho-corporeal in action and practice, and its results are diversified as per the adept's conceptual and logical framework.

In the end, I would again like to say that the present article is a brief statement on my forthcoming book and so my future plan is to develop its theme by focusing on various types of the Buddhist doctrinal formulations, analysis, exploration of the inner world, psycho–physical–phenomenological method, skilful management and practice. The Buddhist conceptual framework comprises of the meditation method, its doctrines and goals, development of the progressive *jhāna*-stages and the attainment of cessation, which finally ends in the state of the cessation of suffering and attainment of *nibbāna*.

References

PRIMARY SOURCES

Sutta and Abhidhamma literature (Pali Text Society edns).

SECONDARY SOURCES

Collins, Steven, 1999, *Selfless Persons: Imagery and Thought in Theravāda Buddhism*, repr., Cambridge: Cambridge University Press.

Cousins, L.S., 1981, "The Paṭṭhāna and the Development of the Theravādin Abhidhamma", *Journal of Pali Text Society*, 10: 22-46. Also reprinted in *Buddhism: Critical Concepts in Religious Studies*, IV, ed. Paul Williams, pp. 52-70, London and New York: Routledge.

Gethin, Rupert, 2005, "Bhavaṅga and Rebirth According to the Abhidhamma", in *Buddhism: Critical Concepts in Religious Studies*, IV, ed. Paul Williams, pp. 159-81, London and New York: Routledge.

——, 1997, "Cosmology and Meditation: From the Aggañña-Sutta to the Mahāyāna", *History of Religion*, 36(3): 183-217.

Hamilton, Su, 1996, *Identity and Experience: The Constitution of the Human Being According to Early Buddhism*, London: Luzac Oriental.

Harvey, Peter, 1993, "The Mind–Body Relationship in Pali Buddhism: A Philosophical Investigation", *Asian Philosophy*, 3(1): 29-41.

Hirakawa, Akira, 1993, *A History of Indian Buddhism: From Śākyamuni to Early Mahāyāna*, tr. & ed. Paul Groner, repr., Delhi: Motilal Banarsidass.

Karunadasa, Y., 2010, *The Theravāda Abhidhamma: Its Inquiry into the Nature of Conditioned Reality*, Hong Kong: Centre of Buddhist Studies, University of Hong Kong.

Nyanatiloka, 2004, *Buddhist Dictionary: Manual of Buddhist Terms and Doctrines*, repr., Kandy: Buddhist Publication Society.

Somaratne, G.A., 2005, "Citta, Manas & Viññāṇa: Aspects of Mind as Presented in Early Buddhist Pali Discourses", in *Dhamma Viniya: Essays in Honour of Venerable Professor Dhammavihari (Jyoti Dhirasekara)*, ed. Asanga Tilakaratne, pp. 169-202, Colombo: Association from Buddhist Studies.

Watts, Jeffrey, D., 1982, "Necessity and Sufficiency in the Buddha's Causal Schema", *Philosophy East and West*, 32(4): 407-23.

Williams, Paul (ed.), 2005, *Buddhism: Critical Concepts in Religious Studies*, vol. IV, London and New York: Routledge.

11

Physical Brain's Self-Awareness of Itself as Physical

A Zombie Who Knows that It Is Not the Real Ego or the I

P. Milan Khangamcha

Abstract: This paper investigates the underlying implications of the so-called objective truth and reductive view of consciousness as physical which innocuously ignores the fact of self-awareness of physical brain of itself as physical as scientific conclusion. This self-reflexivity of physical brain implies intentional act of regressive or backward reference to the highly complex cognitive activities of those very scientists of creative genius to see new patterns of scientific truths as gap among data which were unknown to other fellow scientists. It is this background awareness, which Śaṅkara had anticipated as the intuitive bare ground (*adhiṣṭhāna mātra*), which is affirmed scientifically by Roger Penrose as non-computational human intelligence or understanding or consciousness. The scientific conclusion that mind or consciousness are bereft of ontological status, but only the functional expression of the physical brain implies that it is the concerned scientist's own physical brain which observes the brain of other persons to be only physical. This is the same as saying that physical brain knows its own physical status. That, a physical brain knows itself as mechanical, natural and a physical automaton means that it is an intentional subjective act. The issue in hand is the act of self-knowing of a physical state of itself as physical reality. What does it entail in epistemic terms? Is it equal to machine intelligence which has self-reflexivity of itself as a machine? The underlying act of inter-intentionality of the inter-subjective process of reviewing a physical theory of consciousness as an objective scientific truth may never cease to have a regressive intentional reference to the said act of inter-subjectivity. The act of knowing of something as an objective truth as the background epistemic subjectivity will always be presupposed by any assertion of a truth as objective. Vidyāraṇya's example of "canvas of painting" (*citra dīpa*) and the "light of theatre" (*nāṭaka dīpa*) in his *Pañcadaśī* as the examples of "pure consciousness" (*cinmātra*) had anticipated Penrose's view that human intelligence or consciousness as the knower of something as algorithmic cannot be algorithmic. Hence, though embodied in the brain, the act of knowing of the truth of science or mathematics as its bare ground (*adhiṣṭhāna mātra*) itself cannot be reduced to the same algorithmic or computational function. Thus, without indulging in self-contradiction, no scientific theory of consciousness can disprove the reality of the non-physical consciousness as the knower of such a theory. Thus, the view that apart from the activities of the physical brain, mind or consciousness has no ontological status but it is only the function of the physical brain is incoherent. A physical brain's self-awareness of itself as physical ends up with the act of proving what it originally wanted to disprove (*arthāntara*).

Keywords: Brain's self-awareness, post-human, pure awareness, bare ground, regressive reference, intentional act, *sākṣī-caitanya, anvayavyatireka, citra dīpa, nāṭaka dīpa, arthāntara.*

Introduction

The lost or scathing criticisms against the ontological status of the traditional philosophical concept of consciousness had its genesis in the separation of philosophy from the sciences became effected in the nineteenth century and early twentieth century due to the impact of the rapid advancement of science and technological know-how. The empirical method of modern science and scientific truth became an overriding method of all the fields of modern knowledge systems. Materialistic growth, glitters, development, affluence, leisure, comforts and hedonistic pleasures provided by modern economy, science and technology, and internalization of these as values having the power of emancipation, perhaps had their negative influence by way of increasing treatment of the traditional notions of mind or consciousness or the spiritual vision of the ancients as dogmas and human nature along with the reality at large became demystified. The direct consequences of such modern atheism and science controlled modernity ("the self-definition of a generation about its own technological innovation, governance and socio-economics". Source: https://www.britannica.com/topic/modernity) are material glitters, selfish hedonistic pleasures, environmentally unsustainable affluences and a life of consumerism. Thc colonial legacy of capitalist controlled modern economic system of demand and supply is inconceivable without all these modern materialistic cultures. No contemporary philosophers have ever thought about the intimate connection between increasing modernity and physical view of mind or consciousness. The factual reason of science and its empirical method is accepted by positivist philosophers as Bible and they are boldly declaring that metaphysics is impossible and an unscientific dogma (Van I., Peter, & Sullivan M., Winter 2021 edition). The crux of the issue is that the reductive view of mind of positivism and the sciences is also related to the modern Western anthropocentrism and individualism as their ideological derivative. They are not aware that the modern Western metaphysical duality between man and nature underlies their dogmatic assertion. Rather, anthropocentrism by nature is an atheistic concept, ethically problematic and it replaces the centrality of spiritual principle in the cosmos. The modern positivist philosophers who have become wedded to science would consider that ordinary human desires, self-seeking nature, tendency to seek the satiation of its wants, needs and longings are natural and therefore they have objective validity. The moral values of selflessness, goodwill, commongood, commonwill, etc. are rejected as subjective fancies and unscientific. One last point to be mentioned is the faith of science that, everything including human nature is natural and only its method can explore the scientific truth behind everything and there is no other truth beyond the realm of science and method. It would require volumes to explain as to how this belief of science is hands in glove with the capitalist political economy of privatization, liberalization and corporatization which leave no hole bared beyond its scope and depth of instrumental using anything and everything as its resources. No contemporary academics of the topranking universities of the world will be willing to speak about the relation between industrialization within this model of political economy and the physical theory of human nature reflected in the rejection of the independent ontological status of mind or consciousness.

The above issue has led to the development of the concept of post-human which blurs the distinction between human being as mental-being and machine. Computational linguistics and computational theory of mind in Artificial Intelligence (AI), neuroscience, cognitive science, and the like, based on the physical theory of consciousness are related to the idea of post-human. The matter is no more about logic, scientific reason and evidence, or theoretical consistency or philosophical merits. The main purpose of modern civilization as a modern colonial legacy is neither the ideal value of oneness of spiritual truth nor the goodness of the human civilization or the biosphere but the creation of the iniquitous anthropocentric creation of private wealth for those very few rich people of the world. Thus, the empirical method of science in its applications for business purposes and their control of the materialistic and Godless global dynamics and its hedonistic glitters and the sway of power which these economic forces have in the world had left those pioneer positivists analytical philosophers with no other options except joining the bandwagon of the findings of scientists involved in cognitive science, neurology, etc. in the late nineteenth and twentieth centuries. The reduction of human mind or consciousness to the natural, mechanical, biophysical and physiological processes of the brain is heavily dependent on corporate funding as its limitless potential for practical applications in the increasingly commercialized world today (Harington 2021). The scope of this paper does not permit to investigate and articulate about to what extent all those complicated existential consequences of such a demystified, materialistic and hedonistic modern world of consumerism which has reduced human nature to the status of a mere bio-physico-natural automata. This process is directly controlled by capitalist economic and political forces. Modern economy as a subject of modern education is directly controlled and dominated by this globalized power. In short, everything is calculated in economic terms and explaining away the extra-physical characteristics of human nature as the function of the physical brain have a direct high-end economic dividend. Therefore, to achieve the ultimate end of the neoliberal political interests, the researches in neurology, neuro-biology, cognitive science and AI in the corporate-controlled world are sponsored by this power. Hence, it is neither the reason of science nor its empirical method and its factual truth which drive the most advanced researches on mind or consciousness. It is with these views in the background that the main highlight of this paper should be read and understood. This is not to circumvent a poor logic or lack of evidence of the traditional philosophical theories of consciousness.

The positivist philosophers and the scientists in these fields are so self-confident that, the reality of mind or "I" or ego, its free will and choices are outdated and therefore it is reduced to the status of pure mechanical natural automata of algorithmic processes. They are not self-reflexive enough to admit that to come to this materialistic scientific conclusion is itself carried out by the intentional act of physical brain which is able to see new gaps by ghostly mirror neurons, visual cells, etc. in between a set of data and see logical flaws in the arguments of the opponents who argue in favour of the ontological status of mind or consciousness as a hard problem. How these neurons and their physiological correlates organize and synthesize those concepts, ideas, and scientific principles, and draw a conclusion without a self with the awareness of counterview of traditional view of consciousness with the ability of discriminative insights and intentionally that directs towards a self-consistent theoretical conclusion? Integrated Information Theory of neuroscientist Guilio Tononi says "conscious experience is irreducible" and Global Workshop Theory which says "consciousness is simply the act of broadcasting information around the brain from a memory bank" of Bernard Baars, a neuro scientist (Ratner 2018), are some of the theories associated with the above question. How can a physical brain know of itself as a physical brain which is not some mystical mind or self? While the physical brain knows of itself as a physical process, how can it be that it is not the *self-awareness* of the same physical process of itself as the physical brain that it is not the so-called extra-physical spiritual entity, called soul? Is it not the case of proving what the scientists have initially set out to disprove (the fallacy of *arthāntara*)? Their firmed official thesis is that it is either an emergent property (Scott 1995) of brain or it is a mere functional correlate of the nano-level intricate functions of the complex neural of networking of the brain. That is, beyond its being an epiphenomenon of the complex brain activities, it has no extra-corporeal ontological status. One may take the help of Physicist Brandon Carter's *Weak Anthropic Principle* (1973) and *Strong Anthropic Principle* (*Encyclopaedia Britannica* 2013) to explain the inner self-contradiction inherent in the fact of human existence governed by the same physical and natural laws of the cosmos which "somehow" has the accidental ability to know the physical world as "what it is". Does not this question raise the further problem whether or not it does not tantamount to saying that in and through human mind or understanding or simply brain as the product of nature functioning as per mechanical and physical laws, nature or cosmos has come to know itself? Is it not the case of self-awareness of nature of itself as nature? The question is – is not the self-awareness of something like nature of itself as nature a case of self-contradiction. It is just like, say, that one and the same thing is both of inert nature and is in a position of self-awareness of itself as nature. Nature, in the present case, is the human brain as an accidental by-product of biophysical nature without which no one can indulge in self-glorification and self-congratulatory creamy remarks of civilizational achievements of the modern human species. How can the modern human species which while being an accidental by-product of nature (*abiogenesis*) has come to undertake a lifelong process of intentional scientific researches in various fields such as neurology, AI, astro-physics or cosmology and quantum mechanics and raise the most fundamental questions about the very first origin of the cosmos and launch themselves as the harbingers of science and hell bent upon showing or establishing that the human species is very much a part of the Godless natural, mechanical and physical world? "Physical Brain's Self-awareness of Itself as Physical", the title of this paper, points to the above ideas as its central issue. All the deliberations of this paper will be centred on these issues.

The Impact of Abiogenesis on the Scientific Theory of Consciousness

The definition of life in biology (Annie Prud'homme-Généreux 2013) and all the scientific explanations in neuro-biology, neurology, cognitive science and AI of the highly innovative cognitive functions of human mind or brain as a mere continuum of all the living non-human species in the biosphere does not give any special place to the creative human intelligence. Yet, the West claims that its science had liberated the modern man from his old dogmas and blind faiths. How will and in what way the act of disproving the traditional philosophical view of consciousness as non-physical can go hand in hand with the claim of the history of human civilization which has come of age in the science-dominated modern world as having reached the apex point of an authorless human civilization? Is it not the self-congratulation of the physical brain which is nothing more than being natural automata just like the falling of stone from a higher plane down the hill? How will it be a mere physical brain while placing itself on the apex point of the animal kingdom and it is so much proud of itself as having conquered nature which is its own origin and used it for its purpose? Gordon C. Mills, Malcolm Lancaster and Walter L. Bradley (1993) in their paper show the glossing over, over ambitious nature and overstatement of the biology textbooks dealing with the origin of life in "Origin of *Life & Evolution in Biology Textbooks: A Critique. The American Biology Teacher*" (pp. 78-83) cites Klaus Dose, "one of the best known origin of life researchers for the past 20 years" (the date of their paper being 1993, their views need to be judged with the latest findings after this year as on date) in support of their arguments that the text books are not revealing the existing theory of the origin of life which is still inconclusive. Dose in his paper, "The Origin of Life: More Questions than Answers" (1988: 348), substantiates the inconclusiveness and the difficult nature of the question of life on the earth from matter gives the following summary:

> More than 30 years of experimentations on the origin of life in the fields of chemical and molecular evolution have led to a better perception of the immensity of the problem of the origin of life on Earth rather than to its solution. At present all discussions on principal theories and experiments in the field either end in stalemate or in a confession of ignorance ....
>
> – quoted in Mills et al. 1993: 78

Yet, Jacques Monod's (1971) book *Chance and Necessity: An Essay on the Natural Philosophy of Modern Biology* cites Democritus' everything existing in the universe is the fruit of chance and necessity (p. vi). The biological theories of *abiogenesis* (Rogers 2022) and spontaneous generation (*Encyclopaedia Britannica*, 2018) still conclude that life had its first origin from matter. Richard L. Thomson's small monograph *Demonstration by Information Theory that Life Cannot Arise from Matter* (Thompson 1977), who did his PhD in mathematics at California State University, USA, attempts to show with mathematical calculation that *abiogenesis* is impossible. In a away, this seems to agree with what Klaus Dose's reference to "chance hypothesis of origin":

> In regard to the *chance hypothesis for the origin* of genetic information, Kuppers (1990: 60) notes: The expectation probability for the nucleotide sequence of a bacterium is thus so slight that not even the entire space of the universe would be enough to make the random synthesis of a bacterial genome probable (ibid.: 80).

The empirical question of the origination of life from matter and thus the human brain or intelligence is its accidental by-product of the trial and error processes of the blind nature cannot deny that it is the same blind physical brain itself which knows itself as physical and this is nothing but the case of physical brain's self-awareness of itself as physical. Ancient Indian philosophers were not unaware of this controversy (Veerachary 2018). Accidentalism (Yadr̥cchāvāda) and naturalism (Svabhāvavāda) were very much the alternative causal theories of the ancient Indian metaphysical debates introduced as *pūrva-pakṣa*. The *pañcamayakośa* (five sheets covering the self) of Vedānta begins with the question whether or not body is the self (*ahaṁ idaṁ śarīram*). And the analysis goes on showing that physical body as self and so on cannot be self. The realist and idealist metaphysical trends abound in the inter-school metaphysical debates among the nine schools of classical Indian philosophy. Hence, it is nothing new.

Some mathematicians, well conversant with philosophical issues and philosophy of science, neuroscientists and quantum physicists (Donald 2007) recently have come on a common academic platform and have debated about the question of realism and idealism as the possible theories behind their works. This writer had listened to a lengthy discussion in the YouTube very recently on this issue among mathematicians, neuro-scientists, philosophers of science and quantum physicists in some other interdisciplinary forum of well-meaning experts in these fields. The crux of the issue is that the physical theory of consciousness cannot escape consciousness itself and, without this subjective phenomenon, the said deliberations could not have even been taken place. This is exactly what is demanded from the scientists dealing with the reductive view of consciousness as a physical, natural and mechanical process only amenable to science and its method. The traditional view of consciousness of philosophers is their punching bag and this is what this paper has set out to debunk. Therefore, the complex issues reflected in the topic of this paper is interdisciplinary and even transdisciplinary in the ways in which it is seen and believed by the author. Hence, the adumbrations of the problems under consideration shall proceed accordingly. There is no disciplinary boundary and no academic discipline is taken as self-explanatory and capable of providing any plausible view of anything, not to speak about self and its self-reflexive capability. Physical brain's self-awareness of itself as physical is a blatant self-contradiction. An attempt is made in next section to show as to how this view which in a way still against modern Western metaphysical duality is existentially and theoretically inconsistent.

Roger Penrose's Non-Computational Human Understanding, and Bhāratatīrtha Vidyāraṇya's Nāṭaka Dīpa and Citra Dīpa

Today's top scientists of the world have not become self-reflective or introspective enough about the so-called scientific objectivity, their task of reviewing of scientific papers and interpretations, inferences and their controlled hypothesis and their ability to see the missing explanatory gaps among a set of given facts are dependent upon a background awareness of all these which reveal all these just as a canvas is needed to enable us to see what are painted on it (*citra dīpa* of Vidyāraṇya's *Pañcadaśī*). Without the canvas all those complicated patterns painted will not be visible. Without the general light of a theatrical play (*nāṭaka dīpa*), none of those characters on the stage will be seen by or shown to the members of the audience. Roger Penrose's conclusion that human intelligence or understanding or consciousness is non-computational, because, it is ever presupposed by everything what the great scientists observe, calculate and interpret as computational (Harington 2021). To think that, the very act of computational thinking of the great minds or mind-brains of mathematicians or scientists serves both as a knowing subject as well as its own object known is illogical. A self cannot itself be one and the same entity which is in a state of being a subject as well as an object of itself. That this state is caused by the superimposition (*adhyāsa)* of the root ignorance on the non-dual *Brahman* as the background pure awareness (*sākṣī-caitanya* or *cinmātra*) is the established philosophical position of Śaṅkara in his thesis of Advaita. The negation of the mutually contradictory and logically irreconcilable dichotomic relation between a knowing subject and the object of its knowledge is interpreted by him as "unconcealed" (Heidegger's terminology used as an appropriate concept to convey the non-relational nature of the transcendental condition) by and also intuitive affirmation of their background "unconditioned of condition" of differenceless and relationless "bare awareness". And given that, if "I", mind or ego of the scientists, is an illusion or unreal which is the case according to their latest conclusion, then the highly complicated works of the scientists had been negotiating among the difficult scientific data and finally comes out with some new scientific discovery are the outputs of their physical brains. Rather, such a conclusion is either the scientific experience of their zombie-like illusory "I-s" or that, having mind or consciousness already reduced to a physical state, they indulge in self-contradiction by their ignoring of the regressive intentional reference to their acts of judgements. No matter how much their critical scientific reasoning has the physical correlates of nano-level intricate networking of neurons and neuro-physiological processes, they can hardly avoid their subjective epistemic phenomenon of the self-awareness of itself as physical. Thus, the contention of the neuroscientists that the mind or consciousness is a functional expression of physical brain and thus it is nothing less than a physical process of mechanical automata defeats itself. The bringing in of animal intelligence as a bio-natural stimulus response system observed in the wild forests must not be equated with a highly complicated and creative task of the workings of the highly imaginative fertile and genius minds of great scientists. Except the human beings, no advanced animals just below the human species in the evolutionary hierarchy have so far found writing poems, novels and asking complicated questions like the "first cause" (*sarva kāraṇa kāraṇam*) (excerpted from *Śrī Brahma-Saṁhitā* of Swami Bhaktivedanta Narayana 2004), "who am I" (*ko 'ham*) and "why the world is what it is", etc. Anthropic Principle in physics considers that the human brain somehow has evolved as a *finetuned* species of biological nature to be intelligent enough to ask the most fundamental questions which the philosophers and the scientists have come to do so far. Their emphasis on the human mind is a source of dismay for some atheistic-minded physicists and rejects it as a potential idea for mysticism. As such, what the scientists' reductive physical theory of consciousness argues on the basis of their empirical investigation is tantamount to saying that the physical brain knows itself as physical brain. Some researchers have also argued that no causal theories of consciousness such as Integrated Information Theory (IIT) can explain consciousness (Doerig et al. 2019). Since consciousness is presupposed by every creative and expert works such as those of scientists and causal theories as one of them also have the same presupposition and thus they cannot be explain consciousness. Pure consciousness is what is behind every advanced human cognitive enterprise. Śaṅkara and all the ancient saints, seers and sages of the Upaniṣadic period before him were aware of the impossibility of the finite and defective human minds and senses ever discovering the supreme truth by relying on their own limited ability, piecemeal, discursive, plodding and faltering epistemic apparatus. His only thesis is that whatever the human mind knows or experiences, there always lies something underneath them as their background condition which they cannot go back and know it as an object, because they presuppose it (in a scientific way, it is also the view of Roger Penrose). The question here is – is the psychoepistemic phenomenon of the intentional act of knowing by a physical process called brain which Anthropic Principle is all about is the same with that of a stone falling below from a higher position? This may be discussed within the ambit of the phenomenological givenness of the intentional act of the process of knownness as a subjective epistemic state. Kant's "logical postulate" of "I think" and mind or "I" of conventional philosophy is implied by this process without which concerned scientists could not have ever arrived at such a daring and challenging scientific conclusion which presupposes a higher-order human understanding (Freitag and Kraus 2022).

That the view of the physical universe as a mechanistic natural automata which the scientists came to understand as explainable by their empirical method does not give any special position to their own intentional acts of knowing as something which is non-algorithmic or extra-physical in nature. Rather, their act of knowing or observing is agent-less, and its reducing to the activities of the mechanical and computational brain still demands explanation. Because, it is this mechanical and natural automata which has no subjective knower and, as such, there is no question of free will that has come to question and answer about itself, and the truth about the natural universe. This is a rampant and glaring act of self-contradiction which would lead one only to its conclusion. How is that all the great achievements of human civilizational history are a natural process created by an illusory sense of mind or ego. All the self-congratulatory claims of achievements as creative jumps of human civilization and all the wonders it has brought to the world will be authorless and non-intentional. David Gomez in *Physical Theory of Consciousness* (2018) and the sixth chapter of his another book *Humans and Machine Consciousness*, 1st edn (pp. 85-92) discusses the complex scientific technicalities of the way how the human consciousness as a pure physical process works. The only argument which may be offered is that, it is possible to look at the human brain as a complex "organic hardware" which can only house the human mind or consciousness as "organic software". In the absence of the Kantian "I think" as the locus of the object directed act of the intentional consciousness which interprets, makes judgement and draws conclusion, David Gomez's highly technical scientific reasoning behind the task of writing his paper, his identity as a scientist and his sense of himself as so and so would mean nothing if they are mere mechanical automata of his brain. All his acts as a scientist such as writing, observing, testing, judging, inferring, etc. require a subjective "I". If not, it is the brain called David Gomez which knows itself as a brain. Even when this state of knownness has corresponding physical, ph ysiological, chemical and electromagnetic correlates, it is only a subjective phenomenon embodied in a necessary organic physical brain which knows or observes facts. Otherwise, all the higher cognitive abilities behind the rapid advancements in the fields of science and technological development which brought a sharp turning point in the human history are thus authorless scripts as the works of the automatic physico-mechanical human brain or that the scientists are mere Zombies. The bereftness of an "owner" or an "I" (No Ownership Theory of David Hume and Anātmavāda of Buddhism) who is supposed to own all these self-congratulatory achievements of the modern scientists demand an explanation was corrected by Kant with his non-ontological but "logical postulate" of "I think" (Hamlyn 1984: 199-200). Otherwise, the goal directed and highly creative works of scientists will be that of the ghost in the machine. Śaṅkara had never agreed that a knowing subject which stands in opposition to what it knows as its object known is ultimately real. Its status of being a mundane reality in the empirical world is related to what it knows as its object of empirical knowledge (*vṛtti-jñāna*) is shown by him as logically problematic as it is grounded on a falsifiable and unstable empirical truth claim. The unstable nature of all forms of ordinary knowledge with the ever-lurking possibility of contradiction by a higher knowledge is explained as made possible by their being manifested by the underlying "witness consciousness" (*sākṣī-caitanya*) ultimately grounded in the background of pure awareness. His analysis of the three states of experiences – waking experience, dream experience and deep sleep experiences with the application of *anvaya-vyatirekī-nyāya*-agreement in absence and agreement in presence – shows the invariable presence of the witness consciousness in both the absence and presence of all these states or their mutual negations.

According to T.M.P. Mahadevan in *Philosophy of Advaita* – a book on the *Pañcadaśī* of Vidyāraṇya Swami – a text meant for students, elaborates and explains so well as to how Śaṅkara brought a grand synthesis of subjective approach and objective approach of which his thesis of non-dual *Brahman* as "pure consciousness" is hinted at as a reality to be intuitively grasped (*aprokṣānubhūti*). The expression "pure consciousness" (*kevala caitanya* or *cinmātra*) was not meant by Śaṅkara as a reality to be understood positively as if it is some ordinary entity of sense experience. No empirical category is applicable to it. Yet, the use of language and logic in the form of *neti, neti* of the Upaniṣads – the via negative method (an expression frequently used by Professor R. Balasubramanian in his classes during 1985-87) were only to indicate the unconditioned condition (Radhakrishnan's terminology in his *An Idealist View of Life*, 1932) of the ultimate truth as the ultimate ground without which no negation would be possible. Every negation presupposes a prior affirmation. Vidyāraṇya employs the examples of *citra dīpa* (the light of canvas) on which the paintings are superimposed and made visible and *nāṭaka dīpa* (the light of theatre; similar to Cartesian theatre) without which the actors or characters in a play will not be visible as the illustrative accounts of the Supreme *Nirguṇa-Brahman* as the *niṣprapañca satya* (acosmic/transcendental truth) condition of the *prapañca* (cosmos or the universe) – the bare ground of the world of space and time. The Upaniṣadic method of *neti, neti* as the *via negativa* method – "not this, not this", indirectly hints at the pure consciousness presupposed by every act of the falsification of empirical knowledge. Sadānanda's *Vedāntasāra* (2014) refers to Adhyāropāvāda – *Superimposition and Subsequent Denial* (tr. R. Balsubramanian) as the application of *neti, neti* only to show that the non-dual reality – the bare ground as pure consciousness, in some way or the other, is presupposed by the entire range of falsifiable (*bādhitattva*) empirical human experiences. On the epistemic plane, negative logic is used in this case by Śaṅkara and Madhusūdana Sarasvatī in his *mithyatā* section of *Advaita Siddhi* (1992). On the question, whether or not either the world or *Nirguṇa-Brahman* is affirmed by the ultimate negation, the Naiyāyikas and Advaitins would differ based on their respective idealist and realist positions (Khangamcha 2018). Any act of negation will be impossible without a prior affirmation of an underlying pure awareness. It is a form of transcendental dialectic.

A little introspective observation of one's own mind would reveal that when one is dissatisfied about one's own writing on a complicated paper, a sense of lack, wanting and dissatisfaction of what one has written, etc. is seen when ones says – "I could have done it better", there is an a priori background criterion (pure awareness) without which the sense of dissatisfaction as an intuitive grasp would be inexplicable. Śaṅkaras's *Nirguṇa-Brahman* is precisely this transempirical or intuitive and transcendental condition of all forms of sense experiences. Will the "bundle theory" of Hume, etc. and *saṅghāta* (aggregate) of the *pañca-skandha* (Wikipedia 2022) of Buddhism help a situation? Both may accept a non-conventional or namesake pragmatic self bereft of a "substantial or essential" metaphysical truth without a unitary self with its ever-present pure intentionality. Yet, Kant did realize the philosophical wisdom of the difficulty of explaining human experience or difficult cognitive operations without the logical postulate of the "I think" (not metaphysical postulate) as the inner reality of the "synthetic unity of apperception" (Pereboom et al. 2022).

The Political Context of the Physical Theory of Consciousness: A Framework of Surreptitious Power

The modern scientists may take shelter behind this idea of a non-substantial pragmatic or a namesake empirical self as a Kantian. I think as a logical postulate and not as a metaphysical postulate. This seems to be what the scientists take their personhood to be and go on conducting all their scientific activities. Started as a powerful colonial political instrument, the know-how of science, technology, engineering, empirical method and their factual truths, and inventions and discoveries of scientists and engineers, medical scientists and highly specialized academic experts in the field are still in the tight grip of global powers (Gascoigne and Maroske 2013: Roy 2018). The cooperative intentional and deliberate goal-directed works of powerful political leaders and scientists cannot be conscious agency-less works of post-human automata. The countries which control science and technology, and global business also control the entire world till today. How will this global political scenario has no master minds? The physical theory of consciousness cannot be an exception and its demystification can never serve any good purpose except its use as a convenient tool of exploitation and power.

Hiding behind scientific evidence, it will be too political and economically inconvenient for the powerful stakeholders of the present world who sponsor the scientific works to accpet any sense of normative human nature constituted by some extra-physical truth like spiritually informed self to lead a life of obedience to the demands of a holistic acosmic intelligent principle of a moral universe. It is simply because, it does not pay and it cannot be instrumentalized for achieving the pragmatic value of political economic gains. To substantiate this argument, the entire history of modern civilization has to be re-interrogated.

The history of modern science and technology is inconceivable without its absolute colonial and post-colonial or neocolonial political, economic instrumentalization. The highly advanced and heavily cost-intensive researches on AI today as the basis of super-computers are in the direct control of super powers and industry collusion. Therefore, the traditional philosophical theory of consciousness is rejected mainly because it does not subserve megalomaniac hunger for power and economic profits. This agrees with the Western anthropocentric world view and materialistic thinking which results in the empirical method of science as per Protagoras – "man is the measure of all the things". This cannot go with the holistic Indian world view and the idea of the spiritual nature of human beings as the inseparable parts of the world and its corresponding view of life. The ongoing neo-liberal capitalist-driven economic theory of demand and supply just does not fit into this internationalized neo-colonial Western project. Modern political economic power founded on the modern Western dualistic metaphysical view of reality with man as a subject ontologically standing in an oppositional and exploitative relation to nature, as self-seeking modern man's object, to be misappropriated, is the mother of all the modern sins. It would go counter to the monistic or non-dualistic metaphysics of Vedānta wherein human self-transcendence from its troublesome embodied existence implied by the alternative name of *Brahmasūtra* as Śārīraka Mīmāṁsā. The act of self-transcendence of Vedānta is the realization of the ever-attained non-anthropocentric acosmic spiritual truth which is holistic or inclusive in nature. The physical theory of consciousness does not have any place in this ancient Indian cosmology. The Anthropic Principle of modern physics which treats human nature as a finely tuned self-conscious epistemic organism to know the truth about the cosmos comes very closer the Vedāntic spiritual pursuits:

> A form of the latter known as the *participatory anthropic principle*, articulated by John Archibald Wheeler, suggests on the basis

> of quantum mechanics that the universe, as a condition of its existence, must be observed, so implying one or more observers. Stronger yet is the final anthropic principle, proposed by John D. Barrow and Frank Tipler, which views the universe's structure as expressible by bits of information in such a way that information processing is inevitable and eternal.
>
> – Wikipedia contributors, 30 January 2023

This may be compared with Martin Heidegger's existential phenomenological process of *logos* or discourse as "letting the self-showing of a thing from itself in itself be seen by the seeing of Dasein as the non-ego being-in-the-world acts as the medium of unconcealing the holistic existential truth (Being) of the worldhood of the world. This is comparable with Kant's

> things-in-themselves are unknowable means that they exist but belong to the transcendent beyond, and they cannot be applied to our perceptual concepts and categories. – Li Tse-hou 1979

Husserl and Heidegger interpreted it differently according to their respective concept of phenomenology. Anthropic Principle of physics does not directly imply Western anthropocentrism, but they may be relatable while the former is the condition of scientific discovery of fundamental empirical fact of science. This holds the view that the modern humans are finely tuned to observe the basic scientific truth about the physical universe. Heidegger's existential analysis of the a priori facticity of Dasein as "the-being-in-the-world" as "the correct mode of access" to have the interpretive understanding of the unconcealment via the non-propositional *logos* of the truth about Being while it does not entail anthropocentrism, he implies that, there is a condition in the nature of human being which acts as medium of the integral truth about the world. At the same time there cannot be any model of knowledge when the dichotomized human nature is the centre of the universe as opposed to the universe as a sum totality of it as the object of man's exploitative scientific knowledge. The physical theory of consciousness is directly linked to this political instrumentalized scientific pursuit which the ghostly intentional acts of scientists reduce human consciousness to the status of physical continuum with the vast physical universe. The traditional philosophical belief of mind or consciousness or self is rejected by the positivist modern analytical philosophers and scientists alike, not on the scientific or logical ground, though it is projected as the justification, but for the ulterior political economic interests of the powerful capitalist neo-colonial countries of the world who fund and support such an investigation for their exploitative factual knowledge. The physical theory of consciousness has a lot of neo-liberal capitalist market potentials in today's increasingly corporate-funded privatized educational sector as one of the public policies of the capitalist political and economic powers which are already keeping the power dynamics globalized in their tight grip.

This author has anticipated the highly likely arguments of the potential critics of this paper who are themselves already in the hands of the unipolar regime of the world and thus in the bandwagon of the stated modern political economic global dynamics that bringing in politics in the matter of the controversies surrounding the theory of consciousness, is extra-philosophical or extra-logical. This is precisely the point which this paper has as one of its objectives. The critics are either unaware or looking at the other way of the fact that the *Technology Colonialism* (Simmons 2015) with high-tech, digital-tech companies have been already controlling the world as some sort of extra-legal power. The basis of the argument of the critics is itself a part of the existential crises of the West-defined modern world and, therefore, it cannot offer any solution to the multifaceted crises of today's globalized world. The science-dominated history of modern knowledge systems within which the physical theory of consciousness falls is never free from its larger and overwhelming colonial and neo-colonial (not post-colonial) control of the world in social, cultural and political terms, and more so culture as soft-power and the unipolar regime dominated globalized political economic dynamics as the hard power. The ignored and sidelined (by the present unipolar regime) findings of the climate scientists of the IPCC, UN, that global warming and climate change are anthropogenic (modern human's political-economic history championed by capitalism) can only be explained in terms of the critical but and paradigmatically different re-interrogation of the history of modern civilization. No domains of modern knowledge, cutting across the three academic disciplines being the continuation of the projects of modern colonial history, can be freed from the original sin that they have committed to the holistic world view of the oriental or Indian civilization as dogmatic, just because, it cannot go along with the Western anthropocentrism and the neo-liberal capitalist view (*The Virtue of Selfishness* (Rand 1964)) of the unanchored modern human self as per the capitalist ideology of individualism as the metaphysical foundation of modern economy. The modern Western philosophy reduces nature as a totality of objects to be exploited. This is precisely what K.C. Bhattacharyya argues that while philosophy contemplates on nature in a spiritual attitude, science sits in judgement (Bhattacharyya 1958: 108) on nature as an object of its tinkering around and exploitation. The demystified view of human consciousness reflected in its physical theory is one of the carefully designed and crafted means for the satiation of the extra-survival (Ayn Rand's survival theory) interests of only very few meritorious rich people who can only win in the globalized and highly competitive "dog eat dog" world of the free-market and sit on the apex point of "the pyramid of economy".

This researcher has been working on the above existential issue line for more than ten years within his original thesis of civilizational arguments and accordingly he has found out that the physical theory of consciousness is only one of the convenient ploys of the powers behind the absolutely commercialized world today. The sky is the limit for the creation of private wealth as the exercise of the natural liberty and right of only a very few competent rich individuals on the basis of meritocratic natural selection from the global population. This leads to the economic theory of demand and supply which is impossible without the irreversible rampant mindless destruction of the physical eco-environment system of the Mother Earth. These issues and many more were discussed at length in the two papers of the author – "The Philosophical Call for a Global Responsibility: New Initiatives, Justice, Peace and Ecology" and "An Alternative Model of Spirituality: The Holistic Approach to Earth Ethics" (already published). Both the papers more or less deal with the aforesaid issues; in the second paper, the inconsistency in the political-economic reason behind the global powers' sidelining of the much more existentially catastrophic anthropogenic climate change while the global powers were so actively concerted in responsive to the threats posed to the human race by the pandemic were analysed using interdisciplinary and transdisciplinary methods. In both the papers and many unpublished papers, the author has adumbrated that the spiritual bereftness, the materialistic and hedonistic anthropocentrism set against an incorrigible metaphysical man and nature duality of the modern Western world view has started causing so many miseries to majority global population of the world today. It can only be cured by the panacea of the holistic ancient Indian world view.

The physical theory of consciousness reduces human nature to the trivialized use and throw physical object. The inconsistency in this theory of science is: who entertains such a theory of science? Is it possible to exercise individualistic liberty and rights mainly in the economic sense to amassing limitless private wealth without a self devoid of free will and the ability to have free rational choices? How will it go along with the neurologists' and AI experts' rejection of traditional idea of spiritual self or "I" and its free will and choices? This materialistic global order has left no more spiritual foundation for the present world. There is no more abiding locus for subjective and a priori phenomenological intentional acts of love, concern, empathy and sympathy, compassion and care. They are left without any self who owns them (David Hume's No Ownership

Theory) which on the global scale only the modern human beings can experience as their self-transcending subjective (hard problem) phenomena. No physical theory of mind or consciousness by its very nature can ascribe this subjective phenomenon to the bio-natural mechanical automata called human brain. As per the idea of post-human, all these inner states will have no sense at all. The active corporate funding of R&D on the political-economic plan to demystify traditional view of consciousness in neurology, AI, etc. is not isolated and benign theoretical and humanistic interests of modern scientists. The ongoing researches on the science of consciousness with its blurring of the line of demarcation between man and machine only aim at its potential instrumentalization for commercial use to aid the increasingly liberalized, privatized and corporatized global structural dynamics of industrialization. This is established on the basis of modern scientific *reason* and "despiritualized" knowledge of amoral or rather for the purpose of the immoral use of empirical facts. Sans subjectivity as the inner source of the two mutually opposite inwardizing and outwardizing intentional acts, how will there be the highly respected and authoritative inward cum outward directedness (intentional acts of Husserl) of scientific observations and judgements of the "I-free" brain be physical reality which reduces mind or consciousness to the bio-physical and mechanical automata called brain? Is not the human brain or the racist egoism of the Western self the conscious intentional creator of the consumerist environmentally unsustainable modern economic model of demand and supply? There is some sort of Western subjectivity lurking as a ghost in the machine of physical consciousness in the individualist capitalist world view. The modern global population is made believe that their emancipation or resurrections lies in their freedom from the bondage of ancient dogma of spiritual holism. They are promised with a philistenic materialistic live. Hence, consumerism is based on anthropocentric and self-centric intentionality of modern notion of reason. Modernity as the prior condition of modern man's unfettered exercise of liberty and rights of the emancipated ghostly self is established on the capitalist ideology of individualism. The powerful majority view of physical theory of consciousness is somehow one of the symptoms of the mega disease of the above materialism without which the above global economic schema cannot exist. Many works of The American Association of Psychology link the materialistic consumer culture to increasing discontents, poor health and lesser sense of well being (DeAngelis 2004) in a modern global society of increasing rich and poor divide. All these have been critically examined by this writer since the last ten years as complex and multidimensional global-scale existential crises which require multidisciplinary, interdisciplinary and transdisciplinary paradigmatic critical investigation and a rereading of the history of modern civilization in an altogether different light.

The apparent or actual digression of this section is only an endeavour to place the question of the pragmatic untenability and environmental unsustainability of the physical theory of consciousness in the larger context of the interests of a dark power which runs the engine of globalization today. Therefore, this paper considers very seriously that the essential truth behind the modern scientists' insistence on a physical theory of mind or consciousness does not lie in science and its empirical method or what is claimed as its objective, but it is to be found in those sinful anthropocentric world view of the West. Thus, the externally undetermined unanchored modern political and economic selves defined consumers desperately need a demystified nature of human life and the world so that, the unethical, raw and brutal Darwinian power and the extra-survival global-scale amassing of private wealth unhindered by any spiritual and moral view of the world could go on till the life-supporting system of the Earth dies. Therefore, it is drastically necessary to carry on asking as to how the physical theory of consciousness which is not amoral or value-free but immoral, materialistic, hedonistic has any sense. Such a self-centric self of anthropocentrism which the scientists reject is the very self which also writes the epitaph of all the living species of the biosphere of the Earth which so far is the only known life supporting planet. It will have a boomerang effect on the very survival of the human race.

The Physical Theory of Consciousness Presupposes Anthropocentrism and a Dualistic Western World View

To begin with, the physical theory of consciousness runs counter to the idealistic orientation of Indian philosophical systems like Buddhism and Vedānta which have an overall world view which is spiritual, moral and non-dual in their respective ways. Both a knowing subject and an object which a subject knows are theoretically and existentially problematic for their different ontological reasons. For Nāgārjuna *dhamma* or *dharma* and *nirvāṇa* consists in the pragmatic realization of the Middle Path (*madhyamapratipada*) which arises out of avoiding the two extremes of eternalism and nihilism, physicalism or spiritualism. His negative logic of abstaining from false beliefs of something as either real or unreal, or both or neither (*catuṣkoṭi*) is due to the above sceptic reason. It means, believing in physicalist theory of consciousness as one of the two extreme ends, despite its so-called empirical evidence is still a false belief. Even if it is scientific, the scientists who observe their scientific facts have become inconsistent in being silent or not saying anything about those intentional acts of subjective observers or discoverers of this objective truth. Either, their biophysical brains themselves are self-observers of their own physical brains or only zombies observe this truth. The Buddhist philosophical ideas of spirituality and morality which reject both egoistic or self-centric finite and eternal soul substances or physical substance as objective facts is different from the reason behind the rejection of a real "I" and its freewill by neuroscience, etc. because, modern science affirms physicalism as the only objective truth. The Buddhist logicians at least admit a namesake conventional or a pragmatic self. The only option left for the scientists of physical theory of consciousness is that they have to admit their own physical brains are the knowers of themselves as physical brains. What does this phenomenological epistemic act of mechanical and physical brains' self-knowledge means? The self-contradiction committed by modern scientists of consciousness and positivist philosophers is that either they adhere to a self-centric self of liberty and rights in economic sense which has self-awareness of itself as physical or they have not asked to themselves as to what their own physical selves' self-knowledge of themselves as physical brains means. Their counterintuitive method of scientific observation is self-contradictory because, intuitive or counterintuitive, they cannot reject their phenomenological sense of the inner intentional act of knownness and knowing. Either this state of knowing as an epistemic phenomenon is a subjective ghost in the organic and mechanical automata of brain or it is a reality without which they will not be able to think, argue, analyse, interpret, see gaps in between empirical data of others' brain states and draw the conclusion that there is nothing like an ontologically real extramental entity called spirit or soul. The Buddhist view of namesake self which is only a pragmatic bundle of mental states (*saṅghāta* of the *pañca-skandha* similar to Hume's *Bundle Theory and No Ownership Theory,* 2000) does not end up in physicalism or its opposite spiritual soul substance. The duality of modern Western world view of man and nature and the scientists' as the said modern men who deprive their own being conscious as an ontological reality but at the same time refutes the traditional ontological self only innocuously affirms their own inner light (*antaryāmin* or *sākṣī-caitanya*) which makes them see what they see as facts. The pattern of scientific finding that physical theory of consciousness is neurological, cognitive and neuro-biological sciences is the automata of algorithmic functions is a blatant logically self-contradiction due to the fact that this finding is self-reflexive functions of physical brain. This is absurd and self-defeating. Still, the dogma of the scientists lies in their irrational dogged refusal to admit the reality of the extra-physical nature of mind or ego or "I" lurking as a ghost in their self-defeating conclusion.

Śaṅkara had also rejected the ultimate ontological reality of empirical self and its finitude and its self-centric sense of being a doer (*kartā*), knower (*pramātā*) and enjoyer (*bhoktā*) for an altogether different reason of his non-dual thesis. But all these which imply dualistic difference between subject and what subject is not are analysed as ignorance of the embodied empirical self (*jīva*). This ignorance ends when the intuitive grasp of the invariable pure awareness (*kevala-jñāna*) underlying all acts of knower (*jñātā*) and known (*jñeya*). This is a one step ontological deepening below what is today beginning to be spoken about as quantum consciousness with an idealist connotation of the ever-present observer in the observed–observer phenomenon. In Advaita Vedānta, the knower and known dependent variegated world of names (*nāma*) and forms (*rūpa*) is a superimposition on the one and non-dual pure consciousness (*cinmātra*). Śaṅkara had interpreted the ordinary human experience in such a world as unreal (*mithyā*) superimposition (*adhyāsa*) on the non-dual *Brahman*, because it has the inherent logical contradiction (*itaretara viruddhatva* and *bādhitattva*) between real and unreal (in *avasthātraya*) or valid and invalid of empirical knowledge. But, the non-existence of the external world of variegated difference is not what is intended (*Brahmasūtra with Śāṅkarabhāṣya* II.28-29). Though, based on scientific reasons, three quantum physicists were awarded Nobel Prize in Physics (2022) (awarded jointly to Alain Aspect, John F. Clauser and Anton Zeilinger) for proving that the universe as it is observed is not locally real, i.e. local conditions of Einstein's space–time relativity is no more tenable and everything at the quantum level is an inexplicable simultaneity which disproves his rule of the speed of light. The fundamental philosophical question is that what is only theoretico-logically unreal presupposes an underlying reality and quantum physcists are right now looking for it. S. Radhakrishnan, elsewhere in his *An Idealist View of Life*, states that whether or not, the fundamental ground on which unreality is superimposed is matter or spirit may turn out to be only a matter of interpretation. There are strong possibilities of the reviving of the traditional debates between a new sort of transcendental idealists and realists in advanced theoretical mathematics and quantum physics pointing to the intelligible absolute frame of reference as the Kantian noumenal as that which makes the sensible world meaningful.

Self-contradiction of the Physical Theory of Consciousness Proving of What One Originally Sets Out to Disprove (Arthāntara)

How are we to explain the findings of the scientists of consciousness or mind that it is the physical processes of brain? They have even come to conclude that the normal human sense of being an "I" or "ego" or self, and its "free will" and choices are all illusions projected in the subjectivity of the non-existent zombie or ghost in the natural, mechanical and physical automata of human brain. These questions are not to be found in the so-called scientific papers of the concerned scientists and the positivist philosophers who piggy ride the findings of the science of consciousness as a mere physical process. Is it possible to suppose that all these technically complicated conclusions of the concerned scientists do not presuppose any inner observer in their own intra-personality realm as a subjective phenomenon? David Chalmers hard problem of consciousness (experiencing red) points to this issue. René Descartes (1986) did say something valid by his *Non-Extended Thinking Substance* (*Res Cogitans*). The science of consciousness which Dennett 1993) argues is obstructed by philosophers who mystify consciousness. He is so vehement that the scientists have already empirically proved consciousness to be the complex functional expression of the physical brain. The following description of Amazon gives us some ideas of this book innocuously favourable to the central contention of this paper:

> ... Cartesianism and Descartes' dualism of mind and body should be replaced with theories from the realms of neuroscience, psychology and artificial intelligence. What people think of as the stream of consciousness is not a single, unified sequence, the author argues, but "multiple drafts" of reality composed by a computer-like "virtual machine". Dennett considers how consciousness could have evolved in human beings and confronts the classic mysteries of consciousness: the nature of introspection, the self or ego and its relation to thoughts and sensations, and the level of consciousness of non-human creatures.
>
> – https://www.amazon.in/Consciousness-Explained-Penguin-Science-Dennett-ebook/dp/B004LLIHIG

What Dennett argues by way of as to how consciousness could accidentally have evolved out of matter in human beings and come to confront its own status of ontological reality is what this paper seeks to unpack and point to its indefensible logical conclusion against itself. While scientists in general opine that the universe and life in it have an accidental origin as a natural process, they do not carry on with its philosophical implication of consciousness or mind as an accidental or epiphenomenal zombie as a ghost in the machine (explained by absent qualia) is adamant to disprove its spiritual or extraphysical ontological status. Without being self-reflective or having a regressive reference to their subjectivity and thus indulging in a glaring case of self-contradiction, they can never disprove that their highly technical domain of scientific researches and extraordinary cognitive functions which argue against the traditional view of consciousness is not that of a ghost or zombie in a machine called the automata of their own physical brains. If the physical brain knows itself as physical and not some extraphysical reality, then they still need to explain as to how the intentional act of knownness of their own physical brains of themselves as physical states as a self-reflexive subjective phenomenon will be accommodated to their physical theory of consciousness? This involves their eventual ending up with proving what they initially intended to prove (*arthāntara*).

The Blurring of Human and Machine Difference: A Response to the Thesis of Post-human

The most influential and popular researches on consciousness are carried out by scientists aided by the state of the art digital technology in the present times of globalization. It will be an act of self-complacency for anyone not to be aware that today, the world is almost totally digitally controlled with the help of advanced AI in supercomputers and Internet. The digitally controlled and manipulated world today has come to a situation where human nature and machine are allegedly the same cybernetical physical processes. This had led to the dehumanizing concept of post-human (Wikipedia contributors, 29 December 2022: Gamez 2018) which has diverse interpretations. This theory proposes that the real line of human–machine difference is untenable and it is influenced by the works of the top AI experts and other scientists who work on it and demystify mind or consciousness as a unique and ontologically real human trait. This is the consumerist approach to the physicalist human nature as the post-human automata. The positivist analytical philosophers' surrender to science, its empirical method impacted by the political economic instrumentalization of them by the post-Second World War unipolar regime is the general background of the "bandwagon attitude" and popular thinking patterns of those pro-physicalist academic experts of philosophy and science who seek to reduce human nature and its best cognitive functions as the objective facts of the science. The use of the state of-the-art science and technological know-how for economic gains and the political control of the world by capitalist global powers is something to do with the economically gainful view of human mind or consciousness as nothing but what the computational physical brain does. That, human being is a machine which can be manipulated, constructed and use and throw it away as if machine equated human nature, is an assembly line products of automata is the basic aim of politics and corporate-funded research on science of consciousness for its potentiality political-economic profits. This is what modern education system wants from students – to act as human machines who will help the globalized machination of capitalist political-economic practices. This is not to argue based on some extra-logical or extra-philosophical assumptions to circumvent the weaknesses of the arguments, but it is something what a closer examination of the direction towards which modern knowledge systems in a fast commercializing world is heading to finally reveal. In today's globalized world, the neo-liberal capitalist economy has come to have a complete control of modern education in general and especially neuroscience in modern medical science, neurobiology, neuropsychology, AI, etc. If human nature is reduced to the status of one of the scientific objects to be tinkered and manipulated which the post-human character of cybernetics has come to exhibit, as a part of these modern phenomena, the privatized, liberalized and corporatized researches and activities of the medical science such as neurology and AI have a lot of profits to gain out of the economically objectified physical nature of human capital as purely physical as devoid any spiritual essence at its core reality. Therefore, the philosophical debates only may not turn out to be the sufficient reasons to bring out the truth behind the for and against ontological status of mind or consciousness as non-physical. Even Dennett while being one of the strong contenders of the scientific view of consciousness is reported to have conjectured:

> ... how consciousness could have evolved (by chance) in human beings (as a by-product of physical nature) and confronts the classic mysteries of consciousness: the nature of introspection, the self or ego and its relation to thoughts and sensations, and the level of consciousness of non-human creatures. – Dennett 1993

That is how the human intelligence or understanding with its self-referring self-reflexive ability which the biologists have concluded, though there is no proof, had its past of the abiogenetic origin of life four billion years ago (Soup Theory) and, thus, as a mere natural and mechanical automata like any other physical or natural phenomena having had a chance or accidental origin, it has come to acquire such a power and explain itself as a physical reality and refute its own spiritual nature believed by the traditional philosophers? If this is not the fact of the self-awareness of nature in and through the human mind–brain as a product of the unintelligent or blind physical nature at large (*pradhāna prakṛti*), then it is nothing. In the terminology of Vedāntic epistemology, it is the blatant case of indulging in the act of proving what the scientists had initially set out to disprove – *arthāntara.*

One thing is quite sure; it will be very difficult to explain as to why human existence governed by the same physical laws and thus as a creature of physical nature, in juxtaposition to its own truth, it has come to investigate the truth behind the cosmos? If it is the conclusion of physical automata, then is it not the same thing as saying that, as a bionatural physical automaton, the physical brain knows itself as physical brain? This is what the conclusion of AI experts and neuroscientists, etc. unwittingly entails. So far as, none of them has ever asked this self-reflexive question to themselves as to how they as physical brain with their illusory "senses of I", "free will" which negotiates among what they observe and highly innovative brainy decisions, etc. which they have done by way of reducing consciousness to the complex neuro-physiological process in the nano-level neural networking of their brain seek to explain their own truth as the physical brain? Why have they failed to notice that their conclusion has the epistemic phenomenon of "knownness" of their own existence as physical? It is an internal and a priori intentional act of psycho-epistemic phenomenon. They cannot deny that while they are observing other fellow human beings' brain indirectly they are also observing their own brains and, therefore, their conclusion that mind or consciousness is nothing more than the physical brain also includes their own brains. While making this scientific statement, they cannot equally say that their scientific subjectivity without which they cannot negotiate among difficult scientific facts and draw out highly innovative and path-breaking scientific conclusions are bereft of a self-conscious

"I". The question of embodiment of consciousness in its bodily encaging is altogether a different issue. Perhaps, the human mind is a subjective-software which needs a compatible correlated organic hardware called human brain with all its mind-boggling neural networking and neuro-physiological processes. Where is the source or locus of the intentional acts of questions whether or not, did Big Bang had its first genesis from nothing or something? This a priori background of intentional structure of consciousness is already presupposed by the inability of the human mind to know as to "why the world is what it is and not otherwise". The same is the case with the non-conclusive debates between Willard van Orman Quine and P.F. Strawson (Hamlyn 1984) which reveal that it is very difficult to decide, whether or not, mind is reducible to body or body to mind. But for Strawson, mind and body constitute as the two inseparable components in a person defined as a "logically primitive concept" and, as such, neither mind nor body is reducible to the other.

In philosophical terms, the via brain "physical nature's knowing of itself as physical nature" brings us back to the original issue of understanding or consciousness itself. How can one ever reduce this nature's awareness of itself as nature to the organic hardware called brain which knows it to be so? Can one interpret mind as a software? Roger Penrose's view is in favour of a non-reductive view of human intelligence or understanding to a computational process. If it is not, quantum physics, neuroscience, AI and positivist philosophy will have to be interpreted as the works of ugly zombies. It is here that a closer analysis of the basic contentions of all the researchers in the above fields may reveal that they have not said anything new than what Śaṅkara had argued in the seventh century CE. No doubt, the majority of the cognitive scientists, neuroscientists and AI experts are still quite confident that Cartesian "mind" and its cognates – "I", "ego" and "self" – defined in terms of consciousness as its innate property or nature is simply the function of physical brain. The thesis of Roger Penrose and his co-investigator American anesthesiologist Stuart Hameroff traces consciousness to a quantum wave function in the neurons (Paulson 2017) and they are favourable to the non-computational nature of consciousness (Dyer 1994). In Śaṅkara's Advaita the empirical-level sense of a discrete knowing self or subject or an I, etc. standing in opposition to the objects or facts of science which the scientists observe is analysed as the denotative powers (*pratyaya*) of *yuṣmat* (thou) and *asmat* (I) superimposed on the pure existence-consciousness-bliss (*sadcidānanda brahma*). All the empirical knowledge has built-in inherent mutual contradictions and thus they are always held in perpetual epistemic shifting sands of falsifiability (Popper's theory has some affinity with the *bādhitattva* of truth of Advaita). This, Śaṅkara did by using negative reasoning and *adhyāropa-apavāda* (Nikhilananda, *Vedāntasāra of Sadānanda,* 2014) – superimposition and subsequent denial derived from the proto-logical Upaniṣadic method of *neti, neti* (not this, not this) (*BṛUp.* 2.iii.5.6, IV.v and *Avadhūta Gītā* 1.25). His view of the logically contradictory relation between knowing subject and objects known by it as superimposition (*adhyāsa* or *adhyāropa*) on the pure or non-dual reality and their subsequent denials (*apavāda*) as false (*mithyā*, but not non-existent) are made possible by an underlying unconditioned condition or a bare ground (*adhiṣṭhāna mātra*) without which, just as Hegel's dialectic idealism came to finally establish his Absolute Spirit, all the ordinary dialectic acts of logical negations will have no (absolute) frame of reference. This is what is implied by the thesis of Penrose's non-computational nature of human understanding or intelligence or consciousness underlying every higher-order cognitive activities. It was this "background field" which is common to all the empirical assertions as this is this or this is not possible. It is the background reality of both presence and absence (*anvaya-vyatirekī*). Śaṅkara's analysis of the *avasthātraya-vicāra* as subjective method and real causation or creationism of the world as objective method (*taṭastha lakṣaṇa* – as secondary nature of *Brahman*) and their synthesis applies *anvaya-vyatirekī* attempts to establish that witness consciousness is the invariable condition of both positive and negative experiences. All the empirical categories coming under names and forms including creatorship, etc. associated with the empirical world, are referred to the *pratyayas* of the identity statement "This is that Devadatta:" "this" and "that" (denotative powers) as literal meaning are negated ("is" of identity in Western philosophy). The non-dual *Nirguṇa* and *Nirviśeṣa Brahman* as the above background condition is its *svarūpa lakṣaṇa* (essential nature). The necessary linguistic evils of existence, consciousness and bliss as the nature of the ultimate reality are respectively interpreted negatively as not non-existence, not unintelligent principle, not pain and suffering, etc. The negation of all the conceivable of empirical categories falling under name (*nāma*) and form (*rūpa*) indicated by *neti, neti* which Śaṅkara had developed into a critical negative logical reasoning which he used to explain as the inner contradictions inherent in all forms of empirical knowledge (*vṛtti-jñāna*) is only to show that all their unstable epistemic states of the falsifiability presuppose an a priori bare awareness underneath them. As such, this unconditioned condition of worldly knowledge can be neither object (*viṣaya*) known by knower nor finite knower (*viṣayī*) itself. That, Penrose's view of human intelligence in its most essential form as the background reality which enables mind to perform all the highest level of mathematical calculations can never be reduced to the same mathematical calculations (Roger Penrose), is the reminiscence of what Śaṅkara had also concluded.

Some Philosophical Affinities of Śaṅkara and Heidegger: Duality in Scientific Objectivity and Non-Objective Holism

Śaṅkara's view which is already referred to that all acts of ordinary epistemic affirmations and negations are only revealed by an all-seeing witness consciousness (*sākṣī-caitanya*) may be discussed with Heidegger's the non-propositional logos as letting the self-manifest from itself in-itself "be seen" by the "seeing" of Dasein as existentially given "the there" ("Da") as the "being-in-the-world". This act of seeing is not that of an "I" which sees as a subject standing in an abject oppositional relation to objects as what it knows. Dasein is brought in here only because of the fact that just like Heidegger came to interpret Dasein as a non-subject or "I" not defined in terms of consciousness centuries after, Śaṅkara had already denied the reality of the subject–object dichotomy inherent in all acts of knowing in his first sentence of the *samanvayādhyāsa prathamaḥ* (*Brahmasūtra, Śāṅkarabhāṣyopetam*, 1998, p. 1). Nescience caused *yuṣmad-asmad pratyaya*, as the denotative power (*pratyaya*) of the incorrigible relation of dichotomy between "I and you" have been treated by Śaṅkara as superimpositions on the *Nirguṇa* and *Nirviśeṣa Brahman* is the source of all the contradictions involved in the relational character of triangular nature of empirical knowledge (*tripuṭī-jñāna* – tripot of knowledge). The scientists have to explain their own subjective epistemic state of scientific observation as an intentional act of what they observe as objective facts which, in fact, is what they as the first-person knowers are not. There has to be a knower of the objective fact of physical brain or the knower which knows that, what the traditional philosophers claim as the non-physical is not as such, but, in fact, it is the physical brain. For him, this inherent inner contradiction of empirical experiences is unconcealed by pure consciousness which from the empirical perspective is technically referred to as witness consciousness. As the background condition of all the forms of ordinary knowledge (*vṛtti-jñāna*) and as the ultimate condition which makes them possible, no empirical knowledge in any form can know it as its object of knowledge.

In the case of Heidegger, no traditional categories like subject, object, mind or I or consciousness as mutually contradictory concepts are used. In his *Being and Time*, he avoids them altogether. He has only used interpretive understanding, seeing of Dasein, etc. The concept of *logos* is letting the self-manifest from itself-in-itself be seen by the seeing what *logos* of Dasein. Ontology as dealing with Being is the process of making explicit of its implicit existential truth underlying the ontical plane of regional ontology. *Logos* is that which makes Dasein's ability of "seeing" the "self-showing" nature of things from-themselves-in-themselves. The interpretive understanding of Dasein who while being not a subject or an I is said to be the only being who can raise the fundamental question of Being and it is also only being which what is unconcealed by *logos* is seen by Dasein's seeing of what is made explicit as self-manifesting truths. Śaṅkara's *bhāti* agrees with it and they can be compared to see their similarity. This corresponds to the nickname *Śārīrakamīmāṁsā* of the *Brahmasūtra* which ends in the non-dual absolute through the critical analysis of the truth behind human reality unpacked by showing embodied-human-beings' being subject as standing in a state of incorrigible relation of dichotomy to their objects known as logically inconsistent and always ends in contradictions. The interpretive understanding is Dasein's but, it is not that of Dasein as an "I" who as a subject comes to know something as an objective propositional truth or objective truth. This view is radical because, it has both theoretical and practical bearings on all the ideas, knowledge systems and scientific truths which are controlling the global praxis. Even the physical theory of consciousness of science cannot avoid the mutual binary opposition between subject and object. Heidegger's rejection of consciousness is based on the fact that it is founded on Descartes' duality between knowing subject and objects as what knowing subject is not. On the conceptual plane only, this is more or less the same conclusion arrived by Śaṅkara in his *Samanvayādhyāsa* as the synoptic account of his *Brahmasūtrabhāṣya* which propounds his monistic thesis. This rejection though admitted on the empirical level by Śaṅkara when it is viewed in the light of the background truth which reveals all those experiences in the empirical world has some affinity with Heidegger's *logos* as letting the non-objective existential truth about the self-showing (similar to the *bhāti* which is also self-manifestation of things) of entities be seen by Dasein's seeing. The self-manifest is a prior state called "for having" after which as the pre-existing entity, it can only be spoken about. Before things are spoken about, they have to have prior existence in some way or the other. It is not something created by thought essences or mind. But the comparison between Śaṅkara and Heidegger cannot be taken too far.

The relevance of the above digression is that while Śaṅkara's rejection of human nature as the discrete I or ego was also came to be done by Heidegger, the concept of truth of the former and Heidegger's Being have vital differences except the commonality of their respective refutations of the bipolar relation between knowing subject and its objects known. Thus, the "worldhood of the world" as a holistic grounding structure of Dasein, the relation "being-in" which grounds Dasein to the "world" is unconcealed by the existential analysis of Dasein as the correct mode of access to their ontological unity indicated by the concept of Being (Stein 1970). On the conceptual level, this view of Heidegger comes closer to Śaṅkara's non-dual reality. From this point onwards Śaṅkara's absolute truth takes a different metaphysical and spiritual trajectory. In stating that without an existentially implicit holistic background reality no ordinary knowledge or empirical experience would come to achieve its empirical validity, his thoughts may be taken as having some affinity to that of Heidegger. Heidegger's interpretative understanding of Dasein as the correct mode of access to the question of Being and Śaṅkara's a priori structure of the ever present (*nitya-siddha*) and self-existent (*svataḥ-siddha*) background pure consciousness (*cinmātrādhiṣṭhāna*) as a non-dichotomic totality seem to have some conceptual similarity. Since physical theory of consciousness is the work of the subjectivity of the scientists, their view only affirms the anthropocentric Western world view which reduces the entire world to the status of an object of exploitative investigation as the other to their intentional act of ghostly knowing which knows their own consciousness as the objective physical reality.

The ontological investigation of Heidegger is only making the implicit non-propositional Truth to become explicit which is his logos. This is explained by his non-presuppositional but ontological "hermeneutical circle". Only what is already there as the "Fore-having structure" of temporal existence on the ontical plane leads to the implicit ontological structure of "beings in general" becomes explicit via his negative or regressive analysis as a sense of lost. Plato's recollection and Śaṅkara's grounding tactics of regressive analysis (adapted from Heidegger) and negative reasoning which ends in affirming the ever-existent *svarūpa-jñāna* once again may have something to do with what Heidegger did as the above.

Can there Be Observation without Observer?

The scientists do not seem to be soul searching and self-reflective to act as introspective enough to reflect on their own inner phenomenon of observations, etc. Some neurologists have concluded that without the quantum field underneath the neurons or the mirror neurons in the neural networking of their respective brains consciousness cannot be explained on the level of neural networking. Yet, they refuse to see the *source* of the self-conscious intentional structure of their expert conclusions that they are able to make and to imagine that it is their brains which do this task is difficult to swallow. Concerning their observations in this way and resulting interpretive task, their mirror neurons and the electro-chemical waves in them will not help. Some empirical or subatomic physical phenomena other than their mirror neurons in the complex neural engineering and networking in their brains are responsible for their ability to draw their well-known penchant conclusion that beyond what they see and understand in their labs, they have not located any phenomenon called mind or consciousness as the subjective correlate of the neural hardwaring of their brains. There has to be some source of creative and conscious subjective intentional act of some somewhere who observes what he or she observes. But their observations are the brains of other fellow human beings including or especially the brains of creative genius. Hence, since the same natural, mechanical and physical laws are operative in all the living organisms right from amoeba, fruit flies to the most advanced post-ape modern human animal called *Homo sapiens* sapiens which belong to a common animal kingdom, they cannot say that what they are investigating is some sort of instinctive response like the non-human animal brains do to the stimuli of their environment. This is most significantly applicable to the neurologists and computer scientists working together in tandem on the computational model of mind as nothing more than the algorithmic AI. This view has also influenced analytical interpretation of hermeneutical understanding of texts as computational in computational linguistics. Even the world of meaning born out of textual interpretations is reduced to as algorithmic operations. This is implied in the debates between the Pūrva-Mīmāṁsakas and the Advaitins on whether or not expression precedes synthesis or vice versa (Anvitābhidhānavāda and Abhihitānvayavāda). This does not touch upon the inner light of meaning thrown up by passionate encounter of existence felt on the planes of deeply-felt feelings and emotions of poets and mystics. In phenomenological terms, how will the intentional nature of feeling of shy, shame, guilt, remorse and ability use symbols and signs to convey indirect meanings, etc. be explained away as computational? The deeply-felt inner light and meanings of poets of creative genius and their language of aesthetic symbolism demand an inward-bound regressive reference to an inner world from which they are originated as outward-directed intentional structure stretching towards all those fictional inner objects (Alexius Meinong's concept of pure object) or contents of their aesthetic experience. Even if they are reduced to their neural coordinates and neurophysiological functions like neural chemistry as electro-chemical waves as physical, their nature of self-conscious intentional acts cannot be easily refuted.

The basic issue raised in this paper is not to delve into the empirical subject matter of science, except the philosophical implications of their conclusions. No philosopher can say anything against the empirical data they observe through their instruments. It is in this situation that the Anthropic Principle of physics to mean the physicists as human observers somehow fined-tuned by nature to know what they seek to know as the truth which modern physicists seek to know in the physical universe is also relevant to scientists' intentional state of desire to know and refute the traditional theory of consciousness. How is it that their deliberate and passionate lifelong struggles to establish their own physical brains as physical is devoid of a real subjective state of intentional act of the passion to know? Either, their physical brains have self-awareness as physical brains or that this state of knowing is a ghost in the machine of their brains. How the brains of scientists and not as I or mind or consciousness already reduced to the said material reality, though living systems are still part of the mechanical natural automata of the cosmos and know them as the physical brain? No scientists can deny that this is what is known as matter knows itself as matter or simply matter's self-awareness. What does this imply? Is it a psychological or an epistemological issue of knowing or knownness of something as something? This question is no more about whether or not mind or consciousness has ontological independence. Hence, it does not anymore make sense to go on with or to go against arguments about any ontological status of consciousness or whatever the arguments might lead to. It is only about the Anthropic Principle being entangled with the intentional act of knowing of whatsoever is the truth which only the human quest has revealed to itself in its search for truth behind the gigantic universe.

The latest book by the neurologist cum science journalist Bobby Azarian, *The Romance of Reality: How the Universe Organizes Itself to Create Life, Consciousness and Cosmic Complexity* (https://nextbigideaclub.com, 24 August 2022, accessed on 28 August 2022, 8:30 a.m.) says a lot about those issues surrounding the basic question being raised in this paper. There are two things of pertinence to this question in the book. First, the universe is a self-organizing automata and next is its ability to create life, consciousness and the cosmic complexity. Cosmic complexity is mirrored in the highly complex micro-level neural networking and neural physiological processes of the human brain. What the author who knows his business very well is – he himself is a mere insignificant speck of brain which according to him and quite reasonably, a human life as one of the top most of the species in the biosphere is endowed with consciousness. According to his own self-reflexive conclusion as a neurologist, despite being an accidental product of nature, a writer writes his book with the help of what his mind sees, imagines and thinks of all those complicated ideas which he has gathered from his field, etc. The "law of conformity" in "the like thing knows the like", which explains the knownness of truths about things in the world by human knowers, is behind the Anthropic Principle. This is because the laws of nature work both in human nature and the cosmos. It is a mystery as to why as a creature of physical nature human beings are driven by a quest to know. If panpsychism which seems to have some parallel with the Necessity of the Intelligent Principle of traditional philosophy is true, then the mystery behind as to why the physical brain of the self-congratulatory scientists whose empirical method and ability to come so far in even claiming to have conquered space as the prowess and creative ability to discern the Godless Objective Physical truth of modern scientific endeavours as the sheer contribution of the West to the modern human civilization may die down. They are so ignorant or deliberately avoiding the root issue for personal motives that they have not paid any attention to the regressive intentional structure of their own inner phenomenon from where all their efforts as psycho-motor acts originates. That, as their firm beliefs, all these are mere physical acts of the natural and mechanical automata of their scientific brains which they describe as epiphenomena or hologram, universal field theory (MacIsaa (n.d.)) bereft of the ontologically real self or "I", its free will (Schlosser 2014) which makes conscious and difficult decisions and makes highly complex and technical logico-scientific judgements are the works of their physical brain, this is a blatant act of self-contradiction. Since, the concept of "consciousness" in the expression "physical consciousness" as their core thesis has been already treated as physical, without self-contradiction, they cannot reuse it as the inner source of the phenomenological regressive intentional process of their lifelong and passionate path-breaking scientific works as intentional goal-directed activities of experts. The theory of consciousness of Vedānta believes in the spiritual matrix of the cosmos and easily explains this epistemic intentional phenomenon of knowing of truth of the cosmos as the manifestation of the said divine matrix (Caldwell 2021; Braden 2007; DeConick 2016). Hence, neuroscientists', cognitive scientists', etc.'s ability to know as an intentional goal-directed acts as discursive, painstaking, rigorous, analytically critical, logical, observational, counter-intuitive, cross-referred, reviewed by fellow scientists who blow the same trumpet, well argued, and deliberations towards establishing their thesis that human mind or consciousness is physical still need explanation. This needs to be analysed in the light of the theory of abiogenesis in biology which argues that life had its first genesis about four billion years ago from today from some primordial material stuff after the Big Bang had taken place 13.7 billion years ago. Not to speak about the origin of life, even the creation of hard or gross physical objects is itself still a difficult issue in physics. On the contrary, to get some hope in the spiritual goodness of life, it would be worthwhile to contemplate on William Bysshe Stein's *The Hindu Matrix of Walden* (1970). *The King's Son. Comparative Literature* (1970: 303-18) which deals with Thoreau's meditation on the poetic location of his inner light sustained by the ancient Indian spiritual wisdom of *puruṣottama*. Thoreau employs the literary imagery of a house as a desperate search for a seat in the world schema for the restless wandering soul based on the Indian ritual concept of *āsana*

(p. 306) – the variable locus of human beings in the invariable Infinite and All-Pervasive Divine Light which makes the cosmos to work as a whole.

In similar fashion as the above, the controversial Anthropic Principle of cosmology in modern physics may be looked at as the inevitable and the only locus of the inquisitive scientific minds just like existential analysis of Dasein and not any other being is the correct mode of access to questions concerning the fundamental existential truth about Being. In short, what theoretical implications underlie the intentional act of the phenomenon of observations and the physical truths the creative genius among the physicists who brought sharp turning points in the history of physics? What sort of locus their intentional act of founding their scientific objective truth about the universe if it is not what Thoreau had found as trans-finite-spiritual locus in the ancient Indian philosophical texts as the locus-less bare ground of the variable seat of his finite existence? This is a far cry from the observed external physical truth of physics and its dichotomic relation to the internal phenomenon of observation of this external objective truth. The present scientists of consciousness as physical have already clubbed the poets, traditional philosophers of consciousness and the unified spiritual vision of the mystics as intuitive dogmatic delusions. Protagoras' "man is the measure of all the things" which undercuts the Western concept of man as his own standard as the anticipation of anthropocentric individualism of neo-liberal capitalism demands that there needs to exist a conscious self who makes choices by his or her free will and exercises individualist liberty and rights and one who possess all the powers to garner all the global wealth into his private coffers.

The above is in stark opposition to Bhartṛhari's exhortation to mankind that to realize the insignificance of finite human life and much against their relentless struggles, the sea of tears are awaiting human beings. Bhartṛhari's *Vairāgya-Śatakam* so well describes the insignificant futility of finite and fragile human life when he says:

> Worldly pleasures have not been enjoyed by us, but we ourselves have been devoured; no religious austerities have been performed, but we ourselves have become scorched; time is not gone (being ever present and infinite), but we ourselves are gone (because of approaching death). Desire is not reduced in force, though we ourselves are reduced to senility. – *Vairāgya-Śatakam* 7

The denial by the scientists of the physical theory of consciousness of the reality of self, its free will, choices to act, to be self-consistent, even if they have their alternative senses of being human, they still cannot have the same with the reason of Vedānta's asking mankind to transcend these false senses of agency. The Western scholars still have a lot of homeworks to do with explaining as to how their amoral or value-neutral characteristics of the natural, mechanical automata of physical brain as the scientific objective truth of human beings would go along with anthropocentric individualism as the foundation of the capitalist-controlled modern world. This is because anthropocentric individualism entails a regressive reference to an internal source of an intentional act of a subjectivity which necessarily is not what an object which it knows and quite surprisingly, just as the history of modern civilization reveals, this intentional act qualified by its atomized liberty and rights moves out towards the external world to conquer its wealth. Whether or not it is extraphysical/non-corporeal or physical, the scientists of the physical theory of consciousness cannot refute the existence of sort of subject and its subjectivity or the other existing in a relation of dichotomy to their objective truth of consciousness reduced to a physical state of brain or about the physical reality of the world. It is this physical self of scientists which makes known themselves as physical selves. This also will be in agreement with the neoliberal defined economic concept of man as a voracious consumer self which will have nothing or very little to do with any sense of spirituality and moral sense. In the absence of this consumerist self, liberty and rights as derivatives of the modern dualistic world view with anthropocentric individualism as its core truth will have no theoretical–practical basis.

When the human observers are observing what they have been observing, they have to remember that while living on this planet called the Earth as its self-conscious human creature, what they are observing also reflects their own truth as one of the species in the biosphere. This perspective is transcendental or intuitive subjective field for each of the scientists and their sense of I as the self-conscious subjective phenomenon intentionally which uses their state-of-the-art scientific labs or instruments may have to be taken into account as the source of their urge to know or their intentional act of inquisitiveness behind their relentless search for truth they have been struggling to know. What they are trying to know also may say a lot about the nature of or truth about their own existence. What it means is, it does not matter what the Anthropic Principle of physics says about this subjective phenomenon, without taking into consideration the philosophical issue of mind or consciousness as the seat of human creative intelligence, the physicalist scientists can never argue, observe scientific data, interpret and draw conclusions as new scientific discovery. These higher-order cognitive activities always have an intentional regressive reference to their inner self as the internal source of their desire and urge to know (phenomenological in the Husserlian sense). While the scientists are observing, analysing, examining and interpreting their hard data obtained with the help of their state-of-the-art scientific instruments, all these as intentional epistemic phenomena, will always underlie in the background of their search for the scientific truth they have been looking for. At a minimum, they have to admit that all the conclusions they have been drawing and which they will continue to do so are based on what they believed to be out there. They create appropriate scientific instruments to look beyond or see the unexplained gap among their pre-existing scientific data or facts suggest or imply. This ability to anticipate the likely outcome, for which they keep on creating newer and newer scientific instruments to go on and on to see beyond the stars and galaxies or those basic sources of energy which are behind the ever-expanding space, is located in the human nature reflected in the Anthropic Principle. Due to its philosophical implications, many of the physicists are dismissal of Anthropic Principle. The essential presupposition of this theory is that though having had only an accidental genesis from matter, the nature of modern humans has evolved as a fine-tuned species which can only know the truth behind the cosmos. Heidegger's existential analysis of Dasein and Vedānta's *Brahmasūtra*, defined as the investigation into the essential truth about embodied empirical self (*jīva*) (*Śārīraka Mīmāṁsā*), are fit enough to be examined and compared with the Anthropic Principle of physics. What the best of the astrophysicists want or expect to see out there always presuppose the background epistemic or scientific quests or desire to know and these are always associated with an emotive condition of the existential passions of those gifted scientific beings. David Hume's statement – Reason is the slave of passion – is explained by him that the history of human civilization is propelled not by reason but by this a priori condition of emotive passion associated with human existence in the world. This is also applicable to the works of the great scientists for the sake of which they dedicate their entire lives. This fundamental passion is impossible without the metaphysical term dynamic existence always moved by a deeper level of inner struggle as the urge to know, an adventurous sense of wonder and inquisitive inner drive which would make those great scientists to spend their entire lives as a continuous search for the truth which they believe will be the case. Beyond this, nothing can be said. Religious or spiritual minds only give a mystical name to this fundamental truth to be realized and they believe that no finite human minds as the products of this world can ever encompass or exhaust this truth. It is too large and complex for the discursive, plodding and piecemeal human intellect to fathom. The irony is that an entity such as human mind–brain with its subatomic neural networking and neuro-physiological processes, while being an intimately connected living entity to the gigantic cosmos, is not only trying to know itself and also by privileging itself as subjective processes of adventurous inner theatre, it also is endeavouring to reach out to the core truth of the universe.

Conclusion

Protagoras might have had the above facts anticipated by his "Man is the measure of all the things". He stated this with reference to moral laws. Neither God or else is the source of values. Man is the only source of what he or she is ought to or ought not do (*kiṁ kartavyaṁ ca, akartavyam ca*) in life. It is necessary to extrapolate this normative criterion to the epistemic context. Ethics and metaphysics do have a mutual relation. What pattern of life mankind has to lead based on what meaning and truth lies behind life or the world is not a pure ethical question. Based on what human beings think about themselves determines how they ought to live. What sort of morality scientists follow? How do they deem the course of actions unwittingly demanded by their scientific truth? Say, for instance, for hypothetical sake there is no God and moreover the cosmos in which human beings found themselves as being thrown into is a sheer accidental happenstance. This scientific belief, reflected in the *Chance and Necessity* of Jacques Monod (1971) which rejects necessity but the world and life in it as a cosmic accidence, need not be totally bereft of some form of morality or the other. But its causal assumption of chance leaves death as the dead end before human beings should make the best bargain out of the absurd world. It is not a wonder that the computer simulation has been increasingly used to make some sense out of the cosmos. Human brain and its entire workings have their ontology within the complex cosmos as a simulation. This model cannot go very far because computer simulation is the works of computer scientists. It would be senseless to believe that the natural and mechanical laws of nature like Big Bang are auto-simulated universe-scale computational machine. What panpsychism believes and the quantum theory of the entire cosmos working on the basis of the subatomic level of the field of quantum wave functions had to wait by change once again for the highly creative extraordinary brain of Einstein to become the only cooperative organic receiver of the most innermost workings of the physical universe. His intuitive grasp of previously unknown truths of physics from among those available theories of classical physics which other physicists could not comprehend may have a truth beyond his brain. Quantum field of energy and its subatomic wave functions fill up the length and breadth of the universe. That is, there no point of space which is a vacuum in the universe or possible universes. It is this background field of electro-magnetic quantum reality of the universe, inferred as a totality constituted by dark matter (23 per cent), dark energy (73 per cent) and stars and galaxies only constitute only 4 per cent European Council for Nuclear Research (CERN), is to be explained with the gravitational theory of supersymmetry to facilitate the unification of fundamental forces of universe as an interlinked whole. This truth perhaps links human brain to the truth it discovers in the cosmos and helps migratory birds with built-in organic GPS to negotiate their ways to and from their place of origin and to destinations of their temporary migrations. Otherwise, the subjectivity of inner theatre of the scientists will not be able to ascribe any objective truth to what they see in and through their instruments. The ability of their mind–brains to develop theories using mathematical language which they believe as what their truth is as scientific truth has an element of self-transcendence. Their ability to say that everything including their brains and functions called mind or intellect is physical as an act of the self-knowing of their very brain itself is a self-representation of their own existential truth.

The extraordinary ability of animals to detect the uncommon eruptions of electromagnetic discharges on the surface of the earth and its most likely presence in the atmosphere as a disturbance of subatomic waves of energy in it shows that biophysics as a discipline reveals a common frame of reference for both living and non-living beings in the cosmos. Should we reduce the Anthropic Principle as a mechanical process just like the help the organic GPS of the migratory birds negotiating their ways back and forth from one corner of the Earth to another? Rather the ability of animals to detect the discharged electrical signals before earthquakes and tsunami take place would not prove that the Anthropic Principle of physics is the same as that of the ability of birds to find directions. Behind the questions as to how and why the conventional scientists come to know any higher order new scientific truths, there might be some fundamental non-objective reality as the ultimate condition of the creative abilities of well-known scientists to know what they know. It might be this fundamental reality which makes the cosmos as an interconnected whole and the scientists of creative genius are only self-directed and self-conscious human beings who know what they have been doing and what they expect to find without which they would not be looking for anything into the vast night sky. Behind their sense of wonder and inquisitiveness, it is highly possible that there exists an underlying metaphysical truth behind their ability to know of what they have come to discover as previously undiscovered truths about the cosmos. This is impossible without a background condition which enables the scientists to discover truths. The basic question is why physical nature in and through its accidental product called man seeks to know its own truth as a self-reflexive process of self-knowledge? This is exactly what the scientists of physical theory of consciousness are doing. While they as essentially physical brains the works of which are not like the mere instinctive stimuli-response systems of non-human animal brains and are knowing their consciousness to be physical, they cannot at the same time deny the subjective epistemic process of their brains' self-knowledge of themselves as physical brains. And for Penrose, this underlying human understanding is not reducible to some mathematical process as the latter presupposes the former.

References

Bhattacharyya, K., 1958, *Studies in Philosophy*, vol. II, ed. Gopinath Bhattacharyya, Calcutta: Progressive Publishers.

Braden, G., 2007, *The Divine Matrix: Bridging Time, Space, Miracles, and Belief,* Carlsbad: New House. https://artifactsjournal.missouri.edu/2015/01/divine-matrix/

Brahmasūtra with Śāṅkarabhāṣya, 1998, "Samanvayādhyāyaḥ Prathamaḥ ।।1।।" Delhi: Motilal Banarsidass (2nd edn).

Caldwell, Z., 2021, Is Life an Illusion?: The Spiritual Meaning of 'The Matrix'" (1 June). https://bahaiteachings.org/life-illusion-spiritual-meaning-matrix/

CERN (European Council for Nuclear Research), *Accelerating Science*. https://home.cern/resources/faqs/facts-and-figures-about-lhc.

DeAngelis, T., 2004, "Consumerism: Consumerism and Its Discontents", *Monitor on Psychology*, 35(6) (1 June). https://www.apa.org/monitor/jun04/discontents

DeConick, A.D., 2016, *The Gnostic New Age: How a Countercultural Spirituality Revolutionized Religion from Antiquity to Today*, Columbia University Press. https://doi.org/10.7312/deco17076

Descartes, Rene, 1986, *Meditation on First Philosophy*, tr. John Cottingham, Cambridge: Cambridge University Press.

Doerig, A., A. Schurger, K. Hess and M.H. Herzog, 2019, "The Unfolding Argument: Why IIT and Other Causal Structure Theories cannot Explain Consciousness", *Consciousness and Cognition*, 72: 49-59. https://doi.org/10.1016/j.concog.2019.04.002

Donald, M. J., 2007, "Realism, the Interpretation of Quantum Theory, and Idealism", The Cavendish Laboratory, Cambridge, Great Britain (accessed on 27 January 2023, through [https://people.bss.phy.cam.ac.uk/~mjd1014/real.html]).

Dose, K., 1988, "The Origin of Life: More Questions than Answers", *Interdisciplinary Science Reviews*, 13(4): 348-56 (retrieved from https://doi.org/10.1179/isr.1988.13.4.348).

Dyer, M.G., 1994, "Quantum Physics and Consciousness, Creativity, Computers: A Commentary on Goswami's Quantum-Based Theory of

Consciousness and Free Will", *The Journal of Mind and Behavior*, 15(3): 265-90. http://www.jstor.org/stable/43853644

Eight Upaniṣads with the Commentary of Śaṅkarācārya, 1989 (repr. 1991), tr. Swami Gambhirananda, vol. 1: *Taittirīya Upaniṣad*, Calcutta: Advaita Ashrama.

Encyclopaedia Britannica, 2013, "Anthropic Principle", *Encyclopedia Britannica*. https://www.britannica.com/science/anthropic-principle

Encyclopaedia Britannica, 2018, "Spontaneous Generation", *Encyclopedia Britannica*. https://www.britannica.com/science/spontaneous-generation

Excerpted from "Sri Brahma-Samhita", by Bhaktisiddhanta Sarasvati Thakura, courtesy of the Bhaktivedanta Book Trust International (Los Angeles), 2003. www.Krishna.com. (Tranlsator).

Freitag, W. and K. Kraus, 2022, "An Expressivist Interpretation of Kant's 'I think'", *Noûs*. 56: 110-32. https://doi.org/10.1111/nous.12350

Gamez, D., 2018, "Physical Theories of Consciousness", in *Human and Machine Consciousness* (1st edn, pp. 85-92), Open Book Publishers. http://www.jstor.org/stable/j.ctv8j3zv.9

Gamez, D., 2018, *Human and Machine Consciousness*, Cambridge, UK: Open Book Publishers (retrieved from https://doi.org/10.11647/OBP.0107).

Gascoigne, J. and S. Maroske, 2013, "Colonial Science and Technology", in *The Cambridge History of Australia*, part II, ed. Alison Bashford and Stuart Macintyre, pp. 438-61, Cambridge: Cambridge University Press. DOI: https://doi.org/10.1017/CHO9781107445758.021; https://www.cambridge.org/core/books/abs/cambridge-history-of-australia/colonial-science-and-technology/1F669EEB6CB616365F065A0A9935BEE5#authors-details (accessed on 1 February, 2023).

Hamlyn, D.W., 1984 (repr. 1998), *Metaphysics*, Cambridge: Cambridge University Press.

Harignton, N., 2021, "Roger Penrose Versus the World", *Project Q Peace and Security in a Quantum Age* (*Q Blog*), University of Sydney. https://projectqsydney.com/roger-penrose-versus-the-world

Hume, David, 2000, *A Treatise of Human Nature*, ed. David Fate Norton and Mary J. Norton, Oxford: Clarendon Press.

Khangamcha, P.M., 2018, "Contemporary Relevance of Advaita's Theory of Truth", in *On the Nature of Consciousness*, ed. Adarasupally Nataraju, pp. 68-105, New Delhi: Bloomsbury.

Kuppers, B.O., 1990, *Information and the Origin of Life*, Cambridge, MA: The MIT Press.

MacIsaa, T., n.d.,"A New Theory of Consciousness: The Mind Exists as a Field Connected to the Brain", *Science and Non-duality*. https://www.scienceandnonduality.com/article/a-new-theory-of-consciousness-the-mind-exists-as-a-field-connected-to-the-brain. (accessed on 29 January 2023).

Mahadevan, T.M.P., 2011, *The Philosophy of Advaita*, Delhi: Bharatiya Kala Prakashan.

Mills, G.C., M. Lancaster, and W.L. Bradley, 1993, "Origin of Life and Evolution in Biology Textbooks: A Critique", *The American Biology Teacher*, 55(2): 78-83 (retrieved from https://www.jstor.org/stable/4449589 in feb.).

Monad, J., 1971, *Chance and Necessity: An Essay on the Natural Philosophy of Modern Biology*, tr. form the French by Austryn Wainhouse, New York: Vintage Books.

Narayana, Bhaktivedanta (Swami), 2004, *Sri Brahma Samhita*, Vrindavan: Gaudiya Vedanta Publications.

Nikhilananda, Swami, 2014, *Vedāntasāra of Sadānanda*, Kolkata: Advaita Ashrama

Paulson, S., 2017, "Roger Penrose on Why Consciousness Does Not Compute", *The Emperor of Physics Defends His Controversial Theory of Mind, NAUTILUS*. https://nautil.us/roger-penrose-on-why-consciousness-does-not-compute-236591/

Pereboom, Derk, Edward N. Zalta and Uri Nodelman (eds), 2022, *Kant's Transcendental Arguments: The Stanford Encyclopedia of Philosophy* (Fall edn), <https://plato.stanford.edu/archives/fall2022/entries/kant-transcendental/>.

Prud'homme-Généreux, Annie, 2013, "What Is Life?: An Activity to Convey the Complexities of This Simple Question", *The American Biology Teacher*, 75(1): 53–57. https://doi.org/10.1525/abt.2013.75.1.11

Radhakrishnan, S., 1932, *An Idealist View of Life*, London: George Allen & Unwin Ltd.

Rand, A., 1964, *The Virtue of Selfishness: A New Concept of Egoism*, New York: Signet.

Ratner, P. Jan, 2018, "Why a 'Genius' Scientist Thinks Our Consciousness Originates at the Quantum Level", *Life*, 15. https://bigthink.com/life/consciousness-at-the-quantum-level/

Rogers, K., 2022, "Abiogenesis", *Encyclopedia Britannica*. https://www.britannica.com/science/abiogenesis

Roy, R.D., 2018, "Science Still Bears the Fingerprints of Colonialism", *Smithsonian Megazine – Conversation* (April 9). https://www.smithsonianmag.com/science-nature/science-bears-fingerprints-colonialism-180968709/

Saraswati, Madhusudana, 1992, *Advaita Siddhi*, New Delhi: Indian Council of Philosophical Research.

Schlosser, M.E., 2014, "The Neuroscientific Study of Free Will: A Diagnosis of the Controversy", *Synthese*, 191(2): 245-62. http://www.jstor.org/stable/24019927

Scott, A., 1995, "Toward an Emergent Theory of Consciousness", in *Stairway to the Mind*, New York, NY: Springer. https://doi.org/10.1007/978-1-4612-2510-2_9

Simmons, A., 2015, "Technology Colonialism", *Model View Culture: A Megazine about Technology and Diversity*, Issue 27. https://modelviewculture.com/pieces/technology-colonialism (accessed on 18 September 2022).

Stein, W.B., 1970, "The Hindu Matrix of Walden: The King's Son", *Comparative Literature*, 22(4): 303-18 (retrieved from https://www.jstor.org/stable/1769577).

Swahananda, Swami, 2012, *Pañcadaśī of Śrī Vidyāraṇya Swāmī*, Chennai: Sri Ramakrishna Math.

Thompson, R.L., 1977, *Demonstration by Information Theory that Life cannot Arise from Matter*, Boston: Bhaktivedanta Institute.

Vairāgya-Śatakam of Bhartṛhari: The Hundred Verses on Renunciation, tr. Swami Madhavananda, 2004, Kolkata: Advaita Ashrama.

Van, I. Peter and M. Sullivan, 2021, "Metaphysics", in *The Stanford Encyclopedia of Philosophy*, ed. N. Zalta (Winter edn). URL = https://plato.stanford.edu/archives/win2021/entries/metaphysics/>

Veerachary, P., 2018, "Dimensions of Mind in Indian Philosophy: An Analytical Study", *International Journal of Creative Research Thoughts (IJCRT)*. IJPUB1802128. https://ijcrt.org/papers/IJPUB1802128.pdf.

Wikipedia 2022 (17 November), "Emergentism", in *Wikipedia: The Free Encyclopedia*. https://en.wikipedia.org/w/index.php?title=Emergentism&oldid=1122434101 (accessed on 27 December 2022 at 16:50 IST).

Wikipedia 2022 (22 October), "Skandha", in *Wikipedia: The Free Encyclopedia*. https://en.wikipedia.org/w/index.php?title=Skandha&oldid=1117506522 (accessed on 29 December 2022).

Wikipedia 2022, "Posthumanism", in *Wikipedia: The Free Encyclopedia*. https://en.wikipedia.org/w/index.php?title=Posthumanism&oldid=1130181390 (accessed on 31 December 2022).

Wikipedia 2023, "Anthropic principle", in *Wikipedia: The Free Encyclopedia*. https://en.wikipedia.org/w/index.php?title=Anthropic_principle&oldid=1136386076 (accessed on 1 February 2023).

12

Dhyāna Bhāṣā or the Language of Meditative Reflection:

Understanding the "Existence" or "Sat"

Adarasupally Nataraju

Abstract: It has been said by an author of a Purāṇa, "Do not bring those things within the range of argumentation which are beyond thought. The nature of a thing beyond thought consists in its being other than the things within nature". Therefore, concludes Śaṅkara, a supersensuous thing (*Brahman or Ātman*) is known only from the Vedic source alone. Since the Self is not a thing in nature, any effort in using naturalistic methods would be a failure. Here is the departure in the Buddha's thought. Since it is a super sensuous thing, it is a futile exercise to understand a permanent Self. Therefore, it is desirous that we focus on what is "knowable". There is nothing permanent about the things of the world. Not even the "self" as we understand. For us, self is nothing but the "Ego" and represents body-mind complex. *Nāma* and *rūpa* constitute matter and mind, and are made up of elements. They are ever changing and are only capable of producing pain. The Buddha's silence points towards the limitations of human reason. However, there is *nirvāṇa* which is a permanent state of affairs. And the Upaniṣads, though speak of the impermanence of the *jīvātmā*, they do uphold a permanent ground for all appearances that we call the world.

Keywords: Meditative reflection, self, metaphysics, transcendence.

The method of approaching *ātman* cannot be through logical propositions and analysis of language. This paper questions all those naturalists, reductionists and other modern schools that speak of the "unknowable" as ever remaining "unknowable". That Self can never be known. It can be known but by a distinct model. It is the language of meditation – *dhyāna* and *nididhyāsana.* What I have done in this chapter is to elaborate on this study of the Self based on meditative reflection, not merely doing what I call as "positive metaphysics". Majority of studies on Self or subjectivity these days rest up on analytic and argumentative skills of the interpreter. The *ātman* is elusive to human reason and argumentation skills. It is "unknown" and remains "unknowable" if one were to adopt the model of natural sciences. The "Self" is studied as though one is studying magnetism or electricity. What I argue in this paper is that the method necessarily has to change. We need to adopt the Vedāntic method of approaching the Self. This method transcends reason, but is not against reason. That we can have access to new knowledge through intuition or awareness which is distinct from deriving knowledge with the combination of sensory data and categories of understanding. The original scheme of doing Vedānta as found in the *Māṇḍūkya Upaniṣad* is to meditatively reflect on consciousness in waking, dream and deep sleep states. And also reflect on five *kośa*s as found in the *Taittirīya.* There is also the famous method of *adhyāropa* and *apavāda* as discussed in the *Bṛhadāraṇyaka. Brahman* was at the centre of their study as a Reality existing out there, *vastu-tantra* not *puruṣa-tantra.*

Several words are used these days to denote some kind of a subjective experience. Subjectivity, Subject, Self, First Person Account, Witness Consciousness, I, Me and so on. I have discussed at length different models of meditative reflection available in Vedānta literature in the following pages. The concluding remarks of this chapter are:

1. It is wrong to approach metaphysical questions by means of an analytic enterprise,
2. it is better to avoid doing "positive metaphysics",
3. the method of enquiry of Self cannot be that of natural sciences,
4. one needs a radically different approach to "know" the Self,
5. the Self is not known but is "knowable" in a sense different from our everyday experiences of our life-world,
6. Vedānta provides comprehensive meditative reflections to filter and distill consciousness to its purest form,
7. suspending or bracketing of the world is possible only by the Vedānta techniques,
8. the idea of a concrete solidified Self is at the root of our problem in understanding the Self or subjectivity, and
9. it is the language of meditation that takes one closer to the "knowing" of the Self, not speculative hypotheses.

I

Let us try and understand what it means to do what I these days call as "positive metaphysics". There are several questions which we try and answer though there are limitations of human reason. Metaphysics is a discipline which tries to answer questions concerning the nature and existence of external reality. This can be (a) a neutral investigation without metaphysical presuppositions, or (b) a speculative positive metaphysics. The first model is what is preferable. The second model is what we get in Eastern and Western philosophies. Mere speculation and reckless hypotheses are what we come across in different philosophers. It is the same case when it comes to understanding the "Self" or "subjectivity". Speculative hypotheses are constructed on the model of doing natural sciences, failing to grasp that this science needs a radically different approach since consciousness cannot be reduced to a natural phenomenon.

Metaphysics answers different sets of questions, some of which are:

1. Metaphysics is some fundamental reflection on the status of reality,
2. metaphysics is a theoretic investigation of fundamental building blocks of reality, and
3. metaphysics is a philosophical engagement with questions of will, existence of God, Self, fate, immortality, death, etc.

Heidegger contends that despite allowing for what it is, metaphysics forgets the ground or Being:

> Philosophy does not concentrate on its ground. It always leaves its ground – leaves it by means of metaphysics. And yet it never escapes its ground. – 1956: 266

Heidegger sees metaphysics as a platform for tallying up many beings and eventually considers this totality to be equal to "Being". This is done when metaphysics, "deals with beings as beings"; and by dealing "with the beingness of beings". He maintains:

> Metaphysics represents the beingness of beings in a twofold manner: in the first place, the totality of beings as such with an eye to their most universal traits but at the same time also the totality of beings as such in the sense of the highest and therefore divine being. – Ibid.: 275

He further maintains:

> To metaphysics the nature of truth always appears only in the derivative form of the truth of knowledge and the truth of propositions which formulate our knowledge. – Ibid.: 268

Meanwhile, throughout the lengthy history of metaphysics, from Anaximander to Nietzsche, the truth of Being has remained hidden.

> Why does metaphysics not recall it? Is the failure to recall it merely a function of some kinds of metaphysical thinking? Or is it an essential feature of the fate of metaphysics that its own ground

> eludes it because in the rise of un-concealedness its very core, namely concealedness, stays away in favour of the unconcealed which appears in the form of beings? – Ibid.

While, for Heidegger, the fact is:

> Metaphysics never answers the question concerning the truth of Being, for it never asks this question. Metaphysics does not ask this question because it thinks of Being only by representing beings as beings. ... It refers to Being and means beings as beings. – 1956: 275

From their inception to their conclusion, metaphysical ideas have been oddly embroiled in a continual misunderstanding of beings and Being. Because of this ongoing misconception, the assertion that metaphysics raises the question of Being is incorrect.

The same critique of metaphysics can be levelled against the Sāṁkhya school in Indian philosophical systems. The glaring display of speculative metaphysics makes one wonder as the Sāṁkhya constructs the notions of plurality of *puruṣas* and existence of *pradhāna* (primordial matter). The theory of evolution is also based on some hypotheses and imagination. The existence of matter and consciousness is all proved with the help of subtle argumentation. If someone else comes with stronger arguments, Kapila's thesis will get defeated. The problem with constructing arguments to prove the existence of metaphysical objects is that there is always a chance to construct opposing views with equal authority and may be more convincing than a Kapila or Kaṇāda. To avoid the pitfalls of argumentative positive metaphysics, one should take recourse to doing it negatively and by employing meditative reflection. Can we not answer metaphysical questions at all? Are we to remain silent, as was the case with the Buddha, on all such questions? Can we be ever certain about our understanding on questions on the Self, life, death and immortality? Can we avoid limit concepts and limit contradictions while answering such questions?

II

No philosopher or philosophical school denies the existence of an empirical "Ego", the definitions of such an ego may vary. The second point is an "ethical self" that again is asserted by all the systems of thought whether Eastern or Western. Vedānta, on the other hand, talks about three types of *ātman* (Self).

a. The empirical ego, *vyāvahārika-jīvātmā.*
b. Real individual Self, *jīvātmā* – eternal spiritual substance, centre of individuality
c. Pure Subject – *sākṣī-caitanya*, underground of experience, eternal, self-shining, etc.

One needs to be careful while talking about Self in Vedānta, the word *ātman* gets used with different connotations. Upaniṣads use *ātman* as a transcendental subject, pure consciousness. Buddhists use it as an "empirical ego". The confusion of "Anātmavāda" arises out of comparing the Self from two different categories. There is a "category mistake" which most of the Buddhist scholars from European continent commit. The transcendental subject of Vedānta cannot be compared with an empirical ego of the Buddhists. To be free from the false notions of "I" and "mine" is the goal of both Vedānta and the early Buddhism. The denial of empirical self is the teaching of the Vedās and the Buddha; the Buddha was indifferent to Vedic teachings, not against them.

So much is written and spoken about the silence of the Buddha on metaphysical questions, volumes are written on silence. What are called as *avyākṛta* (inexpressible) fourteen questions. Questions about matter, soul and God were answered in silence by the Buddha. What are we to understand from this silence? Can we say (a) He did not have answers, (b) He was uninterested, (c) He was pragmatic, and (d) He wanted to counter Vedic philosophy. In *Majjhima Nikāya* I.63 (*Chūla-Māluṅkyasutta*), the Buddha compares a metaphysician to that foolish person whose heart is pierced by an arrow and, instead of taking it out, he speculates on the origin, size, metal, maker and thrower of that arrow. The man would die before there are any satisfactory answers. In *Dīgha Nikāya* 9 (*Potthapādasutta*), the Buddha compares search after metaphysical entities to a foolish lover, who has fallen in love with the most beautiful damsel, whom he has never seen and about whose existence, residence, colour, age and beauty, he knows nothing. The Buddha says:

> He knows these metaphysical views, but they are not conducive to spiritual life, do not lead to knowledge, illumination, peace and *nirvāṇa*. – *Dīgha Nikāya* 9

What is negated *śūnya* is a world of plurality, all views, all theories, all thought-constructions, all *svabhāvas*, etc. Thought constructions cannot give satisfactory answers about the nature of *tathatā* (real). We are reminded of the Upaniṣadic statement: words, along with the mind, return unable to reach the Real.

Let me now come back to the discussions on the Self from the Upaniṣads. As I have mentioned above, Vedānta talks about three kinds of selves: *vyāvahārika-jīvātmā*, *jīvātmā* and *sākṣī-caitanya*. One has to be ultra-careful when one talks of the Self from the Vedic literature. As such, these texts comprise of insights on the workings of the transcendent Self; but the word *ātman* gets used in different senses.

These Upaniṣadic meditations are intended to break the shackles produced by the laws of natural processes. Nature has its grip on our lives, it is *karma* that binds us. To break the bondage of *karma* is the running theme both in Buddhism and Vedānta. Techniques of meditation help us to break this bondage created by the laws of nature, "affirming a reality independent of what really is, is called the ego" (Swami Krishnanda). That works as the centre of personality. It is a myth, yet the whole life revolves around this mythical self. The "Anātmavāda" of the Buddha is meant to counter this mythical self, not the transcendent Self.

Something separate from the organic structure of this universe is: what our personality is? Our belief that we are unique, that we are distinct from all that is outside of us. This is the cause of suffering and sorrow of the humans. This is a separate "ego". Births and deaths follow one another in succession to bring the *jīva* back to its original goodness. Universality of Being is deprived because of this false sense of ego, to get back to universal consciousness is the work of the Vedas. Meditations lift us above the ordinary experiences and lift us above this phenomenal world. To take us back to our original state of Being, that is at once universal and is the ground of everything that exists. This journey is *adhyātma vidyā*.

III

The Language of Meditation

By hearing the word *vedānta* one is generally reminded of some of the theoretic problems that Vedānta schools discuss: problems such as the relation of individual *jīva* and *Brahman*, nature of the external world of objects, nature and means of liberation, theories on *avidyā*, *adhyāsa*, *māyā*, *Īśvara*, *svarūpa lakṣaṇa* and *taṭastha lakṣaṇa* of *Brahman*. All most all *ācārya*s who wrote commentaries on the *Brahmasūtra* have touched upon the above-mentioned topics. Since they held on to divergent understanding of these topics, different schools were established with committed followers. They have also discussed several meditation techniques. Seldom our discussions seem centred on *upāsanā paddhati*s (techniques of meditation). Unless one is initiated into religious practices of a particular school, one does not know the practical applications of *upāsanā*s discussed in Upaniṣads and elsewhere in commentarial tradition.

Third chapter of the *Brahmasūtra* discusses *upāsanā paddhati*s based on Upaniṣadic sources. These are in a way different from *upāsanā* models of Bhakti tradition where *iṣṭa devatā* is meditated upon. The principle followed is *tam yathā yathā upāsate, sa tathaiva bhavati* (As one meditates, so does one become). Ending of suffering and acquiring of bliss are the *prayojana* of Vedānta.[1] There is no

---

[1] Dharmarāja Adhvarīndra in *Vedānta Paribhāṣā* explains *prayojana* of Vedānta as *duḥkha nivṛtti* and *ānanda prāpti*.

becoming or achieving something which is not there, it is the purpose of these meditations to make one aware of what is already there (Sastri 1942: 153).

Expanding the individual consciousness and to break the shackles of limitations imposed by ignorance seems to be the implication of all such meditations. The *Kena Upaniṣad* says: "That is adorable, one should meditate on it as 'adorable'."[2] This paper aims to closely look at the implications of Vedāntic meditations as found in the *Brahmasūtra* and *Chāndogya*, *Kaṭha*, *Praśna* and other Upaniṣads. The contention of the paper is that the *upāsanā paddhati*s are all most relegated to the background and Vedānta came to be treated as conceptual analysis and deliberations on metaphysical theories. Vedānta, at least in ancient times, was not constructing positive metaphysics, but was following some rigorous methods in arriving at an understanding of the Truth. After *avasthā-traya-vicāra* and *pañca-kośa-vicāra upāsanā paddhati*s play a decisive role in the culmination of *Brahman* knowledge which ends human suffering.

Traditionally, there has been a long debate among the Vedāntins over the means of realization. That by hearing the *mahāvākya*s at once one can enter into *mahāsamādhi* and attain the realization of *Brahman* is held by some of the followers of this tradition, whereas, others believe that some kinds of *upāsanā*s are essential to realize *Brahman*. That these meditation techniques help one purge the impurities of the heart and loosen the bondage brought about by the sins of countless previous births of the *jīva* is the traditional belief supported by the scriptures. There is hardly any instance in known human history to show that by hearing Vedic statements on *Brahman* one enters into union with supreme consciousness. On the contrary even all the *ācārya*s seem to have undergone all the hardship, practised various *sādhanā*s to attain freedom of the self.

Like in the case of Ramana Maharshi who answered a question that he must have done great *sādhanā* in previous births to have

2 See the *Kena Upaniṣad* for more details on meditation models.

attained realization at such a young age. The question was whether he attained Self-realization without any *upāsanā* or *sādhanā* techniques. In the case of Buddhas and Śaṅkaras, it is recorded in the books that there was a period of intense religious practices that eventually led them to freedom. I do not think it is a strong theory to hold that by hearing *mahāvākyas* once, of course a soul of pure nature, enters into *mahāsamādhi* and attains *mukti*. *Krama-mukti* is what is supported by reason as well as historical evidence. By *krama-mukti* I mean attainment of freedom by undergoing some form of *upāsanā* or the other. *Sadyo-mukti* is understood by me as the Self experiencing its identity with universal Spirit by hearing the *mahāvākyas* only once. There is a long tradition of debate on immediate release verses long time span of *niṣkāma karma*. Purifying the *antaḥkaraṇa* which then leads to the realization of *Brahman*.

According to Swami Krishnananda, "Meditation is the practice of *Brahman*; in Sanskrit it is called *brahmābhyāsa*" (2020: 63). We get a definition of *brahmābhyāsa* in *Pañcadaśī* 7.106:

> *tat cintanam tat kathanam*
> *anyonyam tatprabodhanam*
> *etadekaparatvam ca*
> *brahmābhyāsam vidur budhaḥ* ।

Thinking only of "That" which one is lost due to beginningless *avidyā*. As though a person has lost his beloved, so he needs to think constantly not allowing any other thought to occur. Talking to people only about *Brahman*, not discussing current affairs as we usually do. Depending entirely on That, where thought, feeling and action get merged in *Brahman* is defined as *brahmābhyāsa*. Whoever meditates on God as being present everywhere enjoys the bliss of *Brahman*, says the *Chāndogya*. The *Upaniṣad* goes on to say:

> *sa eva adhastāt* (He is below); *sa upariṣṭāt* (He is above); *sa purastāt* (He is in front); *sa paścāt* (He is behind); *sa dakṣiṇataḥ* (to the right); *sa uttarataḥ* (to the left); *sa eva idam sarvam* (He is all this).
>
> – *ChāUp* 7.25

This kind of meditation obviously is distinct from thinking about God as located in *vaikuṇṭha* or *brahmaloka*, etc. The all-pervading supreme pure consciousness is all that exists is the concluding teaching of the Vedānta. Division between meditator and *Brahman* has to be maintained for meditation to take place.

Defining "Upāsana"

In the *Vedāntasāra* of Sadānanda it is stated:

> *Upāsanā* is a kind of mental process relating to the qualified *Brahman* (*Saguṇa-Brahman*) such as, for instance, the *Śāṇḍilya-vidyā*.[3]

This definition is not comprehensive since this excludes *Nirguṇa-Brahman upāsanā*. There is a distinction made by the author of the text between *saguṇa* and *nirguṇa upāsanā paddhatis*. This is not the view of the Upaniṣads. In his commentary on *Bṛhadāraṇyaka* I.3.9, Śaṅkara defines:

> *Upāsanā* is mentally approaching the form of the deity or something of that sort, as it is presented by the praising portions of the Vedas relating to the objects of meditation, and concentrating on it, excluding conventional notions, till one is completely identified with it, as with one's body, conventionally regarded as one's own self.[4]

The above definition is comprehensive, the object of meditation may be any form of a deity or any object or it may be *Brahman*. It is a mental process as mentioned above by Śaṅkara and its aim is identification with the object of worship. So, the *Vedāntasāra*'s definition is not in accordance with Śaṅkara's understanding. There seems a difference between *upāsanā* and knowledge. There is also the factoring of faith in *upāsanā*; faith in the scripture, on

---

[3] *Vedāntasāra* 12. For more details, see *ChāUp* III.14.1 and *BṛUp* V.6.1.

[4] See also Śaṅkara's introduction to *Chāndogya* and commentary on *Brahmasūtra* I.1.4.

the deity and on the process itself. Knowledge is determined by the object and *upāsanā* is dependent on the subject is the view of *Pañcadaśī* IX.74-82.

In *Bṛhadāraṇyaka Upaniṣad* II.4.5, commenting on *nididhyāsana*, Sureśvara makes a clear distinction between *upāsanā* and *nididhyāsana*. *Upāsanā* is a preliminary stage that may lead to *nididhyāsana* in which there is no thought process, but an awareness that falls short of *aparokṣānubhūti*; an awareness without thinking activity or conscious will. It is the identification with *Brahman*. An element of faith seems to separate *upāsanā* from *vicāra* (thoughtful reflection) on the one hand and *nididhyāsana* on the other which is a special kind of awareness. In the *Upadeśasāhasrī*, Śaṅkara talks about that special kind of awareness which is not about involving some kind of action. An awareness where the observer–observed distinction is absent. Such an awareness is what Sureśvara is calling as *nididhyāsana*. Therefore, there is a clear distinction between *upāsanā* and *nididhyāsana*. *Śravaṇa* is also a form of *upāsanā*. *Upāsanā* involves a meditating person, an object of meditation and a continuous stream of thought, like uninterrupted oil poured from one vessel to another.

Different Upāsanā Paddhatis

Removing all conditioning factors that make feel a soul finite is the goal of all *upāsanā*s of the Upaniṣads. The limitations are a result of space–time matrix. The only thing that is beyond these categories is *Brahman*. Realizing that everything that exists is *Brahman*, and to also realize that the *jīva* is identical with *Brahman* is the conclusion reached by Advaita Vedānta. Bhakti schools, on the other hand, speak about four types of *mukti*: *sālokya*, *sārūpya*, *sāmīpya* and *sāyujya*. There is no question of identity of the individual soul with the Supreme Lord. The duality is always maintained in some form or the other.

The ultimate dictum from the Upaniṣads is *yo vai bhūmā tat sukham* – where we do not see the other; where we do not hear the other; where we do not comprehend the other is *Brahman.* This is established not by logical reasoning, analytic prowess or by any other means. For Vedānta, it is scripture alone that is the proof of *Brahman* as the *nimitta-* and *upādāna-kāraṇa* of the world. *Brahmasūtra* III.2.22 establishes that *Brahman* cannot be apprehended by any other proof than the Vedas. *Muṇḍaka Upaniṣad* III.i.8 says: "He is not apprehended by the eye, nor by other sources, nor by penance, etc." and *Kaṭha Upaniṣad* II.iv.9 says: "His form does not exist within the range of vision; nobody sees Him with the eyes". The very third *sūtra* of the *Brahmasūtra* establishes scriptural authority when it comes understanding the nature of *Brahman.*

Pratīkaupāsanā and *para-brahma upāsanā* are the two models that we come across. Apprehension of *Brahman* is attained by constant practice. Vāmadeva and other *ṛṣis* experienced like that "I have become Manu, the Sun, etc." (*BṛUp* I.4.10). Non-sentient world is spoken of as a form of *Brahman* in the Upaniṣads.

> There is both difference and non-difference. Difference in name and form, and non-difference in substance.[5]

If *Brahman* Itself exists as the non-sentient world, as snake has its coils, then *Brahman* has to undergo change. Whereas, texts declare *Brahman* to be changeless. If there is identity, *Brahman* is contaminated by the imperfections of the world. Therefore, says *Brahmasūtra* III.2.27, their relation is as between light and its substratum. While they are different, yet they are non-different as fire. Even so the non-sentient world a form of *Brahman*, definitely not an illusion as over-enthusiastic Advaitins want us to believe. This still has some problems, so explaining difference and non-difference is the most vexed, hard problem for the Vedāntins till date.

Chapter III, section 3 of the *Brahmasūtra* considers in detail whether meditations such as the *vaiśvānara-vidyā* constitute one meditation or are there many meditations? There are no different

---

[5] Rāmānuja's commentary on *Brahmasūtra* III.2.26.

meditations since they all aim at attainment of *Brahman.* The two words used in the texts – *vidyāt* (he should know) and *upāsīta* (he should meditate) – are common in all texts. The same injunction "he should meditate on Vaiśvānara" is repeated in the *Chāndogya* and *Vājasaneya.*

Vaiśvānara-vidyā meditation is to be found in the Upaniṣads and is equally emphasized in the *Brahmasūtra.* This is also termed as *bhūmā-vidyā.* Swami Krishnananda says:

> Everyday sit and think deeply. This is briefly *bhūmā-vidyā* or *vaiśvānara-vidyā*, the highest kind of meditation one can think of. The great trouble with us is that we feel it is not possible. "It is not possible for me. I am not fit for this." "I have many problems; I have difficulties of many kinds." All the difficulties will melt away. Mountains of sins can be destroyed by the Flame of Knowledge.
> – 2020: 85

What is referred to here is that knowledge burns all the *karmas* and the attendant sins as we see the reference in the *Bhagavadgītā.*

Sage Raikva in the *Chāndogya Upaniṣad* develops *saṁvarga-vidyā* which is a reversed process of meditation as practised in Vaiśvānara *dhyāna.* At length I will quote Swami Krishnananda on this meditation:

> In the usual concept of the *vaiśvānara-vidyā*, the exercise is in identifying oneself with everything. Here we have a slight modification; You absorb the sun into yourself; "I am blazing like the sun; I am resplendent like the sun"; Absorb the moon into yourself; Absorb all space into yourself; Absorb the whole world into yourself; Absorb all the people in the world into yourself; Absorb all the divinities in heaven into yourself; Absorb all the fourteen worlds into yourself – and stand like a Mighty Emperor of the Universe. This is the *saṁvarga-vidyā*, the art of absorbing everything into oneself, so that one becomes everything.
> – 2020: 86

The implications of such an Upaniṣadic meditation is that one becomes everything that is, one is in fact identifying with "Vaiśvānara" or waking state universal consciousness. This is the best form of Advaitic *upāsanā* that we come across. The Upaniṣad goes on to say that good deeds of everyone converge on to this person and the virtues of everyone accrue to him. A person is called a *kṛpaṇa* in Sanskrit, who leaves this corporeal body without realizing *Akṣara-Brahman* here in this life. *Pratīka upāsanā* or *saguṇa upāsanā* leads to the desired deity, there are elaborate descriptions on the fate of the soul in liberation in the fourth chapter of the *Brahmasūtra*. The soul does not merge in God or in Viṣṇu. It enjoys the glory of the Lord. With such an *upāsanā*, one is inseparable from God, but he is not himself Nārāyaṇa. Such is the interpretation of the *Brahmasūtra* by Rāmānuja. Let me quote Swami Krishnananda:

> One of the things that comes out on a close analysis of the real meaning of the *sūtras* themselves is that it seems to be favouring Ācārya Rāmānuja's interpretation of God and the world; it does not seem to be favouring Śaṅkarācārya fully, but Śaṅkara is bent upon seeing that his thought is there. – 2020: 88

The cells out of which our body is made are inseparable from the body, and the body is unique in itself.

Ācārya Śaṅkara does not agree with such a conclusion. Krishnananda further says:

> "Relation" means accepting the existence of two different things. If there are two different things, they cannot become one; If the two cannot become one, duality will persist; If duality persists, there will be no universal experience. Therefore, Rāmānuja is not right and Śaṅkara contends that the *Brahmasūtra* says that the soul merges in God in an Identity of Universality. – Ibid.: 88-89

By bringing in both the *ācāryas* into this discussion, I am trying to show two things.

A. The differences in the models of meditation have a significant bearing on the metaphysical commitments of the Bheda, Abheda and Bhedābheda schools of Vedānta philosophy.

B. That the interpretation of Rāmānuja Ācārya is more in tune with the Bādarāyaṇa's *Brahmasūtra* than Śaṅkara's interpretation of the text. The second point is not the concern of the present paper. Obviously the metaphysical commitments of *ācāryas* have influenced their interpretation of the *Brahmasūtra* is beyond doubt.

Concluding Remarks

Ātman cannot be understood by merely constructing formal hypotheses and Vedānta is purely anti-metaphysical. A formal construction of the Self is rampant in today's academia. The faculty in philosophy departments across the continents indulge in giving hypotheses which are only some logical propositions, they have nothing to do with a reality existing out there. This is what Vedānta calls as *bāhya-dṛṣṭi*. Different from this is what is called as *antara-dṛṣṭi* which is turning away from everything that is external to consciousness and instead focusing attention on what is internal to consciousness. It is rather coming face to face with pure consciousness without the presence of objects. Self is self-shining and does not require objects for its existence. It is self-conscious, self-subsisting and self-contained. The different methodologies that I have discussed in the above pages help one in realizing the true nature of the Self. There is no hardened, concrete "Self" in Vedānta. The "empirical ego" is not a permanent abiding self, it is a combination of loosely knit elements, that transmigrates and is a *kartā* and *bhoktā*. The transcendent Self is neither an agent nor an enjoyer, it is an onlooking witness consciousness. Non-playing captain of the team. *Mithyātmā* which is full of *ahaṁkāra* and *mamakāra* is denied with equal force by both the Vedāntins and the Buddhists alike.

The reality of ultimate absolute "Self" is not denied by the Vedānta. The ground of all that exists, what modern-day physics calls as "unified field" is upheld by the Vedas. It is the language of meditative reflection that takes us to the shores of the "Self" not naturalistic methods. Empirical ego, individual soul and transcendent Self are all discussed in the Upaniṣads, but their interest is to reach at pure consciousness that is the ground of all that exists. This is made possible by taking recourse to meditation techniques and not by logical analysis and naturalistic method is the concluding standpoint of the Vedas.

References

Heidegger, M., 1956, "The Way Back into the Ground of Metaphysics", in *Existentialism from Dostoevsky to Sartre*, ed. W. Kaufmann, New York: Penguin Group.

Krishnananda, Swami, 2020, *Analysis of the Brahmasūtra*, Hrishikesh: Divine Life Society.

Sastri, S.S. Suryanarayana (ed. and tr.), 1942, *Vedānta Paribhāṣā* of Dharmarāja Adhvarīndra, Chennai: The Adyar Library and Research Centre.

13

Consciousness, Subjectivity and Self

A Study with Special Reference to Pañcadaśī

Munmun Chakraborty

Abstract: This paper would like to address the problems related to the concept of consciousness specifically from the Advaitic standpoint. Particularly, it intends to examine some of the intricate concepts associated with the concept of consciousness, such as self, subjectivity, ego and mind in the light of well-known text *Pañcadaśī* of Swāmī Vidyāraṇya. There are two reasons for choosing the text. First, the aim is to investigate the post-Śaṅkara views and techniques for exploring the nature of consciousness. Though there is no fundamental divergence from Śaṅkara Advaita yet the problems related to consciousness, selfhood or subjectivity have received a detailed and meticulous treatment in the hands of later Advaitins. Second, the text has addressed the questions and issues related to self, mind, subjectivity and witness consciousness from a critical perspective. Instead of blindly holding the authority of scripture, Swāmī Vidyāraṇya has succeeded to provide a logical ground of the Advaitic theories. Henceforth, a deeper purpose of this paper is to understand its contemporary relevance in consciousness studies. Since, any traditional theory of consciousness is significant and pertinent as long as it can contribute adequately in the contemporary debate and discussion. The claim is not to resolve the problems of consciousness but to offer an Indian perspective to comprehend the modern problems.

Keywords: Consciousness, subjectivity, self, *kūṭastha, cidābhāsa, Pañcadaśī.*

Introduction

THE trend that has gained popularity today among modern thinkers of consciousness is that either they will deny the existence of consciousness or they will abuse it as a mystery. Certainly, both these two approaches are extreme and disputable. The experience of which we are intimately and immediately aware and also the prerequisite of all experiences is self-evident. That cannot be a mystery nor can it be denied. Since denying it is the same as denying our own existence, the being "I am". The dilemma for any researcher of consciousness studies is that the object of study is nothing but the subject itself or the very first-person experience. It cannot be known the way one can see a tree, a fan or a book on the table. But it is more obvious than any object of our experience.

This paper would like to address the problems related to the concept of consciousness from the Advaitic standpoint. Particularly, it intends to examine some of the intricate concepts found associated with the concept of consciousness such as self, subjectivity, ego and mind in the light of the well-known text *Pañcadaśī*[1] (hereafter *PD*) of Śrī Vidyāraṇya Swāmin.[2] There are two reasons for choosing the text. First, the aim is to investigate

---

[1] I have followed the English translation of *Pañcadaśī* of Śrī Vidyāraṇya Swāmin published by Sri Ramakrishna Math, Chennai.

[2] Śrī Vidyāraṇya Swāmin, also known as Mādhavācārya, is one of the most eminent teachers of post-Śaṅkara tradition. Particularly, he belongs to the Vivaraṇa tradition of Advaita. He was the head of the Śṛṅgerī Maṭha established by Śrī Śaṅkarācārya. Some of the notable works of Śrī Vidyāraṇya Swāmin are *Vivaraṇaprameyasaṁgraha, Dṛk-dṛśya-Viveka, Sarvadarśnasaṁgraha, Śrī Śaṅkara-Digvijaya, Jīvanmukti Viveka* and *Upaniṣad Dīpikā.*

the post-Śaṅkara views and techniques for exploring the nature of consciousness. Though there is no fundamental divergence from Śaṅkara Advaita yet the problems related to consciousness, selfhood or subjectivity have received a detailed and meticulous treatment in the hands of later Advaitins. And second, the text has addressed the questions and issues related to self, mind, subjectivity and witness consciousness from a critical perspective. Instead of blindly holding the authority of scripture, Śrī Vidyāraṇya Swāmin has succeeded to provide a logical ground for the Advaitic theories. Henceforth, a deeper purpose of this paper is to understand its contemporary relevance in consciousness studies. Any traditional theory of consciousness is significant and pertinent as long as it can contribute adequately to contemporary debate and discussion. The claim is not to resolve the problems of consciousness but to offer an Indian perspective to comprehend modern problems.

The Problem of Consciousness

The hard problem of consciousness as coined by David Chalmers is the problem of explaining the subjectivity or self-awareness that seems distinct from the physical body and the material world. While the body is completely physical, the first-person experience or the sense of "I" is subjective, inner and private. The challenge in front of the dualists, materialists and scientists is how to explain the causal relationship between consciousness and the body which are diametrically opposed from each other yet found attached and united in all our experiences. The popular approach is defining this conscious experience or first-person awareness through brain functions or physical activities. Surprisingly, the reductionists have pleased most of the modern minds. However, for many philosophers including Chalmers, reductionism is unacceptable. The problem of reductionism is the rigidity of conceiving consciousness as something non-existing, non-essential, derivative and opaque. Hence, the question is: can there be any other alternative yet rational method to deal with the hard problem instead of going back to reductionism? It is herein, Advaitins' position can be considered as one traditional yet rationally appealing approach to overcome the limitation of reductionism.

The Process of Discrimination

Like the mind–body distinction popular in Western philosophy, Indian philosophers have gone further to distinguish consciousness from both the body and mind. Our ordinary experience that is intentional or object-directed is never captured without an object. All our mental states have an internal or external object towards which it is moving all the time.[3] Not only our sensory experiences that reveal the external physical objects through touch, sound, perception, taste and smell, we have numerous inner objects that keep revealing the inner states of the mind like the states of happiness, anger, love, desire and imagination. While all these objects are different from each other because of their uniqueness and functions, the awareness of these objects which manifests simultaneously in the inner and the outer world remains the same, one and homogeneous (*PD* I.3). Śrī Vidyāraṇya writes:

> The perceived objects are transient and in the waking state they seem permanent. So, there is difference between them. But the (perceiving) consciousness in both the states does not differ. It is homogeneous. – *PD* I.4

The series of experiences one undergoes in waking and dream states point towards these numerous transient objects and the dynamic nature of the mind that keep on moving and transforming over time.

---

[3] This object-directed nature of conscious experience is called intentionality by contemporary thinkers. While for contemporary phenomenologists and analytic thinkers this intentionality is the essential structure of consciousness, for the Advaitins it adheres to our psychological states which are distinct from consciousness *as such*. Consciousness is essentially self-luminous or reflexive and not intentional. For an elaborate discussion on the intentionality and reflexivity thesis in Advaita, please see Jha et al. 2017.

Following Śaṅkara, Śrī Vidyāraṇya here initiated both the rational and phenomenological methods to discern the nature of consciousness from its subsequent objects, physical body and mental states. A phenomenological study of the three states of experiences followed by an analysis of the seer–seen distinction (*dṛg dṛśya viveka*) is the most cogent tool to affirm the unique and indivisible nature of consciousness. The claim is: that which is the seer of our experience cannot be seen. To put it in a different way, that which is the subject or knower cannot be known and thus essentially distinct from the latter. The sense organs being the perceiver can alone see the objects and their forms, shapes, colours, etc. Yet, the former cannot be a perceiver in true sense as they are also perceived by the mind, the inner eyes. But, the mind along with its psychosis is the object of cognition to the witness consciousness that alone is unperceived but of which one is immediately and intimately aware. The dilemma is that even if there is no doubt in admitting the mind as a subject and knower of the senses, there is disagreement in accepting its objectivity. As the mind creates its own image as an agent and knower, it is apparently difficult to affirm it as an object. However, the mind and its different modes and states are also directly and immediately known to us and thus it becomes an object too. Describing the nature of the object, R. Balasubramanian states:

> The object is one that is referred by consciousness and by nature present to it; it is something beyond consciousness and dependent on the former to be cognized. Whereas, that which is revealing the object by recognizing it is termed as the subject.[4]

The mind is known when it is happy or sad, bright or dull, loves or hates, desires or fears and so on. Just as the way, the mind perceives external objects and their features including the physical body, the mind is perceived and apprehended by the consciousness that observes all its modes, transformations and functions in all

[4] For more details please see Balasubramaniam 2004.

the three states (waking, dreaming and deep sleep states). If it is denied, there will be a perpetual problem of knowing one's own mind along with other minds.

In *Pañcadaśī*, Śrī Vidyāraṇya has taken up a rigorous method to differentiate consciousness from anything different and given to consciousness. Particularly in chapters one and three, he offers a thorough analysis of the five sheaths that represent the gross body, subtle body and causal body. Through the technique of seer–seen distinction he argues that not only the "physical sheath" but also the "vital sheath", "mental sheath", "intellectual sheath" and the "bliss sheath" are objects of consciousness as they appear in and through consciousness. Just as the material object is known and given to consciousness, the physical body is known and given to consciousness. The difference is this physical body appears more intimate than the external objects but the former is not nearer than the vital air and the inner organ or mind. Nevertheless, they are too known and witnessed by consciousness.

Again, the objectivity of the mind and the physical body which are always found allied with consciousness and constitute the subjectivity becomes obvious through the phenomenological study of waking, dreaming and deep sleep experiences. In all our ordinary experiences and activities, the mind enjoys some level of privacy and authority over the physical body and external objects due to its dynamic and internal nature. But the mind too is an external and distant object that can be distinguished from consciousness. Though the task seems difficult in waking states, it is evident in the dream and deep sleep states. According to Śrī Vidyāraṇya, the variable and transient nature of the physical body is proved in the dream state when the mind alone acts without the involvement of the body. Likewise, the mind too is absent in deep sleep where consciousness alone persists. Affirming the striking similarity between mind and object, he writes:

> So we see there are two kinds of objects, the "material" and the "mental". The "material" is the object cognized by mind being

> modified, by the form of the material object. And the "mental" is cognized by the witness consciousness. – *PD* IV.31

It is important to note that Advaitins never considered the mind as a substratum of consciousness or a regulator of consciousness but it appears conscious due to its subtle and mirror-like nature. There are several arguments to justify the material and objective nature of the mind. The mind, though the material, is fit to reflect consciousness unlike any other physical object. Being a subtle matter, the mind moves and goes out to the object and also adopts the form of the object just as water takes the form of the container. The distinguishing feature of the mind is its ceaseless association with some objects either material or ideal or imaginary. Not only in the waking state even in dreams the mind gets attached and directed towards some objects. In fact, the dream is one very important proof to recognize how the mind plays the role of an agent and knower even without the aid of the body. But as the mind becomes dormant in deep sleep, the object too remains absent in that state and what persists at that time is the one indivisible consciousness that keeps revealing the "sheath of bliss" along with the general ignorance. The statement one makes after waking up that "I had a sound sleep" or "I was not aware of anything" would not be possible unless we do accept the being of consciousness at that state. Thus, through the method of discrimination and the method of negation, the being of consciousness can be affirmed that is distinct, unmodified and objectless.

Self, Subjectivity and the Sense of "I"

One very persistent problem in consciousness studies is how to explain the concept of self or the subjectivity or the sense of "I" that we all retain. If conscious experiencing is changing and evolving who is that unchanging, one and indivisible being that keeps an identity over the ages? To put it precisely, there is a simultaneous experience of endurance and transformation which together comprise our personal identity. When the body is growing and transforming over the ages, the mind too is constantly moving, growing and generating new ideas, memories and thoughts leaving many old memories behind. But there is a sense of "I" that is incessant and uniformly present in all ages and throughout all transforming experiences. We cannot claim that the body retains the identity because it is diametrically evolving from the time of birth till death. Nor it can be the mind. But there is still one who observes all these modifications and due to which one claims, "It is my body" or "I used to think like this". Ordinarily, the mind is considered as one that retains the individual's identity over the ages but a deep examination of mental states shows how the mind itself is changing and growing regularly. The child who visited the wildlife park at the age of 5 and had a memorable experience has grown up and is a college student today, she definitely will not undergo the same experience even if she visits the same park once again at the age of 18. Although she may remember her childhood experience clearly and say, "I visited the wildlife park when I was 5 only and I enjoyed a lot". There is an obvious difference between the girl who visited the wildlife park at the age of 5 years and the girl who is soon going to cross her teenage. They are not one or the same but they are also not two completely separate individuals. Hence, the question is, "what is the ground of our identity?" or "why the individual considers herself the same person even after fifteen years?" Dan Zahavi, who strongly challenges the no-self theorists of this era and advocates the idea of a minimal self or experiential self has argued that it is the first-person perspective that remains the same, unaltered and generates the sense of *mineness* or *I-ness*.[5]

---

[5] By first-personal perspective, Zahavi did not mean that self is the perspectival owner or possessor of thought or experience. It is neither the perspectival owner nor the personal owner. The minimal self or the experiential self lives in and through the experience and is always present in the first-personal mode. In contrast, the idea of ownership presupposes a sense of distinction between self and the consciousness making the former an independent spectator of everything.

Self is not something an abstract or isolated entity beyond our head and mind, but the very experiential self that endures in and through this conscious experience but remains open to transformation and expand over times. Interestingly, Advaita too advocates an experiential self as Zahavi, yet the former seems to go far beyond this account of minimal self. For Advaita, the experiential self is not the one that gets involved in this phenomenal world. It is the unceasing consciousness that witnesses both the appearance and disappearance, creation and destruction, continuity and disruption instead of becoming a part of it. The one who is the ground of our identity and due to which the person does not assume herself or himself as two separate individuals who observes all these modifications of mental states and body yet remains unaffected and unaltered. It alone is unremittingly existing behind all transformations and thus justifies the unity of our experiences.

The controversy surrounding the nature of the self is a century old. There are strong critics of the concept of self both in classical and contemporary times. But, Advaitins, following Upaniṣads, have proposed a very robust account of self that challenged and questioned many no-self theories. There are two very extreme views that often pleased the advocates of no-self theories. Either they have conceived self as a mysterious trans-personal entity who is beyond our ordinary experiences or there is an effort to define it as an upshot of multiple constituents including the mind and the body. Advaita rejects both the views. The self is not assumed as an isolated and mysterious being behind individuality nor it is a by-product of some elements but one that manifests the body, the mind, the ego and also the external objects. Here, again, one should not get confused about the relationship between consciousness, body, mind and self. The self of our individuality is nothing apart from the consciousness that "reveals at one and the same time the agent, the action and the external objects" and which is also known as "witness in the Vedānta" (*PD* X.9). To put it precisely, the consciousness that witnesses the five sheaths is nothing but the self. It is not identical either with the body or the mind or the intellect as these are the object of this self that witnesses their functions, appearance, disappearance, etc. Being the subject of all these objects, internal or external, the self cannot be the object yet its existence is undeniable and realized in all experiences unlike an object. As stated in *Pañcadaśī* III.27:

> That which is the subject cannot be an object of the senses. But as it is the very Self of everyone, it cannot be said to be beyond the ken of perception.

In the strict sense, even for Advaitins, the self is unknowable but it is never non-existent (*PD* III.13). Describing the nature of witness S. Radhakrishnan (2011: 560) writes:

> Though, this witnessing consciousness arises with the experience of objects, it is not due to the experience, but is presupposed by it.

So, the very radical claim of Śrī Vidyāraṇya and other Advaitins is that the self being the experiencer alone can never be the object of experience and thereby any attempt to apprehend it as an object like a cup or a book is a category mistake. Nevertheless, it does not prevent the scope of knowing the self because it is most immediately and directly realized in all our acts and experiences. Yet, not as an object of experience.

Śrī Vidyāraṇya Swāmin refutes all contrary views that challenged the being of self and proposes a series of arguments to establish the being of self. The self is neither momentary nor it is void, for it is the witness that perceives the momentary appearance of the "I-consciousness" or ego. He argues that even the illusion or the void cannot be proved unless the being of the self is admitted as a witness by the Buddhists (*PD* VI.76). The self is also distinct from the intellect because the latter is perceived by the self. Criticizing the views of the Naiyāyikas and the Digambaras, he argues that the self "is neither atomic nor of medium size, but is infinite, partless, and like *ākāśa* all-pervasive" (*PD* VI.86). He goes further in refuting the position of Prabhākara and some logicians who define the self as a bliss-sheath (*PD* VI.94). He staunchly denies the claims of the followers of Kumārila Bhaṭṭa who assume the self as both conscious and unconscious, or luminous and dark like that of a fir-fly (*PD* VI.97). Thus, Śrī Vidyāraṇya refutes all illusory and distorted accounts of self but not the being of self.

What is central about the Advaitic concept of self is its non-objective, non-relational and non-personal nature. The self is not only beyond cognition but also not an agent or a doer who is bound through bodily features and mental apparatus.

> It is the consciousness or knowledge itself and is different from both the known and the unknown. – *PD* III.18

Being the foundational consciousness the self is unmodified, immutable and association-less. It is called *kūṭastha*[6] by Śrī Vidyāraṇya which must be differentiated from the *cidābhāsa* (reflected consciousness) or the individual self.

The Three Implications of "I"

Even if the self or *kūṭastha* is association-less and pure awareness only, it is accidentally identified as an individual being or *cidābhāsa* who is involved in the worldly process, acts as an agent and aspires to the pleasures of this world and heaven. Unaware of its true nature the individual finds itself bound by the laws and desires of this empirical world. The detached *kūṭastha* finds itself attached to the gross and the subtle bodies and acquires the sense of "I" within. This "I", says Śrī Vidyāraṇya, has three different senses, of which one is primary and the other two are secondary (*PD* VII.9).

One primary meaning of "I" is when an ordinary individual uses it by identifying the *kūṭastha* with the *cidābhāsa* – the reflected

---

6 According to Swāmī Swāhānanda, the literal meaning of *kūṭastha* is the immovable, the immutable that is like a fixed unchanging iron piece on which the blacksmith works. It is like the top of a mountain that is unchanged and undisturbed and on which individual personality is superimposed (*PD* VI.22).

awareness due to mutual superimposition (*PD* VII.10). However, the "I" has two other meanings when one wisely utters "I am going to market" and "I am unattached or pure self". While in the first statement, he uses the "I" in common sense and means the *cidābhāsa* only separating it from the *kūṭastha*; in the second statement, he refers to the *kūṭastha* – the unattached self. As uttered in *Pañcadaśī* VII.12-13:

> From the conventional standpoint, the wise use the expression "I am going", meaning *cidābhāsa*, differentiating it from *kūṭastha*. However, from the philosophical standpoint the wise mean by their "I" the pure *kūṭastha*. In this they say: "I am unattached".

Further, *Pañcadaśī* talks about the seven phases of an individual being from ignorance to knowledge. *Cidābhāsa* who creates an artificial identity along with its psychophysical body and is immersed in worldly affairs is not aware of its essential nature. An individual being thus passes through these several stages – ignorance, obscuration, superimposition, indirect knowledge, direct knowledge, freedom from ignorance and unrestricted bliss (*PD* VII.33). *Cidābhāsa*, being the reflected consciousness, gets influenced by these seven phases from the time of birth until freedom. Due to ignorance, the individual keeps superimposing all features of this phenomenal world and remains unconcerned about exploring its true nature. The real self or *kūṭastha* is concealed till the individual starts discriminating its essential self from the no-self. To put it explicitly, the individual being denied its autonomous identity as ignorance obscures the knowledge of the *kūṭastha*. It keeps superimposing the features of no-self on itself as one continues to impose the qualities of a snake on a rope and gets affected by the losses and gains of the world. The dilemma here is that the individual being is both the victim of this constant superimposition and also a product of this superimposition. However, the *kūṭastha* is technically detached from all these phases as they belong only to the *cidābhāsa*.

Distinguishing the nature of *kūṭastha* from the *cidābhāsa*, Śrī Vidyāraṇya further affirms that the *kūṭastha* that shines like a light reveals every act, cognition and all modifications of intellect that appear and disappear subsequently. It keeps illuminating both the external and internal objects of the mind and persists even when they are absent. As stated in *Pañcadaśī* X.12:

> The witness consciousness lights up the ego, the intellect and the sense-objects. Even when ego, etc. are absent, it remains self-luminous.

It is important to clarify that the so-called difference between external and internal objects must be understood in relation to the body and the mind, and not to the self or *kūṭastha* which is the mere witness of all including the absence or non-existence of the ego and world.

Conclusion

It is worthy to note that throughout the text, Śrī Vidyāraṇya Swāmin has rigorously applied the method of discrimination and reason to establish consciousness and its unique nature, i.e. untouched, motionless, distinct, unmodified and objectless. He affirms that discrimination as a method has not only philosophical significance but also spiritual significance in Advaita (*PD* X.5). Going far ahead of the scriptures, he employs the rational and analytical attitude of Advaitins to discard the assumptions of the opponents and to affirm their position on firm ground. It is imperative thereby to admit the text is not only a mere repetition or description of the earlier Advaita works but an extremely insightful work that has addressed and answered the problems related to the concepts of mind, self and consciousness through rigorous logical analysis and an extensive phenomenological study of our different states of experience. The core arguments of Śrī Vidyāraṇya as elucidated in *Pañcadaśī* can be summarized as follows:

First, it must be noted that the search for a self, in Advaita, is not an inquiry for an independent and isolated self but to identify the self who is self-aware, self-evident and the witness. This self is not the owner or regulator of this psychophysical body. It is also not identical with them nor does it inhere in them. The self, says *Pañcadaśī*, is neither the internal modification or *vṛtti* of the mind that presumes the form of "I" nor it is the external modification that adopts the form of "this" (*PD* X.7). Hence, the "I" or the ego or the agent is the mere construction that grows and performs its role as long as the internal organ does not subside and reflects the awareness of the self.

What is important to note is that the whole effort of Advaita is to show that the self who is the mere witness consciousness is distinct from the object, the physical body and the mind, yet not separate from either of them. Just as the way the waves cannot be separated from the ocean, yet the former is not the ocean. The ocean is the basis that allows the waves to appear and disappear, in a similar manner, the self is the awareness in which the ego, mind and objects emerge and where again all these get dissolved. But the self does not dissolve, it persists even in their absence. Thus, the process of discrimination is just a method to ascertain that the no-self cannot be mistaken as self. Self is not an illusory nor a trans-experience personality but the very consciousness that reveals the world.

Further, it is observed that the account of consciousness that Advaita endorses may satisfactorily resolve the "hard problem" of consciousness without reducing or eliminating its essential existence. Consciousness is not the product that emerges from the mind–body union. But the ever-present motionless witness which is self-luminous like "the light in the dancing hall uniformly reveals the patron, the audience and the dancer" (*PD* X.11). And it does so even in the absence of all. Advaita does not deny the intrinsic and inward essence of subjectivity but eliminates the apparent "I" that creates the sense of *mineness* or individuality and points towards the inner consciousness, the witness (*PD* VII.88-89). It is this apparent "I" or the *cidābhāsa* that acts, craves, loves, hates, evolves, expands, communicates, enjoys and also suffers all the results of the worldly life. As a part of this phenomenal world, the "I" lives in the world, it appears along with the world and gets influenced by the gains and losses of the world. Yet, it is not the inner consciousness that pervades everything and reveals itself autonomously. It is this witnessing consciousness that explains the unity of our experiential states.

In short, following the core principle of non-dualism, Śrī Vidyāraṇya Swāmin discards any attempt to naturalize consciousness. He also avoids proposing any causal explanation since consciousness is not a product nor a quality that can be ascribed to the physical body. But the one which illumines all including the non-existence. Answering the opponents, he thus describes it as "nothing" that witness not only the name and form but also their abolition and void (*PD* III.31). Precisely, consciousness is not a "thing". It is neither a gross nor a subtle entity. Hence, any attempt to categorize it either as a thing or a substance would be an unscientific and futile effort that will certainly trap us in some form of naturalism or dualism or reductionism.

References

Balasubramaniam, R., 2004, "Advaita Vedānta on the Problem of Enworlded Subjectivity", in *Phenomenology and Indian Philosophy*, ed. D.P. Chattopaddhyaya, L. Embree and J.N. Mohanty, pp. 77-93, New Delhi: Indian Council of Philosophical Research.

Nataraju Adarasupally and Munmun Chakraborty, 2017, "Intentionality and Reflexivity of Consciousness: Advaita Perspective", in *Vedānta Ānvīkṣikī Science and Philosophy in Contemporary Perspective*, ed. Girish Nath Jha, Sukalyan Sengupta, Bal Ram Singh, New Delhi: D.K. Printworld.

Radhakrishnan, S., 2011, *Indian Philosophy*, vol. 2, 2nd edn, New Delhi: Oxford University Press.

Śri Vidyāraṇya Swāmin, 2012, *Pañcadaśī*, Swami Swahananda (trs), Chennai: Sri Ramkrishna Math.

Contributors

Biswas, Saumya Kanti, Assistant Professor, Karimganj College, Karimganj – 209502, Assam; [*e-mail:* <saumyakanti.biswas@gmail.com>; *Ph.:* 9435073918].

Chakraborty, Munmun, Assistant Professor, Department of Philosophy, Assam University, Silchar – 788011, Assam; [*e-mail:* <munmunchakraborty58@gmail.com>; *Ph.:* 8724092142].

Ghosh, Raghunath, Former Professor, University of North Bengal; [*Address:* 1/4 Basera Apartment, B.M. Sarani, Siliguri – 734001, West Bengal; *e-mail:* <ghoshraghunath3@gmail.com>; *Ph.:* 9434715403].

Khangamcha, Milan, Professor, Department of Philosophy, Manipur University, Imphal – 795003, East, Manipur; [*e-mail:* <pmilamuni@yahoo.com>; *Ph.:* 9366730947].

Nataraju, Adarasupally, Professor, Centre for Philosophy, Jawaharlal Nehru University, New Delhi – 110 067 [*e-mail:* <adinatraj@jnu.ai.in; *Ph.:* 9435522161].

Poudyal, Sindhu, Assistant Professor, Department of Philosophy, Tripura University, Suryamaninagar, Tripura West – 799022, Tripura; [*e-mail:* <sindhupoudal@tripurauni.ac.in>; *Ph.:* 9969058449].

Pradhan, R.C., Retired Professor, Department of Philosophy, University of Hyderabad [*Address*: 93, Doyens Township Serilingampally, Hyderabad – 500019, Telangana; *e-mail:* <rcpradhan@iias.ac.in>; *Ph.:* 9440052901].

Prasad, H.S., Former Professor and Head of the Department of Philosophy, University of Delhi [*Address:* Ireo Victory Valley, Tower D 25-001, Ground Floor, Golf Course Extension Road, Sector 67,

Gurugram – 122101, Haryana; *e-mail:* <prof.hsprasad@gmail.com>; *Ph.:* 9015778772].

Shakuntala, Associate Professor, Department of Philosophy, Gauhati University, Guwahati – 781014, District Kamrup, Assam; [*e-mail:* <shakuntalabora@yahoo.com>; *Ph.:* 9954065796].

Sharma, Arup Jyoti, Assistant Professor, Department of Philosophy, Tripura University, Suryamaninagar, Tripura West – 799022, Tripura; [*e-mail:* <sarma.arupjoti7@gmail.com>; *Ph.:* 8638382447].

Singh, R.P., Former Professor, Centre for Philosophy, School of Social Sciences, JNU, New Delhi [Address: F 001, Ruhil Residency, Sector 3, Bahadurgarh, District Jhajhar, Haryana; *e-mail:* <rpsinghjnu@yahoo.com>; *Ph.:* 9868061209].

Thoibisana, Akoijam, Associate Professor, Department of Philosophy, Gauhati University, Guwahati – 781014, District Kamrup, Assam; [*email:* <akoithoi@gmail.com>; *Ph.:* 6001794848].

Timalsina, Sthaneshwar, Professor, Department of Religious Studies, San Diego State University, United States [*Address*: 11289 Silver Buckle Way, San Diego, CA 92127, USA; *e-mail:* <timalsin@sdsu.edu>; *Ph.:* +1 (619) 672-261].

Index